CLINIC of HOPE

Clinic of Hope

The Story of Rene M. Caisse and Essiac

Donna M. Ivey

THE DUNDURN GROUP
TORONTO

Copy-Editor: Jennifer Bergeron
Design: Andrew Roberts
Printer: University of Toronto Press

Library and Archives Canada Cataloguing in Publication

Ivey, Donna M.
    Clinic of hope : the story of Rene Caisse and Essiac / Donna M. Ivey.

Includes bibliographical references.
ISBN 1-55002-520-1

    1. Caisse, Rene, 1888-1978. 2. Essiac. 3. Cancer--Alternative treatment. 4. Herbs--Therapeutic use. 5. Herbalists--Canada--Biography. I. Title.

RC271.E68194 2004   616.99'4068'092   C2004-903136-8

1   2   3   4   5   08   07   06   05   04

We acknowledge the support of the Canada Council for the Arts and the Ontario Arts Council for our publishing program. We also acknowledge the financial support of the Government of Canada through the Book Publishing Industry Development Program and The Association for the Export of Canadian Books, and the Government of Ontario through the Ontario Book Publishers Tax Credit program, and the Ontario Media Development Corporation's Ontario Book Initiative.

                    J. Kirk Howard, President

Printed and bound in Canada.
Printed on recycled paper.

www.dundurn.com

Dundurn Press   Gazelle Book Services Limited   Dundurn Press
8 Market Street   White Cross Mills   2250 Military Road
Suite 200   Hightown, Lancaster, England   Tonawanda NY
Toronto, Ontario, Canada   LA1 4X5   U.S.A. 14150
M5E 1M6

To Nony

TABLE OF CONTENTS

FOREWORD

by J. Patrick Boyer

Ask anyone from Bracebridge and you're sure to hear a story about Rene Caisse. Many people far beyond this central Ontario town likewise consider themselves highly knowledgeable, perhaps even experts, about this remarkable nurse and her "Essiac" cancer treatment. They'll all now want to read this intriguing book.

Growing up in the same town where the protagonist of this medical adventure story operated her last-chance cancer clinic, I was one of those who typically thought I pretty much knew the whole story. I even thought I had an insider's understanding of the *real* version of Rene Caisse's twisting tale. So to underscore the significance of this new book by Donna Ivey, I should explain why.

Back in the pre-television 1950s when I was growing up, Bracebridge was like every other kid's town — a place to be out and about directly observing and participating in the relationships at play in one's community. We knew where the town's two newspaper offices were, the stately town hall, and, across a narrow laneway behind it, the squat stone jail and its various prisoners we'd "interview" through the iron bars of their tiny window. We ourselves were highly knowledgeable inmates of the cavernous Bracebridge Public School, and we knew most of the town's numerous churches, too. We'd learned the smells and patterns of the hockey rink, the baseball diamond, the candy counter at Elliot's five-and-dime store, Cale's butcher shop, and the aromas of each of the town's three bakeries (Waite's, Haight's, and Muriel's), Jack's subterranean pool hall, and the inspiring treasures of Shier's sporting goods store.

Our rounds gave us wide-eyed awareness of the dwelling place of the local prostitute and rendered us closely informed about the town's bootlegger. Of course it was a given that we all knew where the lady with the cancer cure lived.

Eventually we discovered that although every self-respecting community had its local swimming hole and movie theatre, not every town had a resident specialist for curing cancer. In this, Bracebridge was both special and rare. Our childhood pride swelled. Boastfully we soon deduced that our town was unique on the whole planet earth.

Not only that, there was something mysterious about it, too. Adults whispered when they spoke about cancer. Our inescapable sense of something clandestine going on was reinforced by all the cars with licence plates from Illinois, New Brunswick, New Jersey, Alberta, and Alabama parked along tree-canopied Kimberley Avenue around Rene Caisse's large home.

All the same, there was something so close and familiar about Nurse Caisse's story that it took us longer to recognize, the more we heard from her supporters and detractors, how distinctive this plucky woman was who stood defiantly against the medical establishment and the mainstream of conventional wisdom.

If we are among all the trees that make it what it is, we don't see the forest itself. For example, Dr. Bert Bastedo, who is closely woven into this book's story as one of the first members of the medical community in Bracebridge to publicly endorse Rene Caisse and her treatment, for reasons Donna Ivey makes dramatically clear, was the same doctor who'd delivered me into the world and whose grave is a mere dozen paces from my own chosen plot in a Bracebridge cemetery at the north end of town. The very first haircut I ever had was given by Rene's nephew Louis, in the same barbershop established by Rene's father. The former British Lion Hotel, where Rene Caisse operated her cancer clinic in the 1930s and 1940s, in utterly remarkable circumstances again documented by Donna Ivey in the pages that follow, was by the 1950s simply another apartment building in town where I delivered copies of the *Toronto Telegram* on my newspaper route. These are reasons that many of us growing up in Bracebridge had difficulty appreciating the exceptional nature of this local story.

In my case, however, the connection got even closer, perhaps making it even harder to see the really big story that now comes across in this valuable book. How close? My grandfather George Boyer had taken Rene as a vivacious young woman to dances in Bracebridge. My father, Robert Boyer, from April 1933, as the then nineteen-year-old editor of the *Muskoka Herald* newspaper, had closely chronicled Rene Caisse's stories, including the opening of her clinic in 1935. Dad continued to have a close association with the "story" over the years and, after 1955, did so both as editor of the *Herald-Gazette* (upon amalgamation of the town's two newspapers), and as Muskoka District's newly elected member of the Ontario legislature.

My most intimate boyhood friend, Douglas Slater, was a great-nephew of Rene Caisse, and we sometimes dropped into her home, which was just across the street from the Slater house on Kimberley Avenue. When my mother, Patricia, my wife, Corinne, and my sister Victoria came to battle tumours each in her turn, Essiac was, in one way or another, part of the story.

Today, as I read Donna Ivey's manuscript to write this foreword, I lift my eyes through the window of my Bracebridge home and see the building that housed Rene Caisse's clinic just seventy yards away across my back lawn. Eight houses north along the street where I live is Rene's former home where patients came, desperate and hopeful, from far and near.

These were further reasons many of us in Bracebridge had difficulty seeing the world-famous distinctiveness of something so closely familiar. It's easier to accord fame to a remote clinic for cancer treatment in Mexico or Switzerland to which Canadians journey at great effort and financial cost, than the other way around.

Rene Caisse's substantial red-brick house, set back from the street, had a large front lawn and a wide white-pillared verandah. Doug and I would stroll through spacious cool dark front rooms and into her extensive "kitchen" area, which had been expanded from the regular kitchen into a windowed back porch with its own steps, door, and reception or treatment area. Up those steps came visitors presenting themselves for an Essiac cure. Large stainless steel pots steamed atop her stove. The place was like a clinic, but also partly resembled the summer kitchen of a busy farmhouse. Most of all, I remember it exuding an atmosphere meant more for adults than kids.

Prior to this era in the 1950s when she dispensed Essiac from her home, Rene Caisse's clinic in the former British Lion Hotel on Dominion Street had been just across from our family's *Muskoka Herald* newspaper office. My Boyer grandparents lived in the immediate vicinity and worked at the newspaper, and Rene and my grandmother Victoria Boyer kept up a close connection over the years, chatting regularly and exchanging news and views, a relationship directly related to our family's newspaper remaining a faithful recorder and steadfast supporter of Rene in her ongoing battles. In time Robert Boyer's routine reporting on the Essiac developments and his intermittent editorials questioning the partisan handling of medical matters would become, as Donna Ivey has told me, an indispensable public record for the research that culminated in this book.

Many people interested in this book have no doubt connected with pieces of Rene's story before. Perhaps like blindfolded people grasping different parts of an elephant, we each thought we understood the whole, coming to a large conclusion from our limited experience holding only a leg, a trunk, an ear, or a tail. By the mid-1970s I came to find myself seized of quite a different part of the Rene Caisse saga. I had fetched up in Toronto as a partner of one of the city's big law firms, Fraser & Beatty, which acted for uranium mining tycoon Stephen Roman through Denison Mines Ltd. and his Roman Corporation. The kid from Bracebridge was again in contact with Essiac, but now in a completely different context.

The entrepreneurial Mr. Roman had become the financial backer of Resperin Corporation, a company headed by David Fingard. Mr. Fingard was a swashbuckler in a pinstripe morning coat with a halo of long white hair and a curving handlebar moustache, looking as if he'd stepped right off the pages of a Mark Twain Mississippi paddle-wheeling riverboat into the imposing wood-panelled boardroom of Roman Corporation, high in the Royal Bank Towers of Toronto's Bay Street. At the flash of a promotional opportunity David Fingard could produce from his bulging coat pockets a sheaf of endorsement letters from duchesses and potentates in far-flung corners of the world. Apart from David Fingard himself, Resperin Corporation had two assets. The first was the remarkable Duke-Fingard treatment for alleviating problems of respiration, which Donna Ivey engagingly and alarmingly explains in this book. The second was Rene Caisse's still closely guarded secret recipe for Essiac.

While the senior partner of our firm, John A. Mullin, QC, and other seasoned and skilled lawyers worked with Stephen Roman and his clear-eyed officials on the complex and rarefied issues of corporate law, resource taxation, strategic minerals, nuclear politics, and a lawsuit against Prime Minister Pierre Trudeau, I inhaled deeply and headed on into the posh inner sanctums of the Roman temple. There, sitting around a highly polished corporate boardroom table, I encountered a world just as exotic in its own ways as that of high-stakes uranium production during the Cold War, which was being addressed down the hall. My role as a professional was to prepare legal documents and research relevant law, all relating to Essiac.

Resperin's board was busily seeking to enter into new clinical trials of Essiac with the Brusch Medical Center in Boston, work out protocols with the Department of Health in Ottawa for controlled dispensing of Rene Caisse's remedy under the supervision of medical doctors in Canada, and generally move Rene Caisse's lifelong quest beyond that of a lone nurse's personal mission into a broad-based, systematically organized, and medically approved operation on a sound financial footing. The boy who had run through Rene's kitchen and gazed with behind-the-scene amazement upon an inner sanctum where pots of brewing Essiac steamed had grown up to draft legal documents for medical protocols and clinical trials in the U.S.A. of the very same herbal tea.

My further encounters with Essiac were again different, but no less real, as a small part of this vast and surrealistic saga traced by Donna Ivey on the pages that follow. In October 1978, when my mother, Patricia Boyer, languished in the Toronto General Hospital following surgery to remove a brain tumour, it was hardly surprising that my younger sister Alison, seeking as any daughter might some method to help her mother fight for her life, arrived in Toronto with a bottle of Essiac. Even when it was restricted, people in Rene Caisse's home-town knew who to see to get a bottle of the magical brew. Upon dis-covering this, the physician in charge of our mother, a Dr. Barnum, summoned our family into an anteroom to imperiously pronounce, "If Essiac comes onto this case, I go off!" Such was the legacy in the world of established medicine of Rene Caisse's treatment.

Two decades later, however, when my wife, Corinne Boyer, was battling cancer of the ovary, attitudes in the world of Canadian medicine were growing more receptive to "non-traditional" meth-ods. Those who so recently had denigrated traditional Chinese medicine had begun crowding into standing-room-only sessions of Canadian Medical Association annual conferences to learn about acupuncture. Who can say how Rene Caisse's long battles against closed-shop medicine contributed to this gradual shift toward greater open-mindedness, as the limits of so-called traditional medical practice became more apparent?

For Corinne by the 1990s, certainly, doctors in Toronto were ready to assist by providing, under procedures established by Health Canada, vials of French scientist Gaston Nassens's 714-X for me to administer through intra-muscular injections at home. There were other "alternate" remedies, too: Tahibo Tea, shark car-tilage, silver bands, reflexology, rearrangement of furniture, re-hanging of paintings, various forms of meditation, new books with humane insights, special pamphlets with cryptic meanings, a universe of spiritual offerings, a smorgasbord of health sup-plements including Muskoka-grown ginseng purchased at source from the farmer, and many other treatments and procedures — including, of course, Essiac.

People seeking a successful treatment against the marauding force of cancer turn to anything and everything. Ever more possibil-ities keep opening up even as previously attempted ones prove futile. Always more believers appear by serendipity wanting to share their zealous convictions and remedies. Patients and their distraught families go through this quest in a twilight bubble with chequebooks open and pens in hand, a reality that provides a necessary subtext for this book and explains the motivation of people in authority who seek to navigate between possible cures and probable charlatans. Fighting cancer is a battleground with many fronts.

Corinne and I bought bottles of Essiac from Kathleen Beers at her home, and it was still a familiar Bracebridge story because this was where years before I'd played street hockey with her son Bill and other neighbourhood boys. Now I had, sadly, moved into that once hushed world kids like me knew instinctively was for adults.

By the 1990s Essiac was readily available. Dr. Gary L. Glum from California had published *Calling of an Angel* in 1988,[*] a high-priced book through which one could in turn buy a tape and acquire the long-secret Essiac recipe, and Muskoka publishers Dr. Edward Britton in his *Bracebridge Examiner* and Douglas Specht in the *Herald-Gazette* had given the full scoop in their newspapers, which you could buy for a quarter. Not only that, but when asked if he agreed with us using Essiac, Corinne's surgical oncologist Dr. Denny DePetrillo in Toronto easily remarked, "Sure, let's try it. It might help." In April 2004 Elwanda Shaw of MacTier, Ontario, told me "I have taken Essiac since my last cancer surgery in 1977. I take it as a herbal tea. I make my own. I get the right plants at the health food store in Parry Sound." She has never had chemotherapy or radiation. When she asked her surgeon in Parry Sound about taking Essiac, he replied, "It can't hurt."

By 1996, when I'd founded the Corinne Boyer Fund for Ovarian Cancer Research and Treatment (today renamed the National Ovarian Cancer Association), and subsequently when I also served for four years on the board of Cancer Care Ontario (the largest single cancer research and treatment organization in North America) and visited many medical schools, cancer research laboratories in Canada and the United States, and worked closely with hundreds of cancer specialists and patients, I had grown even more familiar with the ongoing search for ways to treat the problem of cancer. Among the many pieces of this puzzle, in the realm of "alternate remedies"

---

[*] Dr. Gary L. Glum, *Calling of an Angel* (Los Angeles: Silent Walker Publications, 1988).

that various authorities sought to evaluate for efficaciousness, remained Essiac. It is a story that will not go away.

More than a quarter-century has now passed since Rene Caisse died. In her hometown a bronze statue of the defiant nurse today stands prominently in the very centre of Bracebridge. Just a block away across the river a museum displays artifacts of her life and headlines from her many front-page stories. A block away in the other direction stands the former hotel where Rene Caisse's cancer clinic operated with the support and encouragement of the town authorities, an historic plaque marking the site.

Today not only tourism in Bracebridge and lore on the Internet keep her story alive, but also the commercial availability of Essiac and products being passed off as the miraculous herbal tea. For example, two contrasting advertisements in the *Old Farmer's Almanac* for 2004, published in Dublin, New Hampshire, demonstrate with rare precision the large issues that dominate Donna Ivey's book. One has a beautiful full-page colour ad for "Essiac® From Rene M. Caisse, R.N." Against a background of bright green dew-moistened leaves, a box and a bottle — one the powder formula, the other the extract of the renowned herbal "tea" — are set in a translucent shimmer of surrounding white light, as is the green and gold name ESSIAC® above. "Original Herbal Formula," proclaims white lettering on the lovely green leaf backdrop, "World Renowned Since 1922." On the labels for both versions of the product is a cameo of the smiling Nurse Caisse and her dates, 1888 to 1978, as well as an authenticating reproduction of her signature. The ad, placed by Essiac® Canada Limited of Ottawa, informs readers that the product is "Approved for use in Canada and for Export by Health Canada (C.F.I.A.)," and warns "BEWARE OF COUNTERFEITS."

The second ad in the same edition of this venerable compendium, published annually since 1792 to bring into farms and homes across North America its weather forecasts, seeding timetables, useful and entertaining information (this year, two *additional* ways to hypnotize a chicken), and more than two centuries worth of health cures and home remedies, is not nearly so professional or colourful. Appearing instead like a news story, with a headline and two columns of type, it reports in the dramatic voice of tabloid newspapers: "Black Listed Cancer Treatment Could Save Your Life." It tells the story of a woman in the world of medicine who decades ago discovered "a totally natural formula that not only protects against the development of cancer, but has helped people all over the world diagnosed with incurable cancer — now lead normal lives."* The claim is made: "As unbelievable as it seems, the key to stopping many cancers has been ... kept out of your medicine cabinet by the very agency designed to protect your health — the FDA."

The story, complete with a number of inspiring testimonials of the same kind that flowed in the wake of Rene Caisse's work, tells how the discovery of the remarkable information "was blocked by manufacturers with heavy financial stakes" and "she is denied publication" by the "giants who don't want you to read her words." In this case, the advertiser, Agora Health Books, is not directly selling a remedy but rather a book, *How to Fight Cancer & Win*, which includes the "banned" information of Dr. Johanna Budwig and other expert minds like hers "who have pursued cancer remedies and come up with remarkable natural formulas and diets that work for hundreds and thousands of patients," and "reveals their secrets for you."

Both ads, and many others this year, just as 50 or 100 or 150 years ago, hold out promise, warn of plots or rival treatments that are ineffectual, and reinforce a cult of underground or alternate health care that can be made available despite the conspiracy to suppress it. They serve not only to highlight the centrality of Essiac and Rene Caisse's adventure in this universe of non-institutionalized healing; they equally show how her efforts took place in a wider and crowded arena where for a very long time treatments have been the subject of guerilla warfare in jungle skirmishes between contending forces of health practitioners, each claiming a technique or substance that, in a universe of medical variables, is asserted to be best.

---

*The Old Farmer's Almanac 2004, p. 105.

Ironically, in a realm known for quack remedies, the Essiac saga itself is replete with a number of colourful and breathtaking episodes that defy the line between truth and illusion. Donna Ivey's text is an antidote to that. To get the story behind the headlines required going beyond the explanations and information even in Rene Caisse's own accounts in the booklet I Was "Canada's Cancer Nurse." Donna Ivey exposes better than anyone else has the "shell game" where covers were constantly moved — by those in health care, the government officials, the promoters, the politicians, the doctors, the medical associations, the patients, even by Rene Caisse herself — so that it was never entirely clear where the hidden pea of truth might be. Drilling down through the hype and the apocryphal tales, the author takes us to the deeper story.

Not only does the problematic handling of "so-called cures" over the decades come into better perspective on the following pages, so does the nature of North American culture in its troubling inability to distinguish between "mainstream" and "alternate" methods of treatment. The epithet "hoax," used by some opponents of Rene Caisse, might just as appropriately have been applied to them, as this book clarifies. The institutional power of professional organizations is documented as well, for instance in pressuring doctors and causing them to reverse their prior independent conclusions about the beneficial effects of Essiac. Donna Ivey lets the facts speak for themselves, too, in documenting how government officials professed to follow a process of public inquiry, although it could as readily be interpreted as an inquisition using the power of the state.

It is clearly time to take fresh stock of what it means to be engaged in healing and what it entails to stand against the mainstream. In the pages that follow, Donna Ivey has pieced together the whole story that none of us had before. Chances are that anyone reading this book will already have a strong interest in cancer treatments, as well as personal experiences to bring to this narrative. Chances are even greater that any reader who knows something about Essiac or Nurse Caisse will, up to now, have possessed only fragments of this story. I know I did. Those isolated bits may have been exaggerated episodes or even misinterpreted "facts." The author's devoted research and assiduous attention to the factual record makes for revisionist writing on several significant features of the Rene Caisse story — her status in the medical profession, for example, or the year and circumstances under which she came to possess the formula, not to mention the complex reasons for secrecy surrounding the formula that make this book read in places like a spy novel.

Never out of controversy, always at the raw frontier of treating victims with tumours by administering Essiac, Rene Caisse repeatedly refused to divulge the secret formula. Her steadfast refusal to give up a recipe previously freely given to her made Rene, in the eyes of some researchers and certain leaders of the medical profession, an obstinate nuisance. Yet she bent over backwards to co-operate with doctors and researchers in all other respects and, as this book makes clear, had very good reasons for taking the course she did. Indeed, the struggle to maintain the secrecy of the formula dominates this story and gives rise to some of its most surprising elements. This book reveals more completely than any other the factual story of Rene Caisse's remarkable, yet tortured, adventure. The journey traced by Donna Ivey takes us along a familiar fear-filled frontier whose uneasy boundary is the nebulous line between life and death, medical politics and alternate treatments, personal turmoil and the hungry hope of thousands seeking to escape cancer's death grip.

This book is as much the history of a battle oscillating between claims and cures as it is the biography of Rene Caisse. The geographic battleground began in central and Northern Ontario, and especially in Bracebridge, the capital town of the District of Muskoka and home of Rene's cancer clinic. Yet it was by no means confined to this region. The campaigns were waged wherever people found themselves diagnosed with cancer and in whatever places people sought to provide treatments and remedies. Rene Caisse's story became the large drama it did because of major involvements, all documented in this book, in the United States of America, especially in such states as Connecticut, New

York, Massachusetts, Ohio, Michigan, Illinois, and California, as well as further afield, from India to representations for cancer-stricken Eva Peron on her deathbed in Argentina in 1952.

In chronicling Rene Caisse's remarkable story, this book traces a series of recurring patterns. A cycle plays out, only to be repeated. The rounds involve support for Rene and threats against her. Endorsements of her work are given, but only as others challenge or attack her efforts and doctors retreat from the very approbations they had previously given. The involvement of politicians is also closely interwoven with the saga of Essiac, from start to finish. Mayors, members of the Ontario legislature, and members of the House of Commons, both during their time in office and in their subsequent careers, seemed inexorably drawn to Essiac and its unique politics. Major political leaders of the day, including Ontario premiers Mitch Hepburn and Leslie Frost, are directly part of Rene Caisse's struggle. So are many members of the Ontario legislature, including those representing Muskoka District, from Frank Kelly to Robert Boyer. Lieutenants-governor of Ontario Herbert A. Bruce and Pauline MacGibbon found their careers woven into the Essiac story. So did Ontario opposition leaders in their turn, such as Leopold Macaulay and John Wintermeyer. It was not just governmental and political party politics that Essiac excited. The politics, intrigues, and infighting of the medical profession, too, are on display at the turning of almost every page of this book.

Rene Caisse's story, now reconstructed by Donna Ivey, presents a who's who of power and prominent people in the medical field with whom Rene interacted — from Dr. Frederick Banting and his research laboratories in Toronto to Dr. Charles Brusch and his medical clinic near Boston, from the Sloan-Kettering Institute for Cancer Research in New York to the laboratories of Northwestern University in Chicago. Although wealthy entrepreneurial Americans, from a Buffalo newspaperman to Harry Oakes and others, sought partnerships with Rene Caisse and were prepared to put up seed funding in exchange for the formula and the opportunity to cure millions while making Nurse Caisse (and themselves) very rich in the process, she took a pass.

Donna Ivey explores the complex reasons for this and some other seemingly inexplicable outcomes and comes closer than anyone ever has before in making them understandable. Rene Caisse's temptation to move to the United States with her formula also provides a recurring background tension throughout this story, but, for reasons Donna Ivey makes clear, "Canada's Cancer Nurse" ultimately chose not to go down that road, although her ongoing and extensive involvements south of the Canadian border provided, in addition to personal exhaustion and cross-boundary customs disputes, timely political leverage in dealing with hard-nosed Canadian health department officials.

The "politics" of Essiac truly were unique. Rene Caisse's sensational story was richly accompanied over the years by the writing and signing of many petitions with thousands of names subscribed to them, including several pleading to ensure that Canada's cancer nurse and her secret formula for treating cancer not be driven out of the country and away from needy patients. Why such a public outpouring of support ran amok in the world of politics is closely probed in this book, with telling results.

Journalists inevitably drawn to this story recorded these dramas decade by decade. Thanks to the retrospective view provided here by Donna Ivey, we see how some episodes moved so confusingly that even the press could not keep up. At one point, a distraught Rene Caisse seemed to change her mind almost weekly — and readers will experience how she was torn between caving in to the pressures and harassment from the Ontario government by closing her cancer clinic in Bracebridge and moving it to the United States and valiantly helping those who journeyed from far and wide to her bustling clinic and keeping it open no matter what. Even after her death, Rene's story and the saga of Essiac attracted journalists, from broadcaster Tom Cherington, whose dramatic television documentary cost him his job, to feature writers Sheila Snow Fraser and Carrol Allen, whose extensively researched article in *Homemaker's Magazine* seemed to distill all the issues in this story into one further real-life drama admirably recounted here by Donna Ivey.

From the day Rene Caisse first learned the formula to the end of her long and eventful life, a dramatic series of events propelled by her valiant determination would touch the lives of hundreds of thousands of cancer patients and their families throughout North America and beyond. Her life became inextricably bound up with the story of this treatment, which is why Donna Ivey must inevitably portray how Rene's personal mission unfolded in a world of fear and hope, rivalry and co-operation, avarice and generosity, standard medicine and alternate remedies, public affairs and health care politics.

The Rene Caisse drama takes on its special aura of surrealism through the secretiveness surrounding the treatment, the clandestine manner of Essiac's distribution, and the colourful cast of characters and personalities who themselves became entwined with the Essiac story during the decades of the twentieth century, when armies of the desperate and legions of the hopeful sought cures for cancer even as increasing numbers died from the many different forms of this disease. The raw edge of this story concerns the human struggle to cope with the approaching prospect of death, and the front-line experiences of Rene Caisse's daily dealing with those who came to her begging for Essiac, and those who conspired high and low to prevent her providing it. Such sharp realities give a timeless immediacy and heartfelt intensity to the events chronicled with comprehensive accuracy in these following pages.

This book presents accurate information about a story that up to now has been surrounded by rumour, legend, and unprincipled hype. It is told with a sensitive human wisdom. Donna Ivey narrates these events with loyalty to their times and love of their place. Her book is being published into a world where cancer treatment continues to be more, not less, urgent. It is also a world where strange things have been said about Rene Caisse and Essiac, and many mixed-up versions of events have been confusingly told and retold and spread now across the World Wide Web to a very wide audience of badly misinformed readers. This book, going further than anything published yet, is based on direct and local sources accurately compiled through patient research and compassionately relayed in a realistic telling of the Rene Caisse story.

As someone who became directly familiar with Essiac in many different contexts over half a century, I want to pay tribute to Donna Ivey for her public service in making this ongoing story and its origins so much more understandable. By researching and writing this significant story in such an engaging and balanced fashion, she removes the smudge of misunderstanding and clarifies the record of a remarkable woman who dedicated her life to healing others, even as it required her to stand against the mainstream to do so.

Bracebridge, Canada
Victoria Day, May 24, 2004

PREFACE

Rene M. Caisse was a Canadian nurse who experienced more drama than anyone could expect from the innocent selection of a healing profession in the early twentieth century. In her own writings and interviews throughout the years, Rene's memory of medical matters was keen, but, like many of us, her recollections of dates, names, and events were not. The incomplete data, and unfortunate errors in fact, necessitated meticulous research, demanding in-depth verification of primary sources held in libraries, museums, and archives in Ontario and in the United States. There has been little anecdotal reliance, although with clues from helpful local residents the author was able to flesh out the story from 1888 to present in more detail than was developed by others for previous publications. The author of this biography knows that certain critical pieces of information originally published and repeatedly reissued are incorrect.

Since the research began for this book, actions of the privacy commissioner in Ontario have limited access to documentation regarding all matters of the former cancer commission and the Rene M. Caisse files within the Health Department holdings in the Archives of Ontario. Files that had been previously searched various times by the author as well as other researchers are no longer open, and the quantity of documents in the record boxes seems reduced for reasons not given. Similar restrictions have been placed on documents in Canada's National Archives by the federal privacy commissioner.

Recognizing the public interest in Rene's activities, Mary McPherson graciously deposited originals and copies of documents from Rene's collection in the Bracebridge Public Library, thereby establishing the Rene M. Caisse Archive. Dr. Gary Glum wrote that in 1985 he was given a large quantity of Rene's records, which he took to his home in California.[*] Someday he will want to place those documents in an appropriate Ontario archive. Unfortunately, the repository of Caisse papers remains scattered.

Almost arbitrary closure has had to be made to this work, simply because I suspect that the complete biography of Rene Caisse can never be finished, by anyone. And this author is aging rapidly. As well, the remarkable nurse deserves as many biographies as writers wish to compile from as many points of view. The herbal remedy she administered to grateful patients also needs more evaluation and acceptance for the benefits enjoyed by so many.

It should be noted that the use of the word "Essiac" throughout this book usually refers to the historical name assigned to the herbal tea and treatment developed and used by Rene M. Caisse from about 1926 to 1978, and is not be confused with the named product that has since been registered as a patent and owned by a private company.

I wish Rene were here to appreciate what I hope is a kindly and appreciative tribute.

---

[*]Glum, *Calling of an Angel*, p. 163.

ACKNOWLEDGEMENTS

My sincere thanks are offered to those who helped me find answers to my endless enquiries. Some persons or institutions may have been omitted but by the author's carelessness.

I owe these individuals my special appreciation: Carroll Allen reviewed the chapters involving the *Homemaker's Magazine* research and gave me her astonishing audio tapes of crucial discussions with Dr. Walde, Dr. Brusch, and Rene Caisse; Mrs. W.C. (Tina) Arnold of Haileybury and latterly Vancouver told me of her doctor husband's respect of Rene during her work in the area; Robert J. Boyer, Patrick Boyer's father, reflected with me the years of reporting Rene's activities in his newspaper, particularly those that were so vital to the record of the cancer commission period; Alice De La Plante introduced me to the Rene Caisse legend and shared her files with me; Murray Ellis gave me a large painting by Rene M. McGaughey; Dorothy Farmiloe of Elk Lake shared her vast knowledge of the Elk Lake history and led me to the photo of Rene at the Elk Lake hospital; Vera Goltz described how Rene dried the herbs in her basement; Hugh MacMillan shared memories of his vain attempt to place all of Rene's personal records into the Ontario Archives; Mary MacPherson told me of many of Rene's activities and antics; E.D. McClelland of Emerson, Manitoba, filled me in on how it was in his town during Rene's time there; Lorne and Heather Minthorn of Thunder Bay and Timmins enlightened me about their grandfather, Dr. Henry Minthorn; the Sisters of Providence in Timmins and Montreal assured me that no records of their Haileybury Hospital survived the 1922 fire; Lionel

Venne of Elk Lake directed me to the town's museum and the photo of a young Nurse Caisse and told me about David Fingard, his cigar, and his prospecting activities in the area; Kathy Ward of the Whitby Mental Health Centre found two important letters that placed Rene as a student there (Ontario Hospital) in 1921.

Others who wished to take no credit for their assistance include those who significantly assisted me in providing valuable clues to Rene's activities and led me to further research.

I could not have done without the skills and enthusiasm of the reference staff of the Bracebridge Public Library. The willing assistance of librarians, archivists, and support staff of the outstanding public, academic, and specialized libraries throughout Ontario and the surrounding area also helped me to retrieve those hundreds of dates, descriptions, details, diaries, documentation, and images. Other colleagues include (an asterisk indicates a significant contribution):

*Archives of Ontario, Toronto
Buffalo & Erie County Library, New York
Canadian Mothercraft Society
City of Cambridge Archives
Cobalt Mining Museum
Cobalt Public Library
College of Nurses of Ontario
College of Physicians and Surgeons of Ontario
*Elk Lake Heritage Museum
Greenwich Hospital, Connecticut, Jean Sudol
*Greenwich Library, Connecticut, Richard Hart
*Haileybury Fire Museum, Chris Oslund
Haileybury Public Library
Highway Book Shop, Cobalt, the Pollards
Latchford Information Centre, Temiskaming
Manitoba Historical Society
*National Archives, Ottawa
National Library, Ottawa
North Bay Area Museum

Acknowledgements

*North Bay Public Library

*Ontario Hospital, Whitby

Ontario Registered Nurses Association, Toronto

Orillia Public Library

Parry Sound Public Library

*Stauffer Library, Queen's University, Kingston

*Queen's University Archives, Kingston

St. John's Anglican Church, North Bay

Timmins Museum Centre

Timmins Public Library

*Toronto Reference Library

University of Toronto, Faculty of Information Studies, Canada-Wide Health and Medical Archives Telephone Information Network

University of Toronto, Robarts Library

University of Toronto, Science & Medicine Library

University of Toronto, Thomas Fisher Rare Books Library

My late friend, historian and author William Kilbourn, would be pleased to know I followed his advice and tried to tell a story of historical importance. I want to thank Nancy Wilson of Bracebridge, who in a friendly and professional manner advised and assisted me in various ways during the long preparation of the manuscript. Certainly I appreciate the many kindnesses of J. Patrick Boyer, who whisked my manuscript off to Kirk Howard of the Dundurn Group and placed it on his desk. Thank you, Patrick, for contributing your recollections and knowledge in the Foreword.

My friends and family amiably put up with my frequent disappearances into my study or out of town, which in some cases over the years of this work may have been for them a pleasant relief. Norma Kelly knew I'd be finished the book sometime, and I'm grateful that she hung in with her understanding support and encouragement, taking part in many of the necessary research trips to archives, libraries, and personal interviews.

INTRODUCTION

This is the story of Rene M. Caisse of Bracebridge, Canada, which describes her extraordinary perseverance to obtain official recognition of the herbal cancer remedy she called Essiac — her name spelled backwards.

Rene Caisse was thrust into a lifelong medical-legal-political controversy that persists today, long after her death in 1978. Rene wrestled with the Hepburn government of Ontario over her use of Essiac and the operation of her Bracebridge cancer clinic from 1935 to 1941. She refused to reveal the secret formula of her remedy, the crux of the battle. Legislation aimed at demanding the recipe forced the closing of the Rene M. Caisse Cancer Clinic in 1941 and was not repealed until 1997. The government in turn was embroiled in the dilemma of ensuring their public favour while at the same time assuaging demanding cancer patients and voters. Rene's remedy fielded protests from the medical brotherhood, with its traditional cancer treatments, and the cancer research industry. Some of the medical doctors who were brave enough to challenge their fraternity permitted their terminal cancer victims to obtain Essiac treatments and documented dramatic recoveries. Many details of the 1939 secret hearings of the provincial commission held to assess cancer remedies are documented in this book.

The research into the life of Rene Caisse exposed a warm and compassionate nurse who many times risked her own health with overwork and stress. Study of her character reveals a stubborn woman who refused to reveal her formula. She rejected Sir Frederick

Banting's government-orchestrated offer to test Essiac in his Toronto laboratories and demanded that her human tests be accepted, insisting there was no need to experiment further on mice and chickens. Caisse challenged cancer research organizations, which appeared to be dragging their feet on spending their funds to locate a cancer cure while defaming other efforts to stamp out the scourge.

Rene Caisse was persuasive. When she needed legal advice, she found supportive lawyers in her own camp. Her federal and provincial government representatives were major champions within their limits. She defended the cause she believed in, and, until her death at age ninety, continued to correspond with major U.S. cancer institutes in an attempt to rekindle their interest in more Essiac trials.

In 1977, the Rene Caisse saga exploded in the national media with an article published in *Homemaker's Magazine*, putting additional pressure on the provincial and federal governments to take action in favour of her remedy. A year before her death in 1978, Rene Caisse gave the Essiac formula to a small firm called Resperin Corporation, which was directed by entrepreneur David Fingard, former Ontario minister of health Dr. Matthew Dymond, and other reputable doctors, as well as uranium guru Stephen Roman, who was the money behind the venture.

An Essiac formula, obtained from a mysterious source, was revealed to the public in an American video in 1988, and the making of Essiac went underground. Facsimiles and embellished herbal preparations that claim to be the Caisse formula are widely available in health food stores and pharmacies, as are the herbs to make the Caisse herbal tea. Thousands of publications and anecdotes, in print and on the Internet, can be read throughout the world about this remarkable woman and her remedy. But this volume is the only accurate, documented, and originally researched account of her struggle to bring her remedy to acceptance.

Rene M. Caisse is known throughout the world. Her legacy to new generations of cancer victims is her herbal tea, for which she never charged, along with her philosophy of hope.

CHAPTER 1

CAISSE FAMILY COMES TO BRACEBRIDGE

It was 1879, and for more than ten years pioneers had been encouraged to set down roots with free land grants in the picturesque region surrounding the village of Bracebridge. Incorporated in Ontario's Victoria County, the community was some 180 kilometres north of fashionable Toronto. The magnificent waterfalls in the heart of the village provided power for its industrious mills and access to the Muskoka rivers and lakes. But the few streets were muddy, and travel in and out of the community was by stagecoach and ox carts.

That year, Joseph and Friselda[1] Caisse, who arrived with their young daughter, Albina, named after Joseph's sister, and infant son, Joseph Jr., were among the first families to wander the new wooden plank walks and explore the young village of 750 souls. Joseph and Friselda had married on October 8, 1876, in Peterborough, situated in the eastern portion of the county, where the children were born. Joseph's father, also called Joseph, grew up in Quebec, as did Friselda's father, Louis Potvin. Both families originated in France and immigrated to Quebec in the 1700s.

The young newlyweds — he was about twenty-three years of age and she twenty-one[2] — stayed for a year or so in Bracebridge while Joseph worked at the Muskoka Leather Company,[3] one of the largest tanneries in the Dominion. In the fall of 1880, after the birth of their second daughter, Permelia, the family returned to Peterborough, where Joseph trained as a barber.

The future of Bracebridge looked bright and expansion seemed inevitable, so after February 9, 1882, when Friselda gave birth to a daughter named Louise to honour her father, Louis, the growing family decided to settle back in Muskoka. They travelled from Peterborough by steamboat, railway, and ox cart,[4] probably rumbling over the treacherous Victoria and Peterson Colonization roads that led into Muskoka Road and Bracebridge. The journey would indeed have been an adventure. Legend has it that Joseph liked to tell the story of their arrival. They had not arranged for accommodation, so apparently the kindly village constable broke into a vacant store, which had its own living quarters, near to their future home, and permitted the homeless family to live there temporarily.[5]

Later that year, Leon was born, named to honour Joseph's uncle Leon who had managed the grand Caisse's Hotel in Peterborough for many years. Joseph Sr. soon opened a barbershop to support his growing family. He became tenant on lots 35 and 36 of Muskoka Road West (later Manitoba Street) near the pork butcher, Henry Hines. Aseline was born in December 1883, Archie in August of the next year, and Lillian joined the family in October 1885. Little Archie died in August 1887.

The handsome and enterprising Joseph bought a wooden house on what was known as lot 32 Manitoba Street in May 1888, and the next spring he opened the J. Caisse Barbering Parlour there. Bracebridge property records at that time were unclear, providing a number of possibilities as to the exact location of the lot. It wasn't until years later that the street name and lot numbers were formalized.

A daughter, M. Rena, was born on August 11, 1888, and baptized Mary Anna in St. Joseph's Church a few days later. The family and official records generally suffer from a bewildering series of spellings. For her first three decades she would be called Rena; later she was known as Rene M. Caisse (pronounced "Reen Case"), the name that endured through a life of fame and frustration. For the purposes of this biography, I will use the latter throughout.

That particular month in 1888 was exciting not only for the Caisse family but also for the village, as the new leader of Canada's Liberal Party, Wilfrid Laurier, and his wife, Zoe, were holidaying in the area. Laurier, who took advantage of every audience, spoke to the party faithful in Bracebridge. Its streets, lit by oil lamps affixed to new iron posts, should have made a favourable impression on the well-travelled visitors. Also, plans were progressing for Bracebridge to become incorporated as a town in March 1889.

To complete the Caisse family, Edward was born in 1890, Victorine in 1892, and Elemere in 1902. A total of seventeen children were born to the family, and each of the eleven surviving children was to experience a solid Roman Catholic upbringing. The boys' names included "Joseph," and the girls', "Mary." It was "a happy and a Christian home, where the love and respect of our fellow man meant more to us than riches," Rene was to recall later.[6]

The family home and Joseph's barbershop with the red and white striped pole were at a prestigious location beside the town pump, and the Bank of Ottawa would begin erecting the community's first chartered bank next door in 1900. Young Joe, who had cut hair from the time he was eleven standing on a platform his father had built around one chair, had by then outgrown his nickname, "the Boy Barber." The hours stretched from seven o'clock in the dark mornings until eleven o'clock at night, and over every chair hung two large coal oil lamps connected by a double reflector to cast a good light.[7]

Photo:Town of Bracebridge

The Caisse children stand at their father's barbershop in the 1880s.

Joseph purchased the adjoining vacant lot to the south in 1895; three years later, friends lifted his house and turned it sideways. He added stores with sturdy plate glass windows fronting on Manitoba Street and upper living space for the family.[8] The early structure, later bricked, still can be seen at the rear of the building, and remnants of the stone wall Joseph built in 1905 to hold back the loose soil are still visible.

Friselda was a fine milliner and seamstress, skills she would pass on to her daughters. The eldest, Albina, opened her own millinery business next to her father's barbershop. As his barbering business grew, Joseph proudly installed a compressed air apparatus, making his shop as "complete as it can be."[9] Being a pipe smoker, Joseph operated a successful smokes business as well.

RENE BEGINS SCHOOL

The Caisse children attended elementary classes at the six-room Central School just south of the Roman Catholic church on McMurray Street. When Rene was ten years old, her father served as a school trustee. At sixteen, Rene was shorter than most of the girls her age and showing the beginnings of what would become a lifetime weight problem. She wasn't among the highest ranking students in the senior classes of the Continuation School, but she successfully passed what were called the "entrance exams" in June 1904.[10]

Caroline J.P. Boyer family collection

Rene stands to the right of her friends in the Entrance Class, 1904.

One bitterly cold evening in February 1905, Rene acted as one of three chaperones when a group of young people drove horse-drawn wagons to Gravenhurst and back. It was a long, frosty, thirty-five-kilometre round trip, but it was a pleasant evening of dancing. Rene delighted in a number of activities, including ladies' hockey. At a benefit for the Citizen's Band in the winter of 1906, she played the winning game brilliantly as captain of her team.[11] She must have shared her father's love of sports. Back in 1883, he was one of the main participants in the first lacrosse match ever exhibited in Bracebridge.[12]

For years, all the family travelled back and forth to Peterborough to visit with Friselda's family, the Potvins, and during the summer of 1906 Rene spent three months with them in their lovely home.[13] For a few months in the fall of 1907, Rene worked at an unknown position in Toronto,[14] returning home in time for Christmas.[15]

Albina, Joseph, Permelia, Louise, Aseline, Lillian, Leon, Rene, Victorine, Edward, and Elemere.

Happily, Rene took the morning train to Gravenhurst on July 6, 1908, to begin a summer job as a stewardess on one of the popular passenger steamers owned by the Muskoka Lakes Navigation and Hotel Company. The newspaper reported that Rene worked on the *Muskoka*, but a steamboat historian records that the crippled vessel had its last active season in 1907 and was succeeded in June 1908 by the new *Cherokee*.[16] No evidence has been found to explain just when the *Muskoka* fully retired, but it seems Rene might have sailed the maiden voyage of the luxurious, four-hundred-passenger steamer *Cherokee* to Bala. Summer cruises on steamers were the delight of thousands of passengers who still enjoy the beauty of the Muskoka Lakes in this manner.

Meanwhile, Rene's brothers and sisters were pursuing their own careers and dreams, and travelled amazing distances to experiment with working and living in Toronto and in Northern Ontario towns. Her older sisters Albina, Permelia, and Louise (who also played hockey) all created fashionable ladies' hats. Albina offered trimmed, handmade hats for the princely sum of two dollars and plain ones for fifty cents in her emporium next to her father's barbershop, while Permelia and Louise (Lou) worked with feathers and bows in Albina's branch shop in Port Arthur.[17] Permelia stayed in Port Arthur for years. When the Bracebridge millinery shop closed in 1908, Joseph used the space to sell souvenirs, sporting goods, and stationery.[18, 19] Lillian (Lily) followed her future husband, Alf Slater, south to sophisticated Toronto, were shops and commerce beckoned. Joe Jr. continued to work with his father in the barbershop, and Aseline, Leon, Edward, Victorine, and Elemere (Babe) remained in Bracebridge.

Bracebridge, with a population of over twenty-nine hundred, was a hub for the adventurer. Bold young men, most without specific skills, some with young families, could venture as far as five hundred kilometres north to the mining camps at Haileybury, Cobalt, Timmins, and the surrounding gold-and silver-rich country. In the "New Ontario," they took various jobs; one or two were young doctors. Some came home with the terrible typhoid, and George Denniss returned from Cobalt thinking it was not "a very desirable place to live."[20] But there was much interest in that area's dynamic development, and everyone in Bracebridge knew someone who was exploring the opportunities in Temiskaming country.

Rene's family enjoyed the best of Muskoka. As the era of grand hotels began to decline, the popularity of the lakeside retreat grew. Every manner of cottage, from the comfortable to the elaborate, began to spring up on shores of the Muskoka Lakes. Prosperity meant that Joseph could also afford to have a summer home, and in 1913 he purchased an island from members of the Beaumont family for $250.[21, 22] Rene would row or canoe on the Muskoka River, right up to the magnificent Bracebridge Falls in town, and dock at her father's boathouses, where he kept his gasoline-powered boat.[23] She spent happy days with friends and family at their cottages near the mouth of the river at Alport, which would become a meeting place over the years for all the brothers, sisters, and extended family for a week, a month, or all of the summer.

RENE CAISSE, THE NURSE

Rene finally took steps towards her lifetime ambition to become a nurse and help what she called "suffering humanity." Family doctor William D. McIlmoyle took surgery courses at New York's Bellevue Hospital and Greenwich City Hospital, Connecticut, before he came to Bracebridge. He might have suggested that she consider training in one of the schools of nursing in the United States, as did so many of the young would-be nurses of her day.[24, 25]

So in February 1909, now in her twenty-first year, Rene left the familiar and secure surroundings of her small town to travel to the exciting islands of New York City.[26] There she visited Brooklyn and crossed the state border into Greenwich, Connecticut, to study nursing at the private hospital run by Dr. Fritz Carlton Hyde.[27] Dr. Hyde and his wife, both young medical doctors from Michigan, shared a strong mutual interest in nursing education, and establishing this course in September 1906 was the fulfilment of their dream.[28]

Greenwich Library

Dr. Hyde's twenty-four-bed hospital in Greenwich, Connecticut.

For Rene it was hard, sometimes depressing work, but she found it satisfying. She enjoyed the patients, and they depended on her. She was taught to respect the doctor; she would recognize later that that respect was actually to the point of total domination by physician over nurse.[29] Among the subjects she studied were the making and application of various poultices and blistering to relieve poisons. She also became skilled at wet and dry cupping, which caused a vacuum effect on the skin to allow bloodletting. Young nurses were not encouraged to read medical books, presumably to leave the practice of pure medicine to the physicians and not overburden "their brains with useless knowledge which she would probably not remember much longer than overnight."[30]

The strict set of rules did not allow for innovation, as the young students were expected to perform each duty with rigid compliance.[31] Rene's long day included prayers at 6:15 a.m. — generally non-sectarian, although praying with a Presbyterian or Congregational minister must have been an interesting experience for the loyal Roman Catholic woman from Bracebridge.

She looked crisp in her blue and white gingham uniform with the bib and seventy-two-inch gathered apron. A smart organdy cap, black lisle stockings, and high black-laced shoes completed her uniform.

Rene would have been one of the last nurses to graduate from Dr. Hyde's hospital in Greenwich, although no records of the school of survive. By now the new Greenwich Hospital, which

Dr. Hyde would head for years as president of staff, had its own school of nursing.

Rene, now a graduate nurse, returned to Bracebridge just over a year later in March 1910.[32, 33] She caught up on family events that had transpired during her absence, including the frightening fire in the spare bedroom that had burned the dresser, its fittings, and several articles of apparel, but thankfully had hurt no one. Rene's mother and father had spent a few days at the lake while the smoke cleared.[34]

Jobs for young nurses at that time were limited to private duty nursing in homes, at least in Ontario. For instance, the few doctors in Bracebridge directed their patients to Mrs. Arnott, who worked full-time making her home available to sick people and assisting in the birth of babies from miles around. It would be at least another decade or so before an up-do-date centre would be run as a Red Cross outpost hospital, but there were other opportunities in Northern Ontario. So, not yet working in February 1911, Rene and her sister Lou took a winter holiday with their family in Peterborough.

While Rene had been away at nursing school, an epidemic of typhoid fever had continued to rage in the Temiskaming region north of North Bay, and Toronto newspapers advertised positions for one hundred nurses to aid the victims for a salary of fifty dollars a month with free board and lodgings. Since 1907 the Red Cross hospitals had been desperate for dozens of courageous nurses to join them in the Cobalt area where the silver and gold mining communities were developing. Prospectors and loggers were opening up the Temiskaming region by crashing roads through its rich wilderness, and the new communities were bursting with people, many of whom desperately needed medical care. Rene decided to help. After all, she had heard about the Northern Ontario excitement from the myriad Bracebridge people who had taken jobs and residences there.

TEMISKAMING, NORTHERN ONTARIO

As she made her plans to go north, Rene took part in the best of the Bracebridge scene. At the winter carnival in February 1912 she was judged Belle of Masquerade Ball, and her sister Aseline shared a prize with Marie Dunn for the best ladies' costume.[35, 36]

Rene travelled on the "Cobalt Express" train to the Temiskaming region and into a world of challenge. It is presumed that she worked in the three tiny outpost hospitals of Elk Lake, Gowganda, and Cobalt, as there were administrative connections among them all and photos appear to place her in at least two of them.

Greenwich Library

Nurse Caisse and an unidentified colleague step into the snow at the Elk Lake Hospital, c1912.

Rene would have jumped from the train at Latchford in one of Northern Ontario's coldest, snowiest winters, travelling through nearly ninety kilometres of bush and rock northwest along the frozen Montreal River to Elk Lake. In the summers, thanks to the Upper Ontario Steamboat Company, she would have been able to travel from Latchford to Elk Lake by a two-storey steamboat, portaging by foot over shallow spots with oxen or horses pulling the cargo.[37, 38] It wouldn't be until February 1913 that the Temiskaming and Northern Ontario Railway steamed into Elk Lake, making life very much easier for everyone.[39] When Rene arrived, the small settlement boasted the J.R. Booth lumbering operations with mill, a blacksmith shop, bunkhouses, and other buildings.[40] The cozy log Red Cross hospital run by Dr. G.L. Cockburn's small medical team served lumbermen and silver miners alike.

The Elk Lake silver mining operations reported to the "mother camp" at Cobalt, as did those at Gowganda. Soon Rene travelled to that community another ninety kilometres past Elk Lake to work in a small field hospital run by the Canadian Red Cross Nursing Outpost Hospital Service in co-operation with the mining companies. During the tough two weeks' journey by sled on the horse and wagon trail,[41] travellers bundled up in buffalo hides, tucking hot

Rene, third from left, top, with nursing sisters at the typhoid tents, c1912.

bricks under their robes and long skirts in the open sleighs drawn by powerful horses, and took refuge overnight in the stopping places that dotted the crude road. Warm scarves would have protected Rene's beautiful brown hair, which was normally topped with spectacular hats made by her talented sisters.

Many of Rene's patients would have been prospectors and silver miners from the Miller Lake–O'Brien Mine six kilometres away,[42] so she and her nursing colleagues would trail through the bush on snowshoes when necessary. The rural outpost had accommodation for one or two bed-patients, but field nursing was the chief work of the nurses.[43] The tiny hospital handled everything from miners' accidents, burns from the frequent fires that would consume homes and bush, to severe typhoid disease. Typhoid wasn't new to Rene, as several young Bracebridge men had contracted it while venturing in the Cobalt area, including Albert Fradette,[44] who suffered in August 1909.

The larger Red Cross hospital in Cobalt was stretched beyond its capacity as early as 1906. And although they didn't own it, the mining companies paid the expenses of the wooden hospital and demanded that miners be assisted first, leaving the townspeople at great risk. Rene arrived just as the typhoid epidemic that was ravaging the miners and residents of Cobalt alike reached its peak. The deplorable unsanitary conditions, which included privies made out of packing cases and an absence of sewers in the mud-covered, rock-faced streets, were slowly being corrected. But the offensive, perilous cases she handled went far beyond the courses taught in the Connecticut nursing school.

As compared with the log bush hospitals, Cobalt's frame hospital, which the provincial Board of Health arranged to be built in 1909, was relatively sophisticated and comfortable. Alongside the hospital were the Boer War surplus tents that accommodated twenty-five beds sent by train from Toronto as the typhoid epidemic grew and hospital space was urgently needed. Here Rene nursed women during childbirth, attended to local merchants, visiting geologists and investors, and dirty, rough itinerant miners. The nursing superintendent, Dorothy May Beebee, ran the hospital with a firm British hand.[45]

Rene travelled throughout the northern territory under difficult conditions because not all patients were hospitalized. However, there were humorous sides to unexpected incidents, such as one that occurred while she was at the home of a young woman awaiting the birth of her first baby. When the two doctors failed to turn up as promised at their designated hour, Rene had to deliver the child. Meanwhile, the gowns they had left were accidentally burned on the hot stove when the pan of water there evaporated. When they arrived at the scene, both doctors were dismayed at the sight and annoyed with her. Years later, she would always smile as she recalled this adventure.[46]

Rene always kept a low profile in Northern Ontario, moving from town to town and from one Red Cross hospital to another to help fulfil the demand for nursing staff for a few months or a year.

RENE'S NEW HOME IN HAILEYBURY

The Cobalt hospital was sold to the Sisters of Providence, who joined the group of nurses already caring for terribly sick typhoid victims. The plan of the sisters to replace the temporary 1908 hospital with a fine new one up in Haileybury was realized in 1913–14 when the Roman Catholic Diocese of Haileybury built an impressive five-storey hospital of Temiskaming greystone overlooking Lake Temiskaming. The gracious homes of the newly wealthy dotted the shoreline in the lovely town about eight kilometres north of Cobalt. Rene took advantage of updating courses offered at the Sisters of Providence Hospital[47] and advanced to head nurse,[48] the usual classification for a graduate nurse employed in a hospital at that time.[49]

In a town that could not distinguish between the seasons, Rene would have noticed that "spring was merely a dwindling of winter, with mud instead of snow and yet an occasional snowstorm as late as the end of May just by way of reminder."[50] Doctors such as John McInnis, Herbert Minthorn, and Charles Hair, who would all take significant roles later in Rene's career, launched their professions in Haileybury during the 1906–1910 period. Dr. O.V. Colbeck, son-in-law of Bracebridge's postmaster, Robert Perry, moved his practice to this town in 1909 and remained there until 1915, when he joined the armed services and left for France. Young Dr. Cliff (W.C.) Arnold, whose hearing impairment had been caused by typhoid, would remain in Haileybury throughout his career.[51] Arthur Slaght, a keen lawyer who also resided there at the time, would later become a politician and take a role in Rene's drama during the 1930s. There was also a bright boy called Leslie McFarlane, who would soon grow up to become one of Canada's most prominent writers and pen twenty-six of the Hardy Boys books under the *nom de plume* Franklin W. Dixon.

RENE LEAVES NORTHERN ONTARIO

Rene Caisse had dedicated a great deal of energy and emotion to the sick and injured of several mining regions in Northern Ontario. Now twenty-seven years old, she was still single. Her homes had been a room in someone's house and a variety of staff residences, and she was a long way from her family. Rene had really had enough of the isolation in the rugged mining country, and life for her had lost its enchantment. She had seen many of the young men of the area, including doctors and Native men, follow their patriotic calling to the Great War in Europe. Some of Rene's Bracebridge comrades had joined the 122nd Muskoka Battalion. Two of her hometown friends, May Bird and Grace Mahaffey, had joined nursing corps and were in Egypt and England. Even Superintendent Beebee of Cobalt had returned to England to be of assistance in her homeland when the war broke out in 1914.[52]

In 1915, Rene arrived at a personal decision to leave the Temiskaming region and re-establish her life. Her sister Louise's husband, Otto Stortz, had been transferred from Bracebridge by his employer, the Bank of Ottawa, to Edmonton, Alberta, and subsequently to Emerson, Manitoba, and Rene missed Louise and her twin nephews. Rene accepted their invitation to join them in the delightful little Red River Valley town, located about eighty kilometres south of Winnipeg on the U.S. border.

While Emerson did not have its own hospital at that time, Drs. Wallace and Ross worked co-operatively with those in the small hospital sixteen kilometres to the north in Dominion City. Seriously ill patients would be sent by train directly to Winnipeg where Rene sometimes worked, or, as local historian E.D. McClelland related, "they simply turned up his or her toes and died."[53] There would have been opportunities for Rene to deliver babies throughout the area, as the busy midwives would have undoubtedly appreciated her experienced hand.

In early April 1916, all members of the family, including Rene and Louise, were summoned to the bedside of their seriously ailing father in Bracebridge.[54] Joseph had become ill three years earlier with heart problems and had been forced to give up some of his activities, including his coveted seat on town council.[55] Rene stayed at the Manitoba Street home to nurse and comfort him. Joseph Caisse Sr. died less than three months later, on July first, at only sixty-one years of age.[56]

Meanwhile, Otto had remained in Emerson to deal with a frightening flood that was forcing its way up the Red River. Although not nearly as severe as others before or after, the rising torrent pushed enough water along Main Street in Emerson to float a boat. The staff at the Bank of Ottawa were fortunately able to raise their cash vault on timbers high enough to escape the unwelcome water.[57]

Friselda spent the winter of 1916–17 visiting her children, many of whom were married and living in distant places, and making soldiers' pyjamas for the Women's Auxiliary of the Red Cross. The cash from Joseph's $1,000 life insurance policy, which he had bought in 1906, allowed her a little financial dignity and freedom to travel.[58] Albina had married George Allen in 1913 and was living in Calgary. Aseline and her husband, Joseph Bagan, whom she had wed in 1914, and her unmarried sister Permelia were in Port Arthur (Thunder Bay), still running her millinery business. Edward worked on lake dredgers out of Buffalo, N.Y., while Victorine (Mrs.

Irving) Walker, Joseph, Leon, and fourteen-year-old Elemere were still living in Bracebridge.

Rene's older brother Leon left shortly for Hamilton, where he worked for the Great War effort in a munitions factory until early 1917, when he enlisted in the Forestry Regiment of Muskoka's 122nd Battalion and departed for France. In June, Joseph Jr. married Ella Fradette and continued to operate his barbershop in Bracebridge.[59]

CAISSE FAMILY MOVES TO TORONTO

It seems that Rene did not return to Emerson, Manitoba, after the death of her father, but following a round of farewell parties in October 1917[60] left for Toronto with her mother and youngest sister.[61] Thus began Friselda's routine of wintering in Toronto and enjoying summers at Lake Muskoka. She rented a home in Toronto at 108 St. Vincent, large enough to accommodate Rene and Elemere. In 1918 she arranged for Bell telephone services, which turned out to be an essential comfort.[62] In the late summer, Rene travelled with her mother and Elemere to the Potvin family summer home in Peterborough for a family get-together.[63]

In October, Army Private Leon returned to Canada after months in English hospitals, where he was being treated for debilitating trench foot, which developed in the terrible battle trenches in France. Unable to walk, he was sent to the Toronto General Hospital, where he underwent surgery and therapy. At that time, the hospital was on Gerrard Street East and served returning veterans. Meanwhile, Rene suffered a bad case of pleuropneumonia, which was in epidemic proportions in the city.[64] The family received tragic word two months later that Rene's cousin Edward Bonhomme had died of war wounds and pneumonia in France.[65, 66] His mother, Albina, was awarded a Silver Cross to honour her son's bravery in the Great War, and now the medal resides in the Central Muskoka Branch 161 of the Royal Canadian Legion, Bracebridge.[67]

Rene soon regained her health. Leon could walk again and decided to live in Toronto, returning to Bracebridge for an occasional visit after his long two years away. Rene lived for a while with some of her relatives in Peterborough in the summer of 1920 and later vacationed with her mother and family at their comfortable cottages at Muskoka Lake.

In late 1920 Friselda moved from central Toronto, as there were plans to close her street and demolish houses to accommodate huge government buildings and a hospital,[68] and rented a larger two-storey house at 17 Parkside Drive overlooking picturesque High Park. While Rene's brother Joseph maintained the Manitoba Street home in Bracebridge, her other two brothers and two of her sisters shared their mother's house as they established themselves with jobs in the city. It is presumed that Rene, who was not listed with the others in the city directory, lived in the three-bedroom house as well. For a period, Edward was a salesman at Aikenhead Hardware, Leon was an Eaton's employee, Elemere worked in a branch of the Bank of Montreal, and Permelia,[69] who had just left Port Arthur, ran a millinery business at Macdonnell and Queen streets.[70] But life for Rene was tedious.

CHAPTER 2

MORE NURSING TRAINING

During the winter of 1920–21, Rene was seriously considering her future, particularly because of pending provincial legislation that would become law in 1922. This new act, the Nurses' Registration Act, encouraged voluntary registration of professional nurses in Ontario, and plans were being made for a compulsory examination to earn an "RN" designation to take place in 1926. Since the sequence of her life was disrupted anyway, in 1921 Rene travelled to Whitby (a town some fifty kilometres east of Toronto) and enrolled in classes conducted by Gertrude Bryan, the superintendent of the School of Nursing at the Ontario Hospital for the Insane.[71] Although she had trained as a nurse in the U.S. and Haileybury,[72] Rene knew that she needed instruction in more recent techniques to prepare for new provincial requirements. Rene was employed as a "nurse in training,"[73] brushing up on first-year subjects such as the cardiovascular system and medical terminology.[74, 75]

The classes took only six hours per week. Even with her responsibilities for the patients, she still had lots of time to write poetry, a hobby that transported her into romance, humour, and fashion. Liquor prohibition, flappers, unrequited love, and the indecency of the dress of young women were among her favourite topics. Her romantic thoughts were expressed in this poem:

Last night I dreamed of you.
I dreamed that your love
For me was true.
I lifted my eyes to heaven above
And begged for love, "dear heart",
And there isn't a thing, dear,
I wouldn't do
To win your heart and
Show you I'm true.[76]

The hospital in Whitby was pleasantly situated in secluded grounds offering peaceful and private patient therapy, but Rene was not enjoying life in this remote country setting. Hoping to add more dimension to her life, she applied for a nursing position at a Toronto hospital. In the spring of 1921 she wrote to Dr. Harvey Clare,[77] the medical superintendent of the Ontario Hospital at 999 Queen Street, which was not far from the family home on Parkside Drive.

In a letter dated April 14, 1921, to his counterpart at the Hospital for the Insane at Whitby, Ontario, Dr. Clare asked Dr. James M. Forster for his recommendation as to her suitability for the nursing profession. The next day Dr. Forster responded enthusiastically, saying, "She was quite a capable nurse, and I will be very glad if you will give her a chance."[78] The Ontario Hospital's records are sealed, so it is impossible to verify if Rene did gain employment there, but evidence later in the year suggests that she remained instead at Whitby to continue her course with Miss Bryan.

After spending a dismal New Year's Eve alone in 1921, the isolation of the hospital in Whitby was now really depressing her. Rene had the dreams most young women have — of a home, a man to love, and maybe children someday — and her loneliness was expressed in many of the poems she wrote. This poem, dated 1921–22,[79] summed up the past few months of a melancholy life:

Tis twelve o'clock,
The year has flown,
And still I'm in my mother's home.
I hope that next year by this time
I'll have a little home all mine.
And if I do, I hope that you
Will help me see the old year through.
The year has flown,
I'm all alone.
I wish to God
I had a home.
If I had one
I'd no more roam.
I'd spend my New Year's Eve
at home.

By 1922, Rene was in her thirty-fourth year and still feeling unsettled, yearning to establish a home of her own.[80] Instead, she left the Whitby Hospital's retraining program by early spring, just missing by a year or so the arrival of Mabel and Hazel Hurlburt from Bracebridge, who came to begin their classes.[81] Rene returned to her mother's house on Parkside Drive, just steps from the whirl and excitement of Toronto's new Sunnyside Amusement Park. During the summer she, her mother, and her sisters Permelia and Elemere enjoyed the Caisse cottage at Muskoka Lake. Sisters Albina and Louise of Winnipeg and brother Leon of Detroit joined the local family members for a traditional family get-together.[82] Soon Rene was working with several Toronto doctors, probably assisting them in an office that smelled of ether. She may have aided them in removing children's tonsils at home on their kitchen tables, when they prescribed tingling ginger ale and soothing ice cream for the patients' painful throats. Dr. Robert O. Fisher, one physician Rene worked with at that time, had a busy practice at his large home at 343 Sherbourne Street; he would become a colleague of hers for many years.

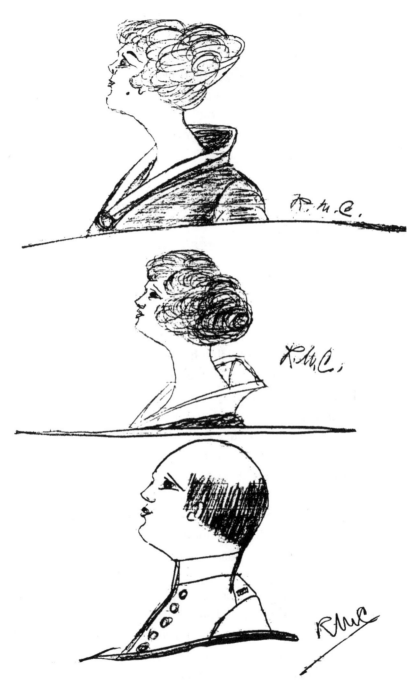

One can only imagine who the fashionable ladies and gentleman were in Rene's sketches, c1922.

SCENE OF RENE'S DISCOVERY DESTROYED

It is is widely thought that 1922 was the year during which Rene learned about an herbal remedy for cancer while nursing in Haileybury. This date has been presumed since the *Toronto Daily Star* first reported her story on January 23, 1932.[83] In 1937 Rene told a Huntsville reporter that "after ten years of steady service to cancer sufferers" she wanted to be recognized.[84] Rene herself narrated the story about her work — "In the mid-twenties I was head nurse at the Sisters of Providence Hospital in a northern Ontario town" — in the 1966 memoir I Was *"Canada's Cancer Nurse."*[85] Eleven years later, at eighty-eight years of age, Rene seemed not to wish to contradict herself and told the authors of "Could Essiac Halt Cancer?" that she was nursing in Haileybury in 1922.[86]

During the autumn of 1922, the year that Dr. Frederick G. Banting, Dr. Charles Best, and their colleagues discovered insulin at the University of Toronto, the people living in Northern Ontario endured a terrifying fire in the Temiskaming district. It was called one of the ten worst disasters in Canadian history and destroyed Haileybury, causing terrible anguish.

In those days, fires were commonplace in the frame and log buildings of mining communities, and while Rene was in the Haileybury area, she would have witnessed a number of raging blazes that instantly levelled homes and businesses. Had she been present on October 4 and 5, 1922, when fire again swept through the Temiskaming district, destroying 90 percent of Haileybury in particular, and leaving eleven of its people dead and three thousand homeless, she would never have forgotten the horror, especially the sight of the Sisters of Providence Hospital being gutted. The handsome stone hospital, in which Rene had worked, was ruined by the fire, its records and equipment destroyed.[87] The nursing sisters heroically carried patients out of the burning hospital, and many patients were transferred at great risk to Lady Minto Hospital in New Liskeard, about six kilometres along the lake to the north.

The Sisters of Providence Hospital, an ashen skeleton after the 1922 fire.

Dr. Cliff Arnold was forced to operate on a patient in a hastily made tent of blankets along the way. Dr. Arnold and his wife were among the families who set up temporary homes in sixty old streetcars that were donated to Haileybury by the Toronto Transportation Commission. The TTC had just introduced their new Peter Witt models, and the outdated streetcars were available for an extended life as protective shelters for fire victims. The homeless residents who weren't fortunate enough to get one of the chilly streetcars were given enough lumber to build a sixteen-by-sixteen-foot dwelling. Desperately needing an office to examine patients, Dr. Arnold was forced to build a shed on the side of their modest streetcar-home.

Bracebridge, Rene's hometown, took a significant role in providing relief to the victims of the fire. The local papers published spectacular stories for weeks, alongside grim lists of deaths — including some former Muskokans.[88,89] Bracebridge lawyer R.M. Best wrote about his experiences during the "holocaust,"[90] and Arthur G. Slaght fled the burning courthouse.[91] Through the encouragement of the Board of Trade and town council, residents raised an astounding $1,000 cash, which was sent north along with an entire refrigerated railroad car full of food and clothing to help their ten thousand destitute neighbours face the winter.[92, 93, 94] Further assistance was requested in December by the Northern Ontario Relief Committee run from the Royal Bank building in Toronto.[95]

There is no record of Rene ever reflecting on the disastrous Haileybury fire of October 1922 during interviews given over the years. The Bracebridge newspapers listed the dozens of Bracebridge individuals and families who were in Haileybury during the fire and Rene was not mentioned. There is no evidence of her working in Haileybury that year, but rather it seems that she was studying nursing at Whitby Hospital and holidaying in Muskoka. She may have still been looking for a hospital job and likely nursing doctors' patients in Toronto.[96] The "1922" dated recollections could have been innocently recalled when, in fact, her discovery of the remedy might have taken place ten years earlier. This would better match the narrative of her life and work in the Temiskaming region as previously related, as well as her uncanny likenesses in various photos of the period. Those memories, a random collage of anecdotal histories, have been perpetuated in countless print and online publications ever since.

The possibility that Rene Caisse may have spent a few weeks in Haileybury in mid-1922 can only be explained if perhaps she assisted at the hospital during the vacation of the head nurse.[97] But within a year or so after the fire, the diocese made the decision not to rebuild their charred, defunct hospital.

Whatever the date, Rene was to recall that she had nursed "a patient up north"[98] and that one day one of her nurses was bathing an elderly patient whose one breast was a mass of scar tissue. Rene related the woman's story in her 1966 memoir as follows:[99]

> "I came out of England nearly 30 years ago," she told me. "I joined my husband, who was prospecting in the wilds of Northern Ontario. My right breast became sore and swollen, and very painful. My husband brought me to Toronto, and the doctors told me I had advanced cancer and my breast must be

removed at once. Before we left camp a very old Indian medicine man had told me I had cancer, but he could cure it. I decided I'd just as soon try his remedy as to have my breast removed. One of my friends had died from breast surgery. Besides, we had no money."

She and her husband returned to the mining camp, and the old Indian showed her certain herbs growing in the area, told her to make a tea from these herbs, and to drink it every day. [A small Temagami band of the Ojibwa tribe had a summer rendezvous at the Hudson's Bay post on Bear Island, Lake Temagami, at that time.[100]] She was nearly 80 years old when I saw her, and there had been no recurrence of cancer. I was much interested, and wrote down the names of the herbs she had used. I knew that doctors threw up their hands when cancer was discovered in a patient; it was the same as a death sentence, just about. I decided that if I should ever develop cancer, I would use this herb tea.[101]

In nursing school, Rene had learned that surgical removal of carcinomas offered little evidence that they wouldn't recur in some other part of the body at some future date.[102] She continued:

About a year later I was visiting an aged retired doctor whom I knew well. We were walking slowly about his garden when he took his cane and lifted a weed. "Nurse Caisse," he told me, "if people would use this weed, there would be little or no cancer in the world." He told me the name of the plant. It was one of the herbs my patient had named as an ingredient of the Indian medicine man's tea!"[103]

In 1932 Rene would tell a reporter, "By elimination, gradually, I discovered what must have been the plant that contained the active principle."[104] These events inadvertently set the course of her working life, spanning almost the next five decades, thrusting her into a medical-legal-political controversy that stretched across the province and into the United States.

RENE'S AUNT GIVEN HERBAL TEA

When Rene's favourite aunt, Mireza Potvin of Peterborough, was in the Brockville hospital for an operation, they took away only enough tissue for a biopsy.[105] She was diagnosed by two prominent doctors as having terminal cancer of the stomach with liver involvement and was given six months or less to live.[106] Apparently the whole stomach was so corrugated with the disease that they simply closed up the wound and left her to die.[107]

Upon being discharged from the regional cancer centre in Brockville, Mireza was taken to her sister Friselda's High Park home to be cared for by Dr. Fisher. Now Rene had an opportunity to try out the Indian herbal remedy, which she had been studying for some time. She asked the doctor for permission to treat her aunt, and he consented because there was nothing else his profession had to offer. Mireza was apparently dying. Rene gave her one drink daily of the freshly brewed decoction for two months until she rallied and went to her home in Peterborough to recuperate.

Rene was greatly encouraged by her aunt's steady improvement, and Dr. Fisher, impressed with the effects of the remedy, asked her to treat more of his hopeless cases. Some patients responded well, and as other Toronto physicians heard of the positive effects of the herbal treatments, they too brought their terminal patients to Rene. Some responded with great improvement.

From her cozy rooms at 27 Breadalbane Street,[108] just around the corner from where she had previously stayed with her mother on St. Vincent, Rene enjoyed going to Dr. Fisher's office on Sherbourne Street. His practice, like that of most doctors at the time, was in his home. It was a two-and-a-half-storey vine-covered brick house, set back from the street behind an attractive wrought-iron fence with inviting gates. The unpaved driveway was originally used by horse-drawn vehicles.[109] Rene would take moments to wander through the spectacular Allan Gardens, directly across the street. One might wonder if Rene realized that the castle-like house next door had been built by Henry and Mary Pellatt in 1898, long before they built their real Casa Loma in 1939. With its splendid homes, Sherbourne Street was indeed elegant Cabbagetown.

FIRST INJECTION

One day towards the end of 1924, a patient with cancer of the tongue and throat was brought to Rene and Dr. Fisher from Lyons, New York. At Dr. Fisher's suggestion, Rene injected the liquid remedy (containing eight herbs) directly into the man's tongue as Dr. Fisher and his young assistant Dr. Ross A. Blye stood by to observe the results.

"Well, I was nearly scared to death," Rene recalled. "The patient developed a severe chill and his tongue swelled so badly the doctor had to press it down with a spatula to allow him to breathe."[110]

This incident lasted about twenty minutes before the swelling went down and the shaking subsided. The cancer stopped growing, and while the patient never received another injection, he was able to live comfortably for almost four years.

After this alarming but challenging event, Rene set up a section of the basement of her mother's house as a laboratory. There she and Dr. Fisher began research on mice inoculated with human carcinoma. They studied the effect of administering the formula by injection rather than giving it orally as a tea. Rene found, "By giving the intramuscular injection in the forearm, to destroy the mass of malignant cells, and giving the medicine orally to purify the blood, I got quicker results."[111]

As they worked together, etiquette of the day would have prevented Rene from addressing Dr. Fisher less formally by his given name, "Rob." Each day Rene would brew a decoction of each of the eight dried herbs for injection into selected mice. Fisher and his colleagues, including Dr. Blye and Dr. E.T. Hoidge, who worked with them

Rene sits on the steps of her mother's house at 17 Parkside Drive.

from time to time, were unaware of the actual contents of the brew. Dr. Blye, whose practice was on Dundas Street East, "sent away to one of the most famous laboratories of the United States and obtained some carcinoma and sarcoma mice." Of eight mice received, four died before Rene could treat them, but "she kept the remaining four alive long after the time they could be kept by ordinary means."[112]

Experiments continued as Rene brewed varying decoctions over several months, eliminating first one herb and then another, until the researchers identified the herb that appeared to most effectively reduce the size of the tumours. By removing its protein content, they found that the substance could now be injected intramuscularly into the hind leg of a mouse, or the forearm of a human volunteer, without causing any reaction. This refinement appeared to carry off the toxins created by the malignancy, purify the blood, and increase the patients' energy and sense of well-being. "I got quicker results," Rene said, "than when the medicine was all given orally." Rene recorded with some pride that the mice implanted with human carcinoma responded well to nine days of herbal injections, until cancer was no longer invading living tissue. The tumours decreased in size and the mice lived longer. [113]

Dr. Fisher probably helped Rene to develop and refine her treatment more than any other physician. He dared Rene to try the injection and assisted her in singling out the herb that reduced tumours. Yet she never, it seemed, revealed to him the properties of the remedy.

Dr. R.O. Fisher helped refine Rene's herbal remedy.

Canadian Mothercraft Society

As word of the new cancer treatment spread, Dr. John A. McInnis heard about it. He enjoyed a very active medical and political life in the mining communities of Porcupine and Timmins, a morning's train ride northwest of Haileybury, which he had left in 1910. Dr. McInnis had been a Timmins councillor during 1916 and 1918 and mayor since 1919. In 1925, his final year in the mayor's chair, he invited Rene to treat a middle-aged diabetic patient with cancer of the bowel. So as not to interfere with its action, the woman's insulin medication was stopped when the herbal treatments began.

During the early treatments, the tumour became larger and harder, until it almost caused an obstruction in the bowel. X-ray pictures were taken during the next few months to see what was taking place. The tumour gradually softened and reduced in size until it was all gone. The treatments were discontinued after six months of weekly injections, yet the patient remained in good health with no trace of either cancer or diabetes.[114]

On or about November 10, 1925, when Dr. McInnis's diabetic cancer patient was almost well again, a group of Toronto physicians brought an eighty-year-old man to Rene.

Mr. Smith's face was eaten away by a malignant growth, and it was hemorrhaging so badly that the doctors predicted he would be dead within a week to ten days. The doctors gathered around Rene and watched her apply a swab of gauze soaked with a special solution containing bloodroot to the ugly open sore. Rene's treatment stopped the bleeding in hours.[115] After several treatments, given orally and by direct application, the growth began to shrink, and the massive sores on his chin started to heal. Photographs were taken before and after the treatments.[116] Mr. Smith's life was prolonged for more than five months, until finally he succumbed to pneumonia at Easter in 1926.

HERBAL TEA BECOMES "ESSIAC"

The herbal brew had been proven to be a viable treatment, and it was time for a name. In an enlightened and quite ingenious moment, Rene selected the name Essiac — her own surname spelled backwards — for the remedy. She had no idea what drama and turmoil the word "Essiac" would create in the arenas of medical science, governmental legislation, and merchandising competition of alternative medicines over the next several decades. And still Rene kept the identity of the herbs in Essiac a personal secret.

CHAPTER 3

ESSIAC IS DEVELOPED

RENE GATHERS SUPPORT

Rene was living in Toronto, thoroughly engrossed in studying her herbal concoction for the relief of cancer patients and working with various doctors at their offices. Since the healing of her aunt Mireza and the improvement of others who had received her treatment, Rene's confidence in her remedy swelled. The support of several physicians was particularly encouraging.

In 1926, the provincial requirement to sit for an examination to obtain an Ontario RN designation came into force. But Rene felt that she had more than proven her qualifications over the past fifteen years, having earned her nursing qualifications in the United States and taken brush-up courses in Haileybury and Whitby. It seems that Rene chose not to sit the exam.[117]

Some of the doctors exposed to the remarkable cancer remissions Rene had brought about felt that she should be given an opportunity to research her remedy more thoroughly. In October 1926, eight determined physicians sent a petition to the Canadian government department responsible for health in Ottawa. They had observed for themselves the effective results while working with Rene and asserted that:

> We, the undersigned, believe the treatment for cancer by Nurse R. M. Caisse can do no harm, and that it relieves pain, will reduce the enlargement, and prolong life in hopeless cases.

To the best of our knowledge, she has not been given a case to treat until everything in medical and surgical science has been tried without effect, and even then she was able to show remarkably beneficial results on those cases at the late stage.

We would be interested to see her given an opportunity to prove her work in a large way.

To the best of our knowledge she has treated all cases free of any charge and has been carrying on this work over the period of the past two years.

The document was signed by R.O. Fisher, R.A. Blye, J.A. McInnis, E.T. Hoidge, Chas. H. Hair, S. Moore, W.T. Williams, J.X. Robert.

Two of the signatories, Dr. Fisher and Dr. Blye, were her Toronto colleagues.[118] Others were local doctors, including Dr. Charles Hair,[119] whom she had probably worked with at the Cobalt Red Cross hospital; he was now a surgeon at the Toronto General Hospital. Then there were her Timmins supporters, Drs. McInnis and Moore.

To investigate this most intriguing petition and its implications under the recent amendments to the 1920 Food and Drugs Act, the federal government sent two employees of the Department of Pensions and National Health to inspect Rene's activities at her home on Breadalbane Street in Toronto. Dr. W.C. Arnold, head of the Pensions Branch, and his associate Dr. Edward H. Wood[120] presented her with official papers to inform her of her responsibilities under the Proprietary Medicines Act and the Food and Drugs Act. The doctors pointed out that she had no licence to administer her remedy, and although some thought she was practising medicine, it was not their role to interfere with the provincial authorities in such matters.[121]

Dr. William C. Arnold (1875–1960) was the doctor responsible for this task. Coincidentally, in Haileybury another Dr. W.C. Arnold (Walter Clifford, 1885–1971), medical officer of health in Northern Ontario, who had known her for many years, would have been eligible to investigate Rene's activities had she had been working in Bracebridge or farther north. This was a parallelism of amazing proportions!

Drs. Arnold and Wood quickly realized that Rene was treating only terminally ill patients with the permission of doctors, and she informed them of the therapeutic properties of Essiac and assured them that they had no reason to be concerned. Instead, the doctors recommended that she further experiment with mice at the laboratory facilities at Christie Street Hospital in Toronto. After Dr. Arnold promised to make arrangements for Rene to work on animal studies, the two men returned to Ottawa, taking the official papers with them. Interestingly, Dr. Arnold, while still in Ottawa, would support her activities in the near future.

DR. BANTING AT CHRISTIE STREET HOSPITAL

The veterans' hospital on central Toronto's Christie Street was actively researching several war injury related ailments and had broadened its interests. For instance, Dr. Frederick Banting had headed the diabetes clinic there since its inception in 1922 as one of the honours bestowed on him after his co-discovery of insulin.[122] Dr. Charles Hair took a role in encouraging Rene to see Dr. Banting at Christie Street Hospital, although he may have not remembered the young nurse. He was to relate years later, "I told her to take her internal medicine as well as the lotion for local treatment to Dr. Frederick Banting, have him definitely use the preparations in authentic cancer cases. If my memory serves me correctly, she did see him. Dr. McInnis of Timmins told me he was interested in it and I recall him telling me that he had one case that apparently had been cured."

Dr. Hair, by then a busy Toronto physician, would also recall that his introduction to Miss Caisse was through a mining man who he felt was interested in promoting a cancer cure commercially.[123] But he said, "I think it was 7 or 8 years ago." That would have placed their first meeting about four years *after* he signed the 1926 petition on Rene's behalf.

Rene recalled how she met Dr. Banting: "I was working with nine eminent doctors in Toronto when Dr. McInnis asked me to treat his diabetic patient in Timmins who had cancer of the bowel. It was after her recovery that Dr. Banting became interested, when Dr.

Dr. Charles Hair played various roles in Rene's career.

Dr. John A. McInnis of Timmins believed in Rene Caisse and Essiac. C1940.

McInnis and Dr. Minthorn prepared their report which they brought to him when the three of us arranged a meeting with him." [124]

However the meeting was initiated, it would have taken place in the latter part of 1926 after Rene's aunt and the diabetic patient in Timmins had recovered from their cancers, along with the dramatic improvement in Mr. Smith's condition. Rene showed Dr. Banting her case notes, X-ray records, and photographs of Mr. Smith's terrible face and remembered that Dr. Banting felt they were the best proof of her work. She was confident this was convincing scientific evidence to present to the medical profession, and who would be more influential than Dr. Banting?

Rene recalled that Dr. Banting said, "Essiac must activate the pancreatic gland into normal functioning, causing the diabetic

University of Toronto Archives

Dr. Frederick Banting shortly after he was acclaimed for isolating insulin, c1923.

condition to clear up. Otherwise, the patient would have had to take treatments for the rest of her life, just as she would have had to take insulin."[125] He continued, "I will not say you have a cure for cancer. But you have more evidence of a beneficial treatment for cancer than anyone in the world."[126]

One would wonder if Banting discussed his personal challenge to find the cure for cancer with Rene, a goal he set for himself after becoming fascinated by the work being done by English researcher William Gye. Gye was working with funds from the Imperial Cancer Research Fund to develop the tumour research with chickens begun by Peyton Rous of the Rockefeller Institute in 1911, and now Banting and his patient research assistant Sadie Gairns were subjecting hundreds of Plymouth Rock chickens to Rous sarcoma.[127, 128]

It was at this time that Dr. Banting advised Rene to apply to the University of Toronto for laboratory facilities to do deeper research. Banting's caution that her secret formula would have to be turned over to the board of governors really made her aware that "they" would then have the remedy. She figured that it would be filed in the archives and forgotten, or be used for university staff research — and her application to do independent research at the university could still be refused.[129]

Rene explained her dilemma: "Dr. Banting was a doctor and a recognized practitioner, so although he surrendered his formula to the profession under the medical code of ethics, he was honored and rewarded. I was in no professional position to secure acceptance of Essiac, or recognition for its discovery, if I surrendered my formula before the merit of the treatment was established beyond all doubt."[130]

Rene decided against Dr. Banting's suggestion and turned down his offer to work with her "after much soul searching and prayer."[131] He approved of her decision and her courage. Although he had discovered insulin, he did not claim it was a cure for diabetes. Similarly, Rene knew that Essiac was a palliative and deterrent.

She explained:

I wanted to establish my remedy, which I called Essiac or my name spelled backwards, in actual practice, not in a laboratory only. I knew it had no bad side effects, so it could do no harm. I wanted to use it on patients in my own way. And when the time came, I wanted to share in the administration of my own discovery. To do such a thing is impossible even today for any independent research worker, due to what I believe is nothing less than a conspiracy against finding a cure for cancer. I decided to prove my treatment on its own merit, without assistance if necessary.[132]

Rene recorded that during 1928–30 she worked on mice inoculated with Rous sarcoma with "Dr. Lockhead" and "Dr. Norich" (referring to Drs. G.W. Lougheed and Arthur C. Norwich) in the Christie Street Hospital laboratories.[133] She observed that mice that received nine Essiac injections lived fifty-two days — longer than anyone else had been able to keep them alive with other remedies. In a later experiment with two other doctors, she kept the mice alive for seventy-two days with Essiac.

In 1930, some 32 doctors and 50 graduate nurses served about 380 patients at Christie Street Hospital, primarily older veterans of the terrible Great War. This was the year, on September 17, that the prestigious Banting Institute, a costly new building across from Toronto General Hospital, was opened. Dr. Banting's department and several others were given quarters there, with his "research kingdom" on the top floor. He would have much preferred to work in a modest out-of-the-way laboratory, one of his biographers wrote.[134]

It appears that Rene shared her time during this two-year period with Dr. McInnis in Timmins, treating patients in his office as well as in her Toronto apartment, as nursing jobs in Toronto were few and far between. In Timmins Rene administered Essiac to a number of cancer patients, including Mrs. George Simpson. On March 16, 1928, Bella Simpson had been X-rayed, and, without a biopsy, Dr. McInnis and two specialists diagnosed carcinoma of the stomach and reported that surgery was not to be considered. She was so sick she could hardly walk around. Within two weeks of receiving the Essiac treatment her condition was greatly relieved, and Dr. McInnis recorded, "The patient was treated by Miss Caisse for a period of about 3 months with very marked improvement." Dr. McInnis told a *Toronto Daily Star* reporter that he fully believed she had a malignant growth, but a positive diagnosis of cancer was not proven.[135]

Mrs. Simpson wrote to Rene in Toronto in January 1930, saying, "I am feeling fine and expect to go to Toronto in the early summer, so will go to see you and also be examined by you.... I wish you could drop in to play a card game."[136] It would seem that Rene's relationship with patients included a bit of friendly occupational therapy. Two of George and Bella's card-playing friends during the long winters were Dr. & Mrs. E.A.F. Day, who spent summers on their picturesque Evergreen Island in Wood Lake, at Bracebridge.[137]

RENE'S MOTHER TREATED WITH ESSIAC

Rene's mother moved to a house a little further north on Parkside Drive in 1928, and by 1930 she returned to her home in Bracebridge, only to become very ill there. (In Rene's 1966 biography, I *Was "Canada's Cancer Nurse"*,[138] as well as during a radio interview in 1977,[139] she recalled that it was "about the time I opened my clinic," which actually would not open until 1935, five years later.) Friselda saw four local doctors who said she had gallstones, but that her heart was too weak for surgery. One of the doctors was Dr. Peter McGibbon, her busy conservative member of Parliament.[140] Even Dr. Roscoe Graham, the Toronto diabetes specialist who consulted with the other doctors, thought that Rene's mother had cancer. Her liver was a nodular mass. When Rene asked how long her mother had to live, Dr. Graham said it would only be a matter of days. Dr. McGibbon was very much against Rene's work and said sarcastically to her, "Why don't you do something?" Rene answered with some confidence, "I'm certainly going to try, Doctor."[141, 142]

Rene immediately started treating her mother with Essiac and told her that the doctor had ordered it for her as a tonic. She administered it daily for ten days, and when her mother improved, she reduced the treatments to three a week, then to two, then to once each week. Friselda would completely recover and live to be ninety. By giving Friselda many years of life she would not have had without the Essiac injections, and adding twenty-one years to her aunt's life by administering Essiac as a tea a few years earlier, Rene was convinced that she had been repaid for all of her work.

CANCER COMMISSION ESTABLISHED IN ONTARIO

While Rene was busy treating cancer patients with her herbal remedy, the Ontario government was recognizing the necessity to manage the increasing activity surrounding the emerging technology and fragmented treatment of cancer.

The Royal Commission on the Use of Radium and X-Rays in the Treatment of the Sick was created by an Order-in-Council on May 29, 1931, to "advise the government on the advisability of establishing cancer research institutes and clinics to facilitate the treatment of cancer through the use of radium and x-rays." They acknowledged the alarming increase in the number of deaths related to cancer since the turn of the century, replacing tuberculosis as the greatest cause of death after heart disease.

The commission was chaired by the Reverend Canon Henry J. Cody, president of the University of Toronto. One member was Dr. Walter Thomas Connell of Kingston, an expert bacteriologist and the father of Dr. W. Ford Connell, medical registrar of the cancer clinic of the Kingston General Hospital. (No relation to Dr. Hendry Connell, who promoted his cancer remedy, Ensol, in Kingston, Ontario, at that time.) Other members of the commission were J.C. McLennan, former professor of physics at Toronto University; lawyer/journalist Arthur R. Ford, managing editor of the *London Free*

Press; Dr. John W.S. McCullough, chief inspector of health for Ontario; and Health Minister Dr. John M. Robb.

The group entered into a ten-month survey of eighty countries to inspect their cancer radiotherapy centres. According to Dr. Cosbie of the Toronto General Hospital, the comprehensive report the commission presented to the legislature, "The Use of Radium and X-Ray in the Treatment of the Sick," "has been the basis for government support of radiotherapy in the province" ever since.[143, 144] "It emphasized cooperation with surgeons, physicians and pathologists in the diagnosis, study and treatment of cancer," Cosbie reported.

Meanwhile, the Ontario Cancer Institute was established in March 1932 to hire skilled personnel, guide research, and set up laboratories. It was to have custody, control, and distribution of government-owned radium for cancer treatment and generally set policies for cancer control.

The first meeting of the commission would not take place until late November 1934, when the new health minister, Dr. Bert Faulkner, called together the group of surgeons, clinicians, physicists, X-ray experts, men concerned a good deal with the treatment of cancer by radium, and a general practitioner. He told them, among other things, "I feel that every root of the Tree of Hope, whose branches we expect to spread over humanity in this Province, will emanate from the vitality, energy and good thought as will be exemplified in this Committee.... Gentlemen, we are having dinner at the Ontario Club and I hope you will all be there for it is costing $1.25 a plate and I am paying for it."[145]

TORONTO NEWSPAPER HEADLINES

A major newspaper story about Rene's discovery appeared on the front page of the *Toronto Daily Star*.[146] The unnamed reporter (possibly Roy Greenaway) had interviewed various unidentified doctors (apparently Dr. Blye, Dr. Fisher, and others) and was most impressed with the dramatic case studies the physicians confirmed. Rene was quoted as having received her Indian herbal remedy from a patient she was nursing up north in 1922, a questionable date that would be published around the world even decades later.

Rene told the reporter that she knew her remedy, not named in the article, was perfectly harmless: "When I was nursing cancer cases, I used to take a dose once in a while myself, and it never did me the slightest harm." Rene confided to him in an unusually candid way, as stories that appeared in his articles had not been related to any other interviewer. He wrote, "Miss Caisse had legal partnership agreements drawn up by physicians who were convinced that she had stumbled on something very important, and wished to obtain the formulas, but she would not sign." This was probably what Dr. Charles Hair was to reflect in 1937 when, although he had no direct evidence of it, he thought Dr. W.C. Arnold of Ottawa was working with Dr. McInnis, possibly to form a company.[147]

"I went to New York to see Ansell Ball, president of the Skin and Cancer Hospital," Rene told the reporter. She said that Ball responded, "Give me your formula and I'll do what's right by you." Nevertheless Rene made the first of her mysterious promises for the safeguarding of her secret recipe and announced that she had made arrangements for her secret to be given to the proper authorities if anything should happen to her. "I will not give it up until I am assured that somebody else is not going to reap advantage of it," she insisted.

Another story, which took front-page prominence on February 24, included details of a letter Dr. McInnis had sent in reply to the Star's inquiry of January 27.[148] Here he described the gratifying results of Rene's herbal treatments on two of his female patients, Bella Simpson and a second with an even more advanced stomach cancer. The Timmins physician said:

> I am convinced that herb treatment relieves pain, reduces the growth and prolongs life to cases of inoperable cancer. Also I believe that in some types of cancer if treated early, the infusion administered by Miss Caisse may perhaps save life.

Further, I am of the opinion that the form of administration can be made much more effective if the active principle of the herbs could be isolated and given subcutaneously and intravenously. In conclusion, may I say that I believe that Miss Caisse has found a very beneficial treatment for cancer, and that it merits the investigation and co-operation of the medical profession.

The *Toronto Daily Star* was first to publish the story of Rene's herbal remedy discovery. This was particularly important because in Roy Greenaway's memoir, published in 1966, he said: "It was a standing rule at the *Star* that all reports of cancer cures were suspect. Someday, when the genuine report appears of a remedy as effective in the control of cancer as insulin is for diabetes, it will be one of the greatest stories ever to appear in a newspaper. It would be worth having spent a lifetime as a newspaper reporter just to obtain an exclusive on that story."[149]

Greenaway also covered the Coffey and Humber cancer clinic story in California later in 1932, but publisher Joseph Atkinson would not print the articles, even though he admired the quality of the reporting. "You make it obvious, I think, that this is just another cancer treatment which offers evidence of a cure. For this reason, I decided not to publish anything that might raise hope and cause a trek of our people over there, which would be useless," Greenaway quoted his boss as saying. The reporter explained, "Later on, although he never mentioned it, I discovered that Mr. Atkinson's wife was suffering from cancer and died soon afterwards." Mrs. Joseph Atkinson, Elmina, was a "pioneering woman journalist who wrote under the name Madge Merton."[150]

Later, in December, a Montreal newspaper reported that a Toronto X-ray expert said, "For several months I have been x-raying patients who have been taking Miss Caisse's herb treatment and some of the results have been uncanny. My deductions are that the herb has some effect on growths and should be studied thoroughly."[151]

Public interest in her work gathered momentum. It seems that a Toronto man named Ernest H. Ashley drew up a lucrative contract that would financially underwrite Rene's costs of operating a clinic, but Rene refused his offer.[152] The unsigned contract was not in Rene's files for review by the author of this biography, but research shows that Ashley was an assistant accountant for a mining speculation firm known as Ventures Ltd. and was looking for "ventures" on behalf of his parent firm run by American mining engineer Halstead Lindsley in Lennox, Massachusetts. It is possibile that this was the "mining man" Dr. Hair referred to earlier in this chapter.

PATIENTS RECEIVE HELP

One grateful patient who received help from Rene was a man named Freeman Maxwell of Beaverton, Ontario.[153] He was carried into Rene's apartment with the necessary written diagnosis addressed to Miss Caisse: "We suspect Mr. Maxwell to have a malignant disease in his pancreas. If he wishes to undertake your treatment, I would offer no objection to him doing so. He is not informed of this." It was signed by F.M. Smith, MD, and dated February 23, 1932.

For a year the patient had been without the use of his arms. He was extremely weak, had no appetite, and had suffered two slight cerebral hemorrhages over the previous eighteen months. After five treatments, he could walk up Rene's stairs alone; on March 30, 1932, Dr. Smith wrote Rene:

Dear Madam:

Mr. Maxwell came to my office Sunday last. Frankly, I was delighted to see such a marked improvement in his general health. He had gained 7 1/2 lbs., his hemoglobin estimated 90%, he moves with a great deal more vigour, and mentally he is very much brighter and alert.... I will watch Mr. Maxwell's progress with a great deal of interest.

Dr. Smith's interest was so great that he also asked Rene questions about her treatment in his letter, such as: "Over what period of time do you believe it should be used?" and "With what conditions do you use it?" Freeman Maxwell responded so well to his Essiac treatments that he was soon running his farm again. This is one case of a seemingly successful Essiac treatment that would challenge the ethics of the medical fraternity in the next few years when Dr. Smith rescinded his judgement under the pressing scrutiny of his medical colleagues in 1939.

FIRST ATTEMPT TO SELL ESSIAC

Rene, like everyone else in the tough economic times of 1932, looked at the necessity of augmenting her meagre income and wondered if she could sell Essiac. In that summer Rene wrote L.F. Teevans, the chief of the Proprietary or Patent Medicine Division of the National Health Department, to ask about the possibility of selling her remedy. In a curt letter to Rene dated August 17, 1932, Chief Teevans bluntly advised her that "medicines for the treatment of CANCER are not legally vendible in Canada." So, she privately presumed, neither would others be able to clone and sell her remedy.

RENE MOVES TO SHERBOURNE STREET

Bay Street was still reeling from the terrible stock market crash that destroyed lives and businesses. In an attempt to cut her travelling expenses, Rene rented an apartment at 387 Sherbourne Street, near Dr. Fisher's office. Thankfully she could stay with her family when she took refresher trips out of the city. But rent in Toronto was very costly. "At the time," Rene said, "I was still nursing 12 hours a day, the customary work day for nurses then. I had only my two hour rest period and my evenings to give to my research work and treatments."[154]

Rene finally gave up her full-time nursing[155] and began treating an average of thirty patients a day, who lined up at her apartment door. Doctors already familiar with Essiac started to send their patients to her place. Soon neighbours complained about the congestion of cars and people, and she changed units within her apartment building in an attempt to appease them.[156] She now had no regular income and accepted whatever patients gave voluntarily. She was not alone, as the depth of the Depression had caused a Canada-wide unemployment rate of some 32 percent. Historian William Kilbourn recorded that no class of Canadian working women was paid more than $1,000 annually,[157] if they had a job at all.

NEARLY ARRESTED IN PETERBOROUGH

Rene moved once again to Peterborough in early 1934, where she found a neat and unpretentious two-storey house to rent near the busy CGE plant at 190 Reid Street.[158] She always felt comfortable in that town — Friselda and her family grew up there, and her grandfather, Louis Potvin, her aunt Mireza, and other relatives were still there. It was a second home to her.

"I was no sooner moved in than the College of Physicians and Surgeons sent a health officer to issue a warrant for my arrest, again the charge was 'practising medicine without a license.'"[159] It is presumed that Rene was treating patients in her home. She insisted that she had letters from the minister of health and the College of Physicians and Surgeons assuring her that they would not interfere as long as she didn't charge the patients for her treatments. "However, I excused myself to go upstairs and get dressed," she said. In the meantime, the man sat down to read the letters and papers, and when she returned he told her that he was not going to arrest her but was going back to talk to his boss, the registrar of the College of Physicians and Surgeons.[160] He was Dr. Henry Wilberforce Aikens, son of Dr. W.H.B. Aikens, former dean of the medical faculty at the University of Toronto.[161]

Rene promptly wrote Minister of Health Dr. John R. Robb, requesting an immediate appointment. Dr. Robb, who had held that position in George S. Henry's cabinet since 1930, was the Conservative MPP from Algoma, a former mayor of Blind River who knew a lot about expressing a daring devotion to one's goal. As a young doctor, for example, he had built and equipped his own private hospital there to serve his patients in the lumbering community. Rene was told that she wouldn't be interfered with again as long as she made no charge for her treatments and had a written diagnosis of cancer from a doctor for each patient. Dr. Robb's philosophy, "The great principal of health is the prevention rather than the cure,"[162] would perhaps unwittingly become one of the medical profession's judgements that would direct primary funding towards the prevention of cancer over the years, delaying the discovery of a cure.

This was probably the last time Rene communicated with Dr. Robb, since the 1934 provincial elections wiped out George S. Henry's Conservatives on July 19, and Dr. Robb lost his job as health minister. One wonders if Rene knew that Dr. Robb and his wife were great supporters of the Canadian Mothercraft Society, where Rene's former colleague Dr. Fisher had just been appointed medical director. That year, Dr. Robb joined the board of directors of the organization, which offered young mothers and children's workers educational and preventative medicine activities.[163]

CHAPTER 4

Clinic of Hope

BRACEBRIDGE TO GET CANCER CLINIC

Despite worldwide research and the advent of caring treatment centres, cancer was still on the increase, and its causes remained largely unknown. Coincidentally, in April 1935, the month a daring plan to challenge the cancer scourge was about to be unveiled in Bracebridge, a discouraging report from the federal government recorded that death by cancer in recent years showed a rapid increase. They noted that there had been advances in treatment, but that a great deal remained to be done in Canadian research.[164] While cigarette smoking was not understood to be a serious issue at the time, it is now notable that the Tobacco Division of the Dominion Experimental Farms in Ottawa proudly announced that month that the tobacco outlook looked bright due to increasing demands on home markets and improved marketing conditions.[165]

While Rene had been living and working in various parts of Ontario, she had not been professionally associated with Bracebridge, except by referral. However, her public notability was enough to rally the interest of her hometown officials, who had begun to believe in the healing power of her herbal cancer remedy. Talk of a possible cancer clinic there started to circulate in early 1935.

Cancer clinics, also called hospitals or institutes, had existed in various countries for centuries; they were not a new idea. For instance, the Middlesex Hospital Cancer Charity had served cancer patients in England since 1792, when the wealthy brewer

Samuel Whitbread bequeathed a generous sum of money to finance it.[166] Closer to home, in Buffalo, New York, a private hospital for the cure of cancer and tumours "without the knife" was operated as early as 1891 by Dr. George H. McMichael,[167] who was born in Waterford, Ontario.

Then there was the small surgery that had been run by the Evans brothers in Cardigan, Wales, for over twenty years. In 1907, they were still dispensing their secret herbal ointments and salves to cancer patients all over Wales and Scotland, much to the horror of the British medical profession. The Evans brothers' method of treatment was to apply an herbal ointment or a decoction to the cancer that, according to them, caused the roots on all sides to withdraw into the original growth, which then fell off, allowing the skin to heal over the wound. They never turned cases away and claimed they had only one or two failures in many years.[168] This interesting report resembled that of Rene's experience with her unidentified herbal decoction and would parallel events to come in the 1950s.

NEW LIFE FOR OLD HOTEL

At a meeting of the Bracebridge council chaired by Mayor Wilbert Richards on April 9, 1935, a respected local physician, Councillor Dr. A.F. Bastedo,[169] moved a simple but momentous resolution, seconded by another councillor, Bert Rawson, "that this Council grant Miss Rene Caisse, the use of the Bracebridge Inn, at a nominal Rental, to be used by her as a Cancer Clinic, and that we give her a Lease accordingly." (It wouldn't be until November that the official By-law #624 was passed, giving Rene a five-year lease for a nominal fee of one dollar a month, including utilities and the use of a janitor.)

The forty-room, three-storey brick building had been vacant for some time after being repossessed for back taxes. Known recently as the Bracebridge Inn,[170] and since the 1870s as the British Lion Hotel,[171] it stood proudly on the northwest corner of Dominion and Ontario streets as an important landmark. Even the town administrators used both names interchangeably in their minutes and documents. Now the handsome building would be easily accessible for patients attending the Rene M. Caisse Cancer Clinic.

Several residents in and around Bracebridge had already sought Rene's help, most of them men with prostate and bowel cancer. Dr. Bastedo clinically diagnosed John Vanclieaf of nearby Baysville and gave him a written diagnosis for Rene Caisse. Using this document as approval, Rene began his Essiac treatments. Dr. Bastedo did not feel that Vanclieaf would survive surgery and had given him thirteen bottles of medicine that didn't help, Vanclieaf later complained, and had Miss Fanny Arnott, a registered nurse, X-ray him. After two weeks of Essiac treatments, Vanclieaf's pain had ceased and he felt better in every way. After seven weeks, another X-ray convinced Dr. Bastedo that the cancer was disappearing.[172]

On April 28, Bert Rawson was given Essiac hypodermically after presenting Rene with Dr. W.G.C. Kenney's written diagnosis of carcinoma. John Tynan of Melissa, near Huntsville, began Rene's treatments for cancer after Dr. A. Ardagh of Orillia had written his wife in January and regretfully told her that her husband's "malignous disease has advanced too far and his strength too much exhausted for any operative procedure to be of any value. In my opinion the only thing now is to give him plenty of hyprolic and keep him from suffering," and the ninety-one-pound patient was sent home to die.[173] The three men showed definite improvement after a few months.

In order to officially arrange the transition from hotel to hospital, Town Clerk Alex Salmon wrote Health Minister Dr. Bert Faulkner[174] on April 15, asking him to examine the Bracebridge Inn and grant permission for a private hospital to be operated from the old hotel building. Rene, about to give up her unofficial "cancer clinic" because she was being threatened by Department of Pensions and National Health inspectors, wrote an urgent letter to the minister from her home in Peterborough. (The threat of a $500 fine or six months in jail hung over her head for administering an unregistered remedy from her home, she recalled.) She assured the health minister that she would be running the private hospital only for the treatment of cancer patients with her successful herbal remedy.[175]

When she moved to Bracebridge in early May, Rene began to work towards the opening of the private hospital and was almost immediately treating even more patients referred by local doctors. Rene probably gave treatments in her family's Manitoba Street apartment, accessed through a back door off Dominion Street, prior to the opening of the clinic. But during the second week in May, the Bracebridge council received a disappointing communication from the Department of Health that refused permission for Miss Caisse to establish a local hospital for the treatment of cancer.[176]

In an effort to create local political pressure, Mayor Richards called upon his peer in Huntsville, Mayor J. Frank Kelly,[177] who was also the member of the legislature for the riding of Muskoka-Ontario, and asked him to set up an appointment with the new Liberal premier, Mitchell Hepburn, to receive a deputation from Bracebridge and area. Residents throughout Muskoka and beyond were encouraged to sign a petition that was available in the office of the *Muskoka Herald* newspaper.[178] The mayor and councillors R. Hines, Bert Rawson, Robert Whaley, and D.J. Hodgson signed the document, supporting the creation of a cancer clinic to be operated by a member of one of the oldest and most respected families in Bracebridge.

A frustrated Mayor Richards also wrote to Premier Hepburn for his intervention on Rene's behalf. This would be the first of several years of correspondence the politician would receive regarding Rene, as his tenure somewhat corresponded with hers. Richards's letter read as follows:

> Miss Rene Caisse, RN, has discovered and developed a treatment for cancer which is showing remarkable results. Among others she has treated John Vanclieaf of Baysville who was given only a few months to live. Now, after a few months' treatment, this man is in better health than he has been for a long time. A local physician diagnosed his case as cancer and x-ray plates showed that his diagnosis was correct and that it was beyond the stage where it could be checked.... This doctor has

stated to me that he is satisfied Miss Caisse has done for this sufferer what he could not do, but he dare not support her openly, for fear of what the Medical Association might do.

Miss Caisse will not make known this treatment at present, as she feels that she is entitled to reap some benefit financially from it. Now a threat has been made to her that if she treats another patient, she will be severely prosecuted. As a result of this, she has had to cease giving treatments to those whom she has been treating, and cannot take any more patients. Consequently, hope has been shattered for a number of cancer victims who otherwise might have been cured....

If this lady cannot continue her work in Ontario, she will go to the US, and in that case this treatment would be lost to our people. A petition is at present in circulation in this district which, when signed, will be presented to you. Your obedient servant, Wilbert Richards.[179]

The statement by the enthusiastic politician regarding her entitlement to reap financial benefits was quite inaccurate and may have done her some harm. The mayor hadn't understood that she never charged for the treatment, and Rene knew by this time that her herbal treatment could not be sold in Canada.

PRIVATE HOSPITAL REQUIREMENTS

During the next few weeks, Dr. W. Mosely, inspector of private hospitals, and Dr. J.W.S. McCullough, chief inspector of health, investigated the rules for operating private hospitals. Their internal memo pointed out that the government was already subsidizing several well-equipped places for the "legitimate" treatment of cancer, referring undoubtedly to the government-funded X-ray and radium cancer centres in seven Ontario hospitals.[180] They noted that "secret cures" only delay the opportunity for the use of proper treatment with disastrous results to the victims of cancer.

On Monday, July 8, Dr. Mosely and another inspector, Dr. J.D. Heaslop, visited the old hotel and agreed with Mayor Richards that it would be most suitable for a clinic. Their visit buoyed those who had worked so hard gathering names on, as one reporter noted, a "largely signed" petition planned for Queen's Park.[181] However, the inspectors insisted that a resident physician would be necessary to oversee all activities, including treatment, should permission be granted to open it. The two men interviewed Bracebridge physicians and some residents. Dr. Bastedo said that he "as a member of the town council was in favour of Miss Caisse establishing in Bracebridge, if she were allowed to establish anywhere."[182] He would not, however, assume any part of the supervision of the hospital or take any responsibility for the treatments given by Miss Caisse, nor would he become a member of the committee that would call on Miss Caisse to establish the new clinic. These remarks gave Dr. Mosely the impression that none of the other physicians in town would be willing to assume that responsibility either.

Even so, Dr. Edward G. Ellis wrote to Dr. B.T. McGhie, deputy minister of hospitals, on July 18 to say that he was anxious to take the position of resident physician of the proposed clinic, but he wanted to know if by taking the position he would endanger his licence to practise.

McGhie responded the next day, and a most discouraged young Dr. Ellis read: "So far, no license has been issued for the operation of this hospital and patients cannot be accepted legally unless a license is granted. This is the only information I can give you on the subject at present."

McGhie fired off a staff memo as well: "Under the date of July 25, 1935, I notified Dr. F.C. Routley that in our opinion this Miss Caisse was practising medicine to wit, treating cancer in Bracebridge without a license and that we refused permit to operate a hospital."

Regardless of this ruling, the first of a series of deputations from Bracebridge arrived at Queen's Park on August 9, 1935, headed by

Mayor Richards. John Vanclieaf was there, along with Frank Kelly and a number of officials who presented a twenty-seven-hundred-name petition to the health minister for the office of the prime minister.[183, 184] (The titles "premier" and "prime minister" were at that time interchangeable. Hepburn's letterhead used "prime minister," while references by his colleagues identified him as "premier.")

Health Minister Faulkner promised to investigate Rene's cancer treatment in order that cancer sufferers be given a chance to recover their health. But permission to open a clinic was not granted. Miss Caisse could open an "office" and continue to treat patients, but she was to work with department doctors who, if satisfied, might eventually consent to her operating a hospital.[185] Grateful for the public's support, Rene thanked the mayor and his council and the thousands of Muskoka people who signed the petition on her behalf in a front-page newspaper "Card of Thanks."[186]

Meanwhile, as arrangements went ahead to prepare the building for the clinic's use, Rene was very concerned once again about being cautioned by medical authorities to stop treating patients.

THE RENE M. CAISSE CANCER CLINIC OPENS

The Rene M. Caisse Cancer Clinic opened on August 26, 1935, and twelve patients arrived for treatments. All in all that day, thirty-four people visited the new clinic, which had yet to receive the necessary approvals from the authorities. Among the patients was Sarah Tibbel, mother of Mary, who would marry Clifford McPherson in June 1937 and become a significant figure in the life and legacy of Rene Caisse. Two cancer patients arrived from Rochester, New York, later in the week. The plan was to open Mondays, Wednesdays and Fridays,[187] but patients encouraged Rene to be more flexible and open various days of the week.

The old hotel had been transformed over the summer. What had been the hotel's large dining room became the reception room and office, with a treatment room in behind. The fresh sparkling white enamel paint gave a handsome, clean appear-

Bracebridge Public Library, Rene M. Caisse Archive

The Rene M. Caisse Cancer Clinic showing the entrance at the south end of the Dominion Street building.

ance. "The council and mayor and a lot of the people around Bracebridge helped me furnish the clinic," Rene remembered. "They were just wonderful — but as my aunt said, I was always just one jump ahead of a policeman. We were right across from the town jail, and Saunders the keeper used to joke that he was saving a cell for me."[188] Rene was always overweight, and Mr. Saunders often joked about having to put another beam in the floor.[189]

People soon appeared from all corners of the province and other parts of Canada as well. It was said that "Dominion Street took on an atmosphere reminiscent of the famous Shrine of Lourdes, as hopeful pilgrims sought a new lease on life."[190] Hopeful cancer patients arrived walking, by ambulance, by private cars — some were even carried. Sometimes sirens would announce the arrival of an ambulance as it pulled into the crowded street. Certainly Rene was seen meeting patients as they were brought to the clinic in very frail condition. Cars were parked everywhere. Patients came from everywhere. The clinic was alive with hope and Rene's remedy was very much sought after.

Some patients came to the clinic without their doctor's knowledge, and after they registered and gave their history in their own words, they were asked to go to their doctor and get their diagnosis from him. Permelia, who had retired from her millinery work and moved back to Bracebridge, helped her sister by signing up patients as they came in.[191] During other periods, Rene's nieces Loretta and Rita helped out. The latter would become a nurse. Another niece, Valeen, often worked with Rene as well.

Rene would not treat a patient without his doctor's permission, as she was very sensitive to the fact that she didn't have a licence to practise medicine. She insisted on written diagnoses that stated the medical health of each and every patient. In some cases, however, patients could not get their doctor's permission to be treated by Rene Caisse because he didn't approve the treatment. But Rene just couldn't accept that these patients had been sent home to die, so occasionally she treated them anyway on the off chance that she could help.

If the busy day allowed, records of each patient were kept, including his or her diagnosis, physical condition, treatment, and results. Some days as many as fifty to one hundred patients would come to the clinic. Patients were treated once a week if possible, and twice a week in some cases, with at least forty-eight hours between treatments. A good number of patients were treated for three months. Some breast cancers, if not too far advanced, would disappear in about six treatments.[192]

In the treatment room, Rene would inject the Essiac into the patient's arm, leg, or hip muscles and follow it with a glass of medicine as a blood purifier. Where there were open sores she would apply a local treatment with gauze, and for hemorrhages she would use a solution for irrigation to stop the bleeding. In cases where the mouth and throat were involved, she administered a gargle she had made and a mouthwash to cleanse. She recommended patients use hers rather than any of the patented mouthwashes because of its healing properties.[193]

The results of the Essiac treatments were often astounding. Even patients whose bodies were irreparably damaged from cancer received some form of relief — less pain, reduced pressure by the shrinking of tumours, as well as great comfort and some hope.

The cancer clinic was functioning with the financial subsidization and moral support of the town, as well as the personal offerings of Rene's patients. She never charged for a treatment, but sometimes she received fresh vegetables, fruit, flowers, jams, or jel-

"ESSIAC"

RENE M. CAISSE
"CANCER CLINIC"

Phones: Office 32   BRACEBRIDGE,
        Residence 80   Ontario

Rene's professional cards promoted "Essiac."

lies as a patient's thanks.[194] Bracebridge was now well positioned to meet the needs of those with chronic and life-threatening illnesses. The Bracebridge Memorial Hospital, the only general hospital between Orillia and North Bay, served the customary ailments and surgery needs of patients.[195] But one would wonder about the relationship between Rene and her peers at the hospital, which was having financial difficulties.

In October the Red Cross Society, which was responsible for the finances and operations of the buildings and equipment of Bracebridge Memorial, was actively raising funds from summer and permanent residents alike to sustain its ledgers. Another mortgage had been put on the property to compensate merchants who hadn't been paid for the materials supplied to build the new hospital wing three years ago. The nurses held a card party to raise funds for more equipment.[196, 197]

The general hospital succeeded, and the town of more than three thousand souls also had its own cancer clinic, which served cancer victims from all over Ontario. But the Department of Health was angry at the audacity of the Bracebridge authority. The clinic was operating in spite of their objections. Health Minister Faulkner had promised that doctors of his choosing would oversee Rene's methods of treatment, but so far that arrangement had not been made. He expected too that the group would co-operate with Ontario's cancer commission. This commission was also expected to form an opinion soon on the cancer treatment that Dr. Connell was developing in Kingston, Ontario.[198, 199] In another Ontario city the *Ottawa Journal* reported that the tumour clinic at the Ottawa Civic Hospital had served 450 cancer patients in its first year, supplying X-ray, radium, and surgery to absolutely hopeless patients.[200]

LETTERS TO ROYALTY

Over the past few months, Rene and others had corresponded with persons they believed could ensure that Essiac would be officially approved. On September 21, 1935, she mailed a letter to the Prince of Wales at St. James' Palace in London, and his assistant private secretary responded on October 2:

> His Royal Highness has read with interest what you have to say regarding your treatment for cancer, but does not feel … competent to comment upon it.
>
> But for the fact that you desired your communication to remain confidential, it would have been forwarded to the Secretary of the British Empire Cancer Campaign in London….This might provide the best means of furthering your claims.

The Prince of Wales' secretary acknowledged Rene's October 12 note on October 24, stating that the first one had been forwarded to the (British Empire) "Cancer Campaign" in accordance with her request. One week later, the general secretary of the enterprise sent this reply to her: "If you will give the full details of the chemicals, which will be treated in strict confidence, together with a note from any registered Medical Practitioner who has had any of his patients treated by you, we will look further into the matter."

His request for the disclosure of her remedy, along with a promise to keep it confidential, was in keeping with those that she would continue to hear throughout the rest of her life. Rene probably didn't bother to answer, for she had no intention of revealing the formula to anyone at that time. No response was located in Rene's files.

Nevertheless, the British Empire campaign did publicly announce that a new cancer serum was being given trials, and that "moving pictures have proved the immunized serum used on rodents kills cancer cells in a few minutes and leaves others unaffected. The discovery is hopeful, but it is definitely not claimed that a cancer cure in human beings is found."[201]

As the extraordinary year was gearing down, a disturbing earthquake rattled dishes and broke plaster walls in Bracebridge the first week of November — it was called the most violent in Canada since 1874. The quake's epicentre was twenty-five kilometres from North Bay, about two hundred kilometres away, and had Bracebridge not been built on rock, dramatic damage could have occurred.[202]

CHAPTER 5

DR. BANTING AND CANCER RESEARCH

NEW PETITION

The popular expression of public opinion, the petition, was once again being circulated throughout Muskoka and other Ontario locations by January 1936. The petitioners were described as being "firmly convinced from personal knowledge of reliable information, the Miss Rene M. Caisse has effected cures of cancer in where reputable physicians had previously diagnosed the patient's ailment as cancer and held out no hope for recovery." The second public plea on Rene's behalf to Dr. Faulkner, Premier Hepburn, and the attorney general read in part:

> Cancer is the greatest scourge of humanity and … therefore anyone who can cure it should be permitted and encouraged to do so.
>
> Wherefore, it be resolved that we very strongly urge that the Honourable Minister of Health fulfil his promise and have this treatment investigated in order that cancer sufferers be given a chance to recover their health.[203]

Plans were made for its presentation during the summer, and Rene launched an aggressive letter-writing campaign. In May, Rene's seventy-eight-year-old mother, Friselda, returned to Bracebridge after several winter weeks in Florida and her children's homes in the Detroit area, having missed the publicity that surrounded her daughter's worries and achievements.[204]

SUPPORTIVE LETTERS

Many cancer victims who received treatment at the cancer clinic attempted to show appreciation for their new lease on life. As an example, the *Bracebridge Gazette* published this letter, written by Mrs. Thos. Leyman of Beaverton:

A TRIBUTE TO MISS CAISSE

I wonder if I might be allowed to have a small space in your valuable paper, for a matter I would like to draw your attention to, one I feel very strongly about, re Miss Rene Caisse's Cancer Clinic.

I wonder if you people do not know of what a wonderful thing it is, or is it in the hurry of everyday life you forget.

I had been given three months to live before I came, the time is past and I have received such wonderful results that I feel I must do my utmost to bring the knowledge to other sufferers of this dread disease, and Miss Caisse has proof she can show of what she had done for me and is doing.

Now, people of Bracebridge and surrounding districts, give your fellow townswoman your wholehearted support in helping her in every way necessary to start her hospital, and put Bracebridge on the map as the place of the most wonderful cancer clinic.

I would also wish it distinctly understood that Miss Caisse did not ask me to write this, but in thankfulness for my own returning health, I felt that if there was anything I could do to let other sufferers know of the wonderful cure it is my duty to do so. Trusting you may find space in the paper for this, and thanking you, I am Yours truly, Mrs. Thos. Leyman. [205]

Mrs. Leyman had been kicked by a horse and developed a carcinoma of the right breast. She was terribly thin and in the terminal stages of cancer when Dr. J. Mason Smith referred her to Rene in March 1936. Rene's treatment caused the mass to loosen from the chest wall and reduced it in size, making her breathing more comfortable. Rene admitted she was not in a physical condition to be cured, but she was at least made comfortable until her death in July.[206]

Meanwhile other patients lauded Rene's treatments. James Summerwill, a Sprucedale, Ontario, notary wrote the *Muskoka Herald* in June about his impression of the rewarding treatments he received, which he felt would provide a permanent cure. He had been taking weekly treatments since November 1935 for a lymph sarcoma tumour diagnosed by the provincial health laboratory. Dr. Connell at Kingston admitted that they had nothing that would be of any use for the sarcoma type of cancer, it being malignant.[207] Mr. Summerwill wrote in his professional style:

> Having heard of a lady in the Town of Bracebridge who had a number of cancer cures to her credit as well as being able to give relief, I made personal application to her. Miss Rene M. Caisse, who kindly consented to treat my case, providing that I had the proper diagnosis and the written consent of my doctor. On production of these I commenced taking her treatments, which was about the middle of November 1935. I have been examined by three different doctors, who have pronounced me O.K. but with the advice to continue my treatments for a very short time, in order to remove any possible chance of a return of the trouble. Today I am fully satisfied that I have received a permanent cure under and by

the treatment of Miss Caisse, and to whom for and on behalf of my family and friends I owe to her a debt of gratitude which money can never repay.

Further, with all due respect to the Government and medical profession, who no doubt take all precautions to protect the public from fraud and fakers, it does seem extremely arbitrary that notwithstanding that Miss Caisse can produce absolute proof that she has abundant proof of her cure, that she is prohibited from advertising or making a charge for her invaluable work, or to let the public know that there is relief from the dreaded cancer affliction.[208]

Other patients wrote intense and articulate letters to newspapers and government officials, all ending up on the desk of the health minister. In fact, Dr. Bert Faulkner was being inundated by letters from appreciative patients and thankful families. So was Premier Mitch Hepburn. The letters related stories of the success of Essiac in making patients feel better and seemingly arresting their cancers, and were signed by patients, their families, and others. They demanded that the Department of Health support Rene's work. At that time, Dr. Faulkner was actively involved in bettering the conditions of patients and improving hospitals for mental defectives,[209] but he took at least a political interest in the demands of cancer patients.

DELEGATION TO QUEEN'S PARK

A second impressive delegation of Bracebridge officials descended on Queen's Park in the terrible heat of July 10, 1936, to state Rene's case. It was so hot that on the following day, a Sunday, ice men were allowed to deliver to restaurants and dairies to keep their food from spoiling.[210] The group was composed of Mayor Richards, MPP Kelly, Dr. Arnold, and a few councillors. Several patients,

Nurse Caisse and her hollyhocks at the entrance of her clinic.

including James Summerwill and John Vanclieaf, were introduced to Dr. Faulkner with Dr. McGhie at his side. Rene presented a huge petition of some four thousand names, the mayor gave an address, and Toronto newspaper reporters were there to hear the health minister promise Miss Caisse a chance to discuss her cancer research cancer with Sir Frederick Banting.

The *Toronto Daily Star* heard the mayor of Bracebridge say, "We want Miss Caisse to get a chance to prove her treatment. If she has something, she has done more than the whole medical fraternity has been able to do. That people have been benefited is evident from the fact that some of those here to-day would have been in their graves otherwise."

Rene told the reporters that she had some distrust of the medical profession and pointed out that in many cases discoveries by laymen were "rediscovered" by the profession.[211]

Dr. Faulkner assured the crowd that the government would certainly get behind her treatment if its success was proven. In a similar report, the *Globe* stated, "Dr. Faulkner said the Government had no money set aside for investigation, and 'we must protect the unsophisticated from being exploited by so-called cures.'"[212] The *Evening Telegram* related that Dr. W.C. Arnold declared James Summerwill cured after Miss Caisse's treatments, and John Vanclieaf, whom doctors had given up on, reported that he was cured.[213] The *Muskoka Herald* delighted in announcing that Sir Frederick Banting would test her cancer treatment.[214] In an undated private letter to Rene following the newspaper coverage of Banting's offer of assistance, Summerwill lightheartedly wrote, "I think the sub-heading on the article above mentioned should be reversed, to read 'Miss Rene M. Caisse offers assistance to Sir Frederick Banting, to prove the cancer treatment.'"

However, Rene was very annoyed with the *Telegram*'s reporter who "passed over lightly" the importance of her work, and she wrote the editor to say so. "No one in the world has ever before cured a lympho sarcoma. I think any surgeon will tell you that this is a fact. Mr. Summerwill's growth is gone and he is in perfect health. What more would any sane person ask than that as proof positive."[215]

Perhaps not coincidentally, on the day the Caisse delegation arrived in Toronto, the *Telegram* editor published a letter from Kitchener's Dr. J.E. Hett, who pleaded for early cancer detection clinics. He pointed to the cancer commission's fund of $420,000 as a possible source for monies and reminded readers that cancer causes the death of one out of every ten persons over the age of thirty-five years.[216]

BANTING DISCUSSES TESTING

Feeling the public pressure to test Essiac, Dr. Faulkner had taken the opportunity to discuss the situation with Sir Frederick Banting (he liked to be called Doctor or just Fred[217]) while at a meeting of the Canadian Medical Association in Victoria, B.C., a few days later. Upon his return to Toronto, on July 23, Banting made a proposal to Rene that appeared attractive on the surface. He did not acknowledge that their paths had crossed at the Christie Street Hospital, when he had been impressed with the behaviour of Essiac on a Timmins diabetic patient and offered Rene the opportunity of sharing his lab.[218] But Banting offered her another chance:

> I have told the Honourable Minister of Health that this laboratory is prepared to do the following:
>
> 1) Provide you with mice inoculated with mouse sarcoma
> 2) Provide you with chickens inoculated with Rous sarcoma
> 3) These animals will be placed at your disposal in the laboratory between the hours of 9 and 5 daily, except Sundays and Holidays, so that you may treat them as you wish.
> 4) You will not be asked to divulge any secret concerning your treatment.

5) All experimental results must be submitted to me for my approval before being announced to anyone, including the newspapers, or published in medical journals.

6) If necessary, special arrangements will be made for the special treatment of the animals during Sundays and week-ends.[219]

This arrangement meant that Rene could treat patients on weekends, work in the lab throughout the weekdays, and, if there were favourable responses in the animals, she would achieve recognition and honour. But many years had lapsed since her first encounter with Banting, and during that time her distrust of the medical profession had increased, as had her desire for recognition for her work, which, she insisted, she had developed unaided.

Banting was no longer an enthusiastic researcher, having reached his pinnacle of inventiveness more than ten years ago, but he had a responsibility to keep his Banting Institute laboratory in the University of Toronto's Department of Medical Research active. Since 1925, he and his staff had been sacrificing thousands of mice injected with mouse sarcoma, and hundreds of chickens inoculated with Rous sarcoma, looking for a cancer cure.[220] Placing these animals at Rene's disposal in his lab, along with certain conditions, could have been an opportunity for Banting to extend his research. Banting stated his hypothesis on cancer in a 1935 radio appeal for the King's Silver Jubilee Cancer Fund: "Research has shown that food is not a factor in production of cancer growth, the tendency to cancer is hereditary."[221] Earlier, he had theorized that "tumour growth was the result of some 'combination of a male and female protein element in such a manner that cells are stimulated to divide.'"[222]

Undoubtedly it was with great pride that Rene's sister notified Frank Kelly to say that Rene had received a letter from Sir Frederick Banting. Kelly dashed off a letter of best wishes and promised to drop in to see her the next time he went to Bracebridge.[223]

The following Monday, five doctors went with Rene to talk to Dr. Banting. "He was very kind," she recalled, then continued:

But he made it clear I'd have to give up my clinic if I went to work with him. I felt it was inhuman for them to ask me to give up treating patients while I showed them whether it would work on mice. I'd already done work on mice.

There was a big uproar about it because the patients were terrified I would leave them, but many doctors said I should jump at the chance to work with Dr. Banting. I said I'd be willing to, but I'm not going to let people die while I do it. It was an agonizing decision, but I refused his offer.[224]

Rene told a local newspaper reporter that she was not in a financial position to go to Toronto to do the research and still clung to the hope that the government would supply her with inoculated animals so that she could do the work in Bracebridge, treating patients at the same time.[225] "Medical science," she considered, "will not accept proof developed on human beings, but will accept proof on mice and chickens shown to have cancer."

In a letter to Rene dated August 11, 1936, Dr. Banting wrote: "I think you will regret that you have not availed yourself of the offer made by this laboratory. However, if at some future time

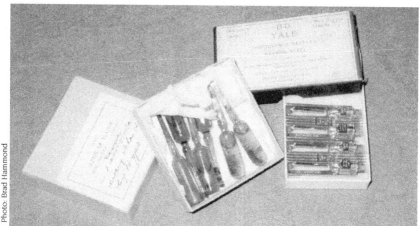

Photo: Brad Hammond

The contents of Rene's medical bag included Yale hypodermic needles and glass ampoules of Essiac.

you again decide to have the treatment investigated, I am sure that Doctor Faulkner and myself would re-consider the matter."

Rene mused that she would do the same thing again, although she was sorry that she had to refuse the incredible opportunity.

Rene was becoming well known throughout the province, and in a warm letter dated August 14, Dr. Gordon L. Hagmeier congratulated her on her great work and on her ability to show the world that she really had something, "irrespective of the scoffers." Hagmeier, who with his brother Dr. John owned and operated an imposing clinic in Preston, Ontario, a treatment centre for nervous diseases with a surgery component and beautiful gardens, wished her "all the luck in the world because the world certainly needs people like you, and your treatment." He offered Rene and her (unnamed) sister his kindest regards.

ROYAL RESPONSES

It was time for Rene to reopen the chain of letters to royalty. The British Empire mourned the death of King George V, who died in his sleep on January 20, 1936, and the enigmatic and handsome Prince of Wales became king for nearly a year.[226] Rene wrote to the yet-to-be crowned king Edward, requesting that he examine her cancer treatment, and in August 1936 she was advised that her letter had been forwarded to her old nemesis, the Department of Pensions and National Health.[227] Dr. J.J. Heagerty responded, and Rene was enraged. In angry frustration she lashed out a return letter:

> I have every reason not to expect recognition from the medical profession for my discovery; since they have never at any time given credit to the laymen who have discovered many of the things used by medical science at the present time to aid suffering humanity.
>
> I can also prove my statement that the dissection of the cancerous section aggravates the growth and

that deep X-ray scatters it and I have personally treated patients badly burned by radium.

I am not expecting consideration from the medical profession, that is why I appealed to His Majesty the King. I hope that for the sake of suffering humanity, he would use his Royal power and give recognition to my work. I might add that I have never charged for treatment.

Rene's files did not contain a response from the Ottawa health bureaucrat, but the "important" cancer campaign continued, and it wasn't until April 1937 that Rene received a huffy note, saying: "I am duly in receipt of cuttings from a number of newspapers relative to a treatment for cancer advocated by you. I would refer to my letter of November 1st and December 16th, 1935 and would remind you that until you supply the full details referred to therein the matter cannot be dealt with." It was signed E. Chapman, General Secretary, British Empire Cancer Campaign.

CLINIC OF HOPE

Over the years Rene told interviewers about the hundreds of cancer patients who travelled weekly to the Caisse Cancer Clinic, where the waiting room was always crowded with suffering people. They endured endless forms of cancer, ulcers, and sores located in every part of the human body. They suffered terribly from debilitating, angry, and painful sores that were devastating to see. All had been given everything their doctors could and were usually considered to be in terminal stages of their disease. But they willingly made their way to Rene's clinic for Essiac treatments, some hemorrhaging badly, and in the fraternity of the suffering they gave each other strength to continue. They trusted Rene, and she gave them hope and comfort. Her treatment seemed to give them relief by way of positive changes in their weakened conditions and reduction in pain.

In fact, Dr. Charles Hair, who had believed in her work in 1926 when he signed the petition to the federal government, reported, "There may be some tonic effects from its use internally, and certainly local cancerous ulcers may improve under her treatments." He also recalled that one of his patients benefited from Miss Caisse's treatment when "locally ulceration was cleaner after treatments."[228]

By 1936, Rene had read everything she could get a hold of on cancer and the detrimental effects of radiation as a treatment. She began to formulate her theory on radium use. "I believe that radium, used in too heavy doses, is a prolific cause of further cancer in burnt tissues," she would write.[229] A patient named Miss Margaret Ann Mitchell of Milford Bay, Ontario, was one example of the harm that was caused by the radium treatments of the day. From 1932 to November 1936, Miss Mitchell had received many hour-long radium treatments to her incision following a mastectomy and to several lumps that occurred sequentially in various parts of her wasting body. Terribly sick, with a diagnosis of cancer of the breast and underarm, she arrived at the clinic on December 5 and was given her first Essiac treatment. There was a large oozing hole in her side, stuffed with a foot-and-a-half of gauze, caused by a radium probe. Within two weeks, her burn was not as angry-looking, inflammation was gone, and there was less discharge and odour. By March, Ann Mitchell was feeling better, gaining weight, and her radium burn was filling in nicely.[230, 231]

Following regular injections of the herbal remedy, Miss Mitchell had improved to the point that on December 7, 1937, she notarized a statement in support of Rene Caisse's treatment with Wilbert Richards, the commissioner of oaths.[232]

Patients continued to congregate at the clinic of hope. And Rene continued to manage her personal finances on donations of money supplemented by gifts of whatever the patients could provide. One day at her clinic two doctors were listening to the conversations of patients and asked Rene how much the average patient would donate. "They give what they can, and if they cannot give, they get the treatment just the same," she explained.

That particular day, as the story goes, one man came over to her and gave her fifty cents. The doctor said, "And you thanked him! Why I would have thrown it in his face!"

Rene replied, "That's the difference between you and me. That fifty cents meant more to that man than a hundred dollars would mean to you."[233]

These were the toughest days of the Depression, and many people were extremely poor. As early doctors would concur, patients would give butter, vegetables, or hand-sewn and knitted articles to compensate the best they could for their kindly medical attention. Rene had a good feeling knowing that she was helping people. Money did not seem important, as long as out of donated funds she could purchase her medical supplies and the ingredients to make Essiac.

Patients and supporters who packed the clinic's waiting room offered each other encouragement. One woman, May Henderson, recalled, "We tried to get our treatment before lunch, have a bite to eat in Bracebridge, and then drive back. It only took a minute to get the injection and drink the tea, and the patients used to exchange progress reports while we waited." Dr. John McInnis considered her tumours malignant and felt it was pointless to treat her. But he heard her say later that year, after she took Essiac treatments, that "the lumps seemed to grow harder, then the turning point came and I discharged great masses of fleshy material."[234]

Rene and her cancer clinic were experiencing uncertain times. Rene was savouring great personal rewards as patients gathered to receive comfort, hope, and beneficial treatment during their worst days. But behind the humane scene medical authorities, government bureaucrats, and potential exploiters lurked, spying on her every movement.

CHAPTER 6

CAISSE TO LEAVE CANADA?

While a number of Ontario's politicians and medical doctors, as well as a few federal bureaucrats, were wrestling with the demands of Rene Caisse's patients and supporters in mid-1936, word of the Essiac remedy was already attracting interest south of the Canadian border. The prospect of becoming involved in a major cancer treatment breakthrough excited entrepreneurial medical doctors and their financiers, and as attractive U.S. offers to Rene began to surface, her Bracebridge patients feared she would abandon them.

Local newspapers had been writing articles about thier Bracebridge heroine totally savouring the recent international attention. In early August, only days after Rene's rejection of Dr. Banting's offer, one published a feature story on a cancer specialist, Dr. W.L. Whittmore of New York City, who had come to investigate Rene's work at the clinic for his boss, Dr. John Gartner. Dr. Gartner, head of the Cancer Control Commission in New York City, was following up on an offer he had made to Rene four years earlier of a fifty-bed ward in his hospital to treat cancer patients — before her notable Bracebridge clinic had ever been thought of. At that time, she hadn't been in a position to accept the offer, and she recognized that the current offer was of more value than the previous one. "I really want to keep this work Canadian, and want it to be considered a Canadian, and not an American, discovery. There is pathological proof of cure from my treatments, and I have previously proved in animal research that I can prolong life, after cancer inoculation."[235] This was only one of many offers Rene would refuse.

News of another "attractive offer" appeared in several newspapers that autumn. On October 15, a local newspaper reported that Rene had met an unnamed Chicago doctor in Detroit to examine a patient of his.[236] She had been persuaded to go to Chicago to meet a number of important doctors and financiers who had assured her of secure financial backing if she relocated there. "A Rochester medical institute has also lately suggested to Miss Caisse that they would be pleased to have her come to them," the story continued. Dr. B.L. Guyatt, instructor of the anatomy department at the University of Toronto, clearly aware of the Chicago offer, was reported to have come to Bracebridge to examine Rene's patients at the clinic on Tuesday, October 13, and then had a hurried meeting with Mayor Richards and councillors J.K. Shier, H. Rawson, and A.W. Tingey. It was obvious that the town wanted Rene to remain in Bracebridge, so a petition was hurriedly composed, to be signed later by a number of influential people.

The story was augmented in a dramatic and detailed interview with Rene Caisse in Toronto's *Globe* two days later. The heading proclaimed: "CANCER 'REMEDY' CLAIMED IN BRACEBRIDGE GOES TO U.S.A."

> On the invitation of G. T. Rich of Chicago, Rene Caisse of Bracebridge, who claims to possess a cancer remedy, left Toronto Friday for the famous Mayo Clinic in Rochester, Minnesota, where she hopes her treatment will receive more attention than it has in Canada. In an interview with The Globe yesterday, Miss Caisse claimed that her sponsor at Rochester would be a "well-known diagnostician of Chicago who was attached to the Mayo Clinic for many years."[237]

The unnamed physician was Dr. Clifford Barborka, and through him Rene was introduced to Dr. Cutting of Northwestern University Medical School and subsequently Dr. John A. Wolfer, the director of the Tumor Clinic.[238]

Rene's connection with G.T. Rich, she stated to the *Globe*, had been established through Dr. Guyatt. Mr. Rich was a millionaire who had promised her financial support, she reported. "I can have $500,000 to open a hospital in which to carry on my work," she declared, "and it does not matter where it is located. Of course I am sufficiently patriotic to want to have it on this side of the line, but if I do not get permission from the government, I will have to leave." Rene related to a *Globe* reporter that she had been treating cancer patients with a series of hypodermic intravenous injections of a "vegetable compound" that she had discovered "'by accident' thirteen years ago, while she was a nurse."[239, 240]

Dr. Wolfer presented Rene Caisse with several case history records to examine. After being assured that she would not have to disclose the nature of her remedy, Rene accepted his offer to demonstrate what he referred to as her "so-called cancer cure" on a group of volunteers, all hopelessly inoperable cancer patients who had previously submitted to radium and/or surgery.[241] The study was to be carried out under the observation of Dr. Wolfer and five staff doctors who would be the sole judges of the results obtained. If anything of value was demonstrated in Miss Caisse's treatment of cancer, he said, then the public as well as the medical profession at large should have benefit of it. This offer stipulated that there was to be no publicity of any sort.

Arrangements were made for Rene to begin her Essiac treatments in Chicago in November. She was provided with distinctive accommodation in the home of the Rich family on affluent Sheridan Road, and George Rich was a welcome guest in Rene's mother's home in Bracebridge in late November.[242] Elmer Rich was president of the Simonize Company, and the family was interested in seeing a cancer cure developed.

The publication of a report in the *Muskoka Herald* October 29[243] claiming that "Miss Caisse would be going to the U.S. every other week" prompted the swift submission of the completed petition to the prime minister of Ontario, minister of health, and the attorney general two days later. Drs. J.A. McInnis and H.L. Minthorn of Timmins, W.C. Arnold of Ottawa, J.E. Richie and E.A. MacKercher of Cobden, and Robt W. Davis of Toronto signed it. Prominent Timmins merchant J.W. Ecclestone of Marshall-Ecclestone, brother of Bracebridge hardware merchant George W. Ecclestone, signed it as well.

To reinforce the earlier appeal to the same politicians, an almost identical petition was submitted two days before Christmas to Dr. Faulkner by nine doctors who had long been impressed with the success of Rene's treatments. Drs. Wm. H. Oaks of Rosseau, M.S. Wittick of Burk's Falls, W. Dillane of Powassan, E.G. Ellis and J.M. Greig of Bracebridge, and F. Shannon of Churchill signed that petition. So did her colleagues Dr. Ben Guyatt and Dr. Robert Fisher of Toronto, and the ever-faithful Dr. McInnis, who had also signed the October document.

Both petitions pointed out that cancer was the greatest scourge of humanity; that Essiac was a treatment that had proven to be a complete control, if not a cure, for cancer; and that Miss Caisse had pathological proof of the effectiveness of her remedy. The doctors openly declared that patients treated by Rene several years ago were still living and well, and that immediate action should be taken to make Essiac available for cancer sufferers. Their major concern was that Miss Caisse might be persuaded to move to the U.S., where she could continue to demonstrate her treatment before American university doctors. They emphasized that "as physicians and doctors of the Medical Profession" they recognized the importance of this treatment and were in favour of keeping it a Canadian discovery, in Canada.

CHICAGO TRIALS

People's fears were not without foundation. Patients and Bracebridge residents were frantic when their Nurse Caisse often

December 23, 1936.

To:

The Honourable the Prime Minister of Ontario,
The Honourable the Minister of Health for Ontario,
The Honourable the Attorney-General of Ontario.

This humble petition of the Undersigned, in the Province of Ontario, sheweth as follows:-

1. That whereas Cancer is considered the greatest scourge of humanity.

2. Whereas Miss Rene M. Caisse of Bracebridge has discovered "ESSIAC", a treatment which has proven to be a complete control, if not a cure for Cancer.

3. Whereas patients treated with "ESSIAC" several years ago, are still living and well.

4. Whereas Miss Caisse has pathological proof of the effectiveness of "ESSIAC", her treatment for Cancer.

5. That we as physicians and doctors of the Medical Profession recognize the importance of this treatment and are in favour of keeping it in Canada.

6. And whereas Miss Caisse is demonstrating this treatment before American University doctors, which will inevitably take her out of Canada permanently if action is not taken to keep her here.

Wherefore be it resolved that we, the undersigned do strongly urge that the Honourable, the Minister of Health take immediate action, to make this treatment available for cancer sufferers, and keep it a Canadian discovery.

And your petitioners will ever pray &c.

Signature of petitioner	Post Office Address	Occupation
W. H. Oaks	Rosseau	Physician
M. F. Kittick	Burks Falls	Physician
A. Hope	Bronson	Physician
E. J. Ellis	Bracebridge	Physician
F. Shannon M.D	Churchill	Physician
B. Guyatt	Toronto	Physician
R. Miller	Toronto	Physician
J. M. Grey	Bracebridge	Physician
J. A. McInnis M.D	Timmins	Physician

Physicians petitioned to the Ontario government to recognize Essiac and allow Rene Caisse to continue her work in Canada.

disappeared from the clinic at regular intervals, for several days at a time. But when at home, Rene would attend her patients during the day, and at night, boil and steep the herbs for a new batch of Essiac, then strain and bottle the decoction early the next morning. She began the exhausting series of trips back and forth to Chicago by train, assuring the patients that "there will always be a cancer clinic in Bracebridge."[244]

The study at Northwestern University's tumour clinic got underway on November 13, 1936,[245] when six patients received Essiac treatments, and by January 1937 there were twelve very sick people for her to treat. All were given Essiac, both orally and by injection, with local applications to the skin.

Rene granted an interview with the *Evening Telegram* in her Bracebridge clinic, and it printed this heading: "Nurse Spurned in Ontario Claims U.S. Clinic Satisfied Cancer Treatment Helpful."[246] The two-column report described her struggle for recognition in Canada. This public revelation of the project that she had agreed to undertake quietly certainly must have upset Dr. Wolfer.

Rene had been commuting across the border to Chicago every other week throughout the first three wintry months with Dr. Wolfer's explanatory letter to get through customs. It read, "This is to certify that Miss Rene Caisse is coming to our clinic at Northwestern University Medical School at frequent intervals to treat cases. She brings with her at each visit essential drugs and remedies which she uses in the treatment of these cases."[247]

Rene's timetable was hectic. After treating her patients in Bracebridge, she would travel to Chicago to administer her Essiac on a Friday or a Monday. Then she made a mid-week stopover on the journey home at the King Edward Hotel in Toronto where she would attend to more people. One day in January, she overheard a bit of very favourable conversation about her work as she passed through the hotel lobby. Then there was a trip to Timmins. While on a train returning home, Rene was exhilarated to listen to an extensive discussion about her between four men at the next dining table. They did not know that the subject of their talk was seated next to them.[248] Ontario newspapers continued to write editorials and articles expressing their regard and concern for the extraordinary human interest events taking place.

Back and forth Rene went, attempting to meet the needs of at least three groups of terminal cancer victims. She was a nurse, but she seldom took time to look after herself. The demanding schedule finally took its toll. In February Rene was taken to her sister's home in Michigan, where the family doctor counselled her to take a complete rest for two to three months for her heart and nervous strain.[249]

There were only six patients left in the Essiac study by February, as one had died and two were hospitalized. Others were removed from the program by Dr. Wolfer.

In her February 26 letter to Dr. Wolfer, Rene had every reason to complain that it was unfair of him to have her spend about one hundred dollars besides risking her health to go to Chicago to treat only six patients. She was really ill, she told him, although she had treated two hundred patients at her clinic a week ago, went on to Toronto to treat fourteen more, then on to Walkerville (where her brother Leon lived) to treat again more. She asked him to tell her candidly if he had lost interest. But Dr. Wolfer assured Rene in his letter of March 13 that he was still "in hopes that we might be able to carry along our work at the Clinic for a sufficient time to provide us with some evidence to enable us to make up our minds relative to your treatment." Two weeks later, on March 25, Rene wrote Dr. Wolfer to say that she was now well enough to return to Chicago, so arrangements were made for her to arrive there on April 4.[250]

This was to be her final trip. As the remaining six patients waited for Rene to administer their Essiac treatments, she could not help but see how much they had deteriorated since early February.

Two men died later that month. Clearly, with her own neglected health and the seriously ill patients failing to respond as anticipated, Rene had no choice but to stop the trials. Treating the Chicago patients as well as several groups elsewhere had proved to be an insurmountable challenge, and Rene could not keep up the demanding schedule.

Rene received a poignant letter from a Chicago patient, May Miller, addressed to "Miss Case, Cancer and Tumor Researcher from University of Toronto, Bracebridge, Canada."[251] While she was concerned about Rene's health, she pressed Rene to return to help her again, since she practically had no pain now. May Miller, who had suffered from pain and swelling for several years, was one of the "inoperable, hopeless" cases included in the Essiac study. Dr. Wolfer was to admit later that this patient "thought she received relief from pain" and "is now in fairly good condition." He noted that she had been last examined at his clinic on September 13, 1937, after another course of radiation therapy, and her condition was little changed.[252]

Retrospectively, perhaps Rene should have left some of her ampoules[253] and tea with Dr. Wolfer to be administered in her absence. Certainly Rene feared that his laboratories could analyze her remedy, although Rene was to learn later while involved in the Essiac study in Cambridge, Massachusetts, that a laboratory there was unable to decipher its contents. But the trials did not demonstrate the beneficial results that Ontario physicians had witnessed.

Dr. Wolfer expressed some doubts when wrote the following words to Dr. A. Moir of Peterborough, Ontario, in answer to his request for information about the Chicago trials:

> I'm sorry that there had been so much publicity about our clinic. The understanding was that when she began at our Clinic, no publicity of any sort should be made.... I fear that Miss Caisse is capitalizing the experience. Due to some personal contact about a year ago, Miss Caisse and her "Cure" were brought to my attention. Because of certain specifications that had been made, we thought it advisable to allow her to try her "Cure" on a limited number of cases.[254]

In Chicago, however, Rene had absolutely no control over the trial. She wasn't consulted, kept abreast of results, or allowed to establish her own controls over the project. No one will ever know what benefits Rene's decoction had on the fragile patients who received Essiac treatments and lived months past the dates the doctors had projected. Although seven of the twelve patients died in 1937, five would still be alive in 1938. Three of them were "in very poor condition" and one was "completely disabled," according to Dr. Wolfer's report to Dr. Robert T. Noble, the new registrar of the College of Physicians and Surgeons of Ontario.[255] One of Noble's first jobs was to pursue the activities of persons such as Rene Caisse, who in his opinion was treading the fine line between her role as a medical practitioner and that of members of the college. The Chicago trials would have been of great interest to him.[256] He wrote Dr. Wolfer in Chicago during the summer to enquire of his knowledge about her and received a reply dated August 31, saying that Miss Caisse came a number of times to the clinic and treated possibly eight or ten patients. In no case did he see any appreciable benefits, he wrote.[257]

Rene gave treatments on these dates:

November 13, 1936, 6 patients   January 11, 1937, 10 patients
November 27, 1936, 9 patients   January 25, 1937, 8 patients
December 11, 1936, 8 patients   February 8, 1937, 6 patients
December 28, 1936, 7 patients   April 5, 1937, 6 patients[258]

It would be published years later that Rene recalled treating thirty patients successfully at that clinic over a year and a half.[259, 260] She maintained that the American doctors concluded that her remedy prolonged life, broke down modular masses to more normal tissue, and relieved pain. "I was proved right. Later, these doctors offered to open a clinic for me in the Passervant [sic] Hospital in Chicago, if I would stay in the United States," she reminisced in her 1966 autobiography.[261] Actually, at the time of the trials, a Toronto newspaper reported that the doctors were "so satisfied with results that the clinic is to be removed to the Passavant Hospital where eventually a new group of patients will be submitted to be under similar conditions of observation."[262]

Rene reasoned that she wanted her work recognized in Canada, and, of course, she didn't want to abandon her Bracebridge patients. The pressures of the trials, travelling, and tribulation seemed to override her full recollection of the stressful events over the years.

RALLY FOR ESSIAC

During the apprehension over the Chicago trials and Rene's frequent illnesses and absence from the clinic, her supporters sustained their momentum. The enthusiasm for maintaining the cancer clinic in Bracebridge continued. The high school auditorium had a good audience for a well-publicized community event that took place March 13, 1937. Residents flocked to hear all about Essiac from doctors who knew its value.[263] Rene's friends Drs. McInnis and Minthorn came from Timmins to speak, as did Dr. Arnold from Ottawa.

Dr. Minthorn, known as the "baby doctor," enjoyed a Bracebridge connection. His son Bill and his family operated the Airport Motor Court until the summer of 1955, when it was sold to Stan and Vivian Einarson. His grandson, John, was born in Bracebridge. Herbert, a

---

You are cordially invited to attend a meeting in the High School Auditorium at Bracebridge, Ontario, on the evening of March 13th, 1937, at eight p.m.

The topic of the evening will be why "Essiac," the Rene M. Caisse treatment for cancer, should be given recognition by the medical world.

Doctors who have visited the Bracebridge clinic and investigated this work, will be there to tell of the results they have seen. Any medical man who has suffering humanity at heart will be interested in this work.

Author's collection

Invitation to the Essiac information rally.

popular name in the Minthorn family, was a second cousin to U.S. President Herbert Hoover; Minthorn's aunt Hulda (Helen) was the Canadian mother of the thirty-first U.S. president.

From the high school stage, Dr. Minthorn claimed that he was no speaker, but a good thinker and worker for Miss Caisse. He told the audience that he'd had occasion to see her work three times, four weeks apart, and said that she is doing good work and has ample proof of the effects of her treatment.

Professor Guyatt was studying for his MD exam and couldn't come. He had received his MB in 1914 and was now updating his credentials at the University of Toronto. Just days before the rally he spoke to the Scouter's Club Smoker at Hart House about sanity and mental health, the consequences of unchecked selfishness and jealousy, and the necessity of accurate information regarding the other party before entering the state of matrimony.[264]

The doctors all told about the successes of Rene's herbal remedy as a cancer treatment. "When it comes to cancer, Nurse Caisse has the key to the situation," Dr. McInnis told the assembly.

Local support came from Dr. Edward G. Ellis; the new mayor, Ben McBride; Wilbert Richards, who was now the town clerk; and W.J. Hammell, an Essiac patient and former member of Parliament for Muskoka. John Vanclieaf spoke forcefully on his successful treatment. "Dr. Faulkner told me I hadn't cancer, but all I've to say is what is the difference between being eaten by a wolf or eaten by a bear. The doctor said he couldn't cure me and that I would die. Miss Caisse cured me in six treatments."[265] According to the newspaper report, Bracebridge's medical community wanted to see Essiac recognized, but, Dr. Ellis said, "We can only think so much and say little as doctors, although as private citizens we are right behind a beneficial treatment."

Following Dr. Minthorn's presentation, Rene arrived at the auditorium after a very busy day, and the crowd welcomed her with an ovation. But she "was unable through tiredness to address the gathering." (Unfortunately, she missed hearing songs sung by Ernest Taylor and William Flatman, which were accompanied by local piano teacher Louise Golden, ATCM.) Thus the informative presentation about Essiac became a rally, generating support for the next delegation from Bracebridge, which would meet with Health Minister Dr. Faulkner in Toronto two days later.

At the event in Toronto, the third people's petition, signed by seventeen thousand citizens, demanded that the nurse be given a licence to practise because of the proven success of her treatments.[266] The Bracebridge contingent included MPP Kelly, Mayor McBride, Town Clerk Richards, Councillor W.E. Hunt, and citizens A.W. Tingey, J.K. Shier, and Jack McVittie. Also present were Drs. McInnis, Arnold, and Minthorn, and his wife, who was a registered nurse in Timmins. Pathologist Dr. Gladstone W. Lougheed, with whom Rene had worked in Christie Street Hospital from 1928 to 1930,[267] was also in the delegation to share his experience with her work. Dr. Faulkner was flanked by his head of hospitals, Dr. B.T. McGhie, and Dr. Noble, who, when he overheard a report that a man who had become ill seven years ago was now working his farm at Beaverton, responded, "All I say is, God bless Miss Caisse, if that be true."[268]

CANCER LEGISLATION PLANNED?

Dr. Faulkner told Rene, "If you feel you have something you should not hesitate to prove it."

"I am not afraid to prove it," she returned, "but there is no reason to work on mice."

Faulkner reminded the group that "Miss Caisse is not the only one who thinks they have a cure," and the medical profession was as anxious to get a cure for cancer as anyone. "We are considering introducing legislation that will give all the people who have the idea they have a cure for cancer an opportunity to submit their cures to test and they will receive such encouragement that will put beyond doubt the nature of the treatment."[269] In fact, the Ontario government was well into quietly drafting legislation for that very purpose.

The mayor, town clerk, and Drs. McInnis and Minthorn had a private meeting with Sir Frederick Banting following the mass presentation. Dr. Banting reiterated his willingness to co-operate with

Miss Caisse, but reminded the visitors that she had not availed herself of the opportunity he had offered. Banting indicated to the delegation that he "had much interest in Miss Caisse's work, but had nothing to do with permitting Miss Caisse to practice her treatments … he was only interested in research."[270]

As requested by the Ontario Medical Council, Rene laboured preparing a report of her work, including revealing case histories during her trips to Chicago. But in Toronto, before she could give it to Dr. Noble, she succumbed to what was reported as a heart attack and stayed with her sister Albina Allen.[271] On April 13, her friend Dr. McInnis presented it on her behalf to Dr. Noble. "Surely this is of vital importance to the whole world and there should be no delay in making it available to every cancer sufferer," the *Muskoka Herald* pondered.[272]

Actually, Dr. Noble was gathering evidence against Rene Caisse and her Essiac treatment, carefully keeping track of patients who had died under her care. And physicians who had provided handwritten diagnoses for their patients to give to the nurse were requested to complete a newly designed questionnaire and return it to his office. Some doctors feared that they could lose their licence to practise medicine should the college disapprove of their faith in Rene's treatment. As a result, her patients became frustrated and frightened when their physicians refused to provide a diagnosis.

CLINIC ENLARGED

Rene's friends knew that she needed more space to accommodate the increasing number of patients in her clinic, so while she was recuperating from her latest illness in Toronto, they enlarged her clinic and give it a fresh new look — with the approval of the property committee of the town council.[273] Upon her return to Bracebridge on April 23, the clinic was redecorated and now filled the whole ground floor of the old hotel, except for one room at the rear still used by the Canadian Legion. Two rooms on the second floor were prepared for her as well.

The bright, attractive office, dispensary, reception room, and five treatment and dressing rooms were suitably furnished by her supporters. The main room was decorated in warm rust, sand, and brown, with floor-length drapes on the three large windows. Furniture placed on a colourful Congoleum rug included a few antique chairs, some tables, and a modern chesterfield, as well as some cozy, comfortable chairs for which suffering patients and their families were grateful. The beautiful paintings that enhanced the walls had been presented to Rene by an appreciative Toronto patient, Albert Moses.[274] And two large glass doors had been installed on the south side of the building so that patients had only a short walk from their cars to the clinic.

With this princely new decor surrounding her, and patients demanding her treatments, Rene must have felt quite confident that her cancer remedy was on the brink of major acceptance.

In early June, Bracebridge citizens were offered an informative article in the *Muskoka Herald*. "When is Essiac for the Rene M. Caisse Treatment for Cancer going to be made available to cancer sufferers all over the world?" the story began. Reading suspiciously like Rene's composition, the two-column article reviewed the many achievements of the past ten years and featured a photo of her in her nurse's uniform standing at the door of her clinic (see page 159). Essiac would be proven as a cancer preventative throughout the world, the story forecasted.[275]

Rene rushed into the newspaper office and bought several copies of the issue containing the article about herself to proudly send to her family and supporters all over the country.[276] In response to this article, a Baysville reader suggested that Rene was being treated as an "outlaw" and that Dr. Faulkner had ignored the seventeen-thousand-name petition he received last March. M.J. Kelly offered to take up the demand to get her a "certificate" to practise her treatment of cancer.[277]

Rene claimed to have recently interviewed Dr. Noble, head of the Ontario Medical Council, but had received little or no encouragement. "These Medical Association representatives would oppose the closing of my clinic, but they refuse, on the other hand, to acknowledge the efficacy of my treatment. That is what baffles me," Rene told a reporter. She insisted that she wasn't concerned about money, but rather wanted full credit for her cancer remedy discovery.[278]

PREMIER'S SUPPORT

On July 13, 1937, Rene sent a CN telegram to the premier asking if he could see her tomorrow, as she had been trying for an appointment for several weeks. Also on July 13, Hepburn replied to Rene in a day letter saying, "Exceedingly regret necessary to cancel your appointment Thursday as I will be out of city."

But Premier Mitch Hepburn did agree to meet with Rene Caisse. In spite of severe pressures on him, including the epidemic of violent labour strikes, a near coalition between the Liberals and Conservatives to fight the challenges surrounding the U.S.-based Congress of Industrial Organizations (CIO) headed by John L. Lewis, and his poor personal health, he made time. Facing still another barrage of letters from Rene and her patients, the premier and Provincial Secretary Harry Nixon met with Rene at Queen's Park on July 22, 1937.[279] This meeting was one of dozens Hepburn had handled on as many subjects that record-breaking hot month.

He told the press: "I am in sympathy with Miss Caisse's work, and will do all in my power to help her." Hepburn was also heard to say that if Miss Caisse's treatment had lessened the suffering and prolonged the life of those fortunate enough to secure it, no human agency should stand in the way of its broader service to humanity. The honourable gentleman promised to pass a bill in the legislature to license her work, if necessary. "The onus is now on the medical profession," he was reported as saying. It "must now either prove or disprove Miss Caisse's claims, and I do not believe they can disprove them."[280]

BANTING TO EXAMINE ESSIAC?

The following week, however, the Toronto dailies carried the story that Sir Frederick Banting would be asked to meet with Hepburn and Nixon to advise them about Caisse's treatments, and that they might possibly license her to legally administer her remedy. "Province Tests Nurse's Cancer Treatment, Sir Frederick Banting to Examine Treatment of Bracebridge Nurse";[281] "Reported Treatment for Cancer is Being Referred to Banting," the newspapers announced.[282]

The United Press (UP) also released the story, which then hit newspapers across the continent. "Banting asked by Hepburn to test Essiac," headlines blared.[283] It seemed Rene was on her way. While no evidence suggests that the celebrated doctor worked

Evening Telegram, July 26, 1937

Rene's treatment gets headline billing second only to world chaos.

specifically in the investigation of Essiac, in a short disjointed column entitled "Banting on Cancer" he stated, "So far, surgery, X-ray and radium are the only means of proven value in the treatment of cancer." Among other assorted topics, he briefly described his institute's work with chickens and Rous sarcoma, its use of the Warburg technique of measuring the respiration of tumour cells, and the 1914 Japanese study of rabbits and malignant tumours caused by painting their ears with coal tar.[284]

Dr. Faulkner admitted that months ago he had set a policy of referring all supposed cures and treatments for cancer to Sir Frederick before committing the government to any opinion or action. But one of Faulkner's Belleville colleagues, Dr. G.J. Forster, wrote him about his own cancer cure that he wanted investigated and was told that he had to go Dr. (J.G.) Cunningham of the hygiene division because the Department of Health had no facilities for testing cancer cures.[285] In another letter to Faulkner, this from Buffalo doctor T. Simpson Burton, breastfeeding was promoted for infants because of his studies that showed that female rats that were not allowed sucking experienced breast cancer, and he wanted funding for further work. Dr. R.O. Fisher took great interest in the matter, which was also brought up for discussion at the Canadian Mothercraft Society.[286]

Rene took time during a two- or three-day trip to Montreal on August 4 to write Mitch Hepburn on Hotel Windsor letterhead telling him that Dr. W.C. Arnold went to Philadelphia at the request of Dr. Ellise MacDonald of the Franklin Institute to discuss her work. But, she reminded him, she wanted recognition from her own country.

Prime Minister Hepburn told the *Toronto Daily Star* a few days later, "We are going to see that she is able to practice. Miss Caisse has established a clinic at Bracebridge, where she treats by means of a herbal remedy cancer patients referred to her by doctors. I am sure that she is doing a good work, but to permit her to continue, we may have to ask the Legislature to give her a license to practise through the means of a special bill." He and Provincial Secretary the Hon. Harry Nixon were very interested in her work.[287, 288]

A SUMMER OF EVENTS

Outside of Rene's extraordinary local sphere, the wider world continued to unfold. Her brothers and sisters were having children, but she had little time to visit her new nieces and nephews when they travelled to Muskoka to carry on the tradition of summers at the lake. Rene's niece Rita, who had been helping at the clinic, entered the nursing school at St. Michael's Hospital in Toronto to fulfil her dream.

During the summer of 1937, poliomyelitis, also called infantile paralysis, was spreading throughout Ontario in epidemic proportions, and Bracebridge was not immune. The iron lung, a "breathing monster" in which the patients were placed to help them breathe, was set up in a farm home known as St. Anne's House of the Sisters of St. Margaret.[289] There Dr. Bastedo, his young assistant Dr. W.G.C. Kenney, and Dr. Fraser M. Grieg worked with the quarantined patients. Bracebridge had only a handful of polio victims, but the annual agricultural fair was cancelled that year. When the Bracebridge Isolation Hospital no longer needed the iron lung, the one-and-a-half-ton machine was stored in a space at the back of the building that housed Rene's cancer clinic.

At a time when major distress was involving so many people, at least the staff of life was being improved. Waite's Bakery announced that it was able to supply the public with sliced bread.[290] In fact, Waite's Bakery was to sell sliced bread and its popular chelsea buns to Muskoka's permanent and seasonal residents well into the 1980s.

CHAPTER 7

U.S. & PROVINCIAL RECOGNITION

AMERICAN DOCTORS COME TO BRACEBRIDGE

Despite what seems to have been a failure in the Chicago trials, plainly the publicity regarding the Ontario government's recent sympathy for Rene's work and Banting's proposed investigation into her remedy brought the subject to national prominence.

While Rene was travelling back and forth to Chicago during the winter of 1936–37, Dr. Emma M. Carson of Los Angeles, California, heard about Miss Caisse's Bracebridge cancer clinic from Professor Henry James Reynolds of the University of Chicago. "Dr. Reynolds is a big man in the American medical world, heading a Federal research committee, and he has taken an interest in Miss Caisse," Dr. Carson said.[291] Several of her professional friends talked about the Caisse Cancer Clinic in Bracebridge, Ontario, and praised Miss Rene M. Caisse's Essiac treatment for cancer that they claimed had become, practically speaking, "world famous" during the past fourteen years. "After listening to their fascinating statements, in whom I had implicit confidence, my curiosity became thoroughly stabilized," she claimed, and so Dr. Carson exchanged letters with Rene, arranging to visit her Bracebridge clinic the following summer.[292]

Apparently Rene notified the local newspapers about Dr. Carson's expected arrival on August 11; the *Muskoka Herald* enjoyed a half-hour's conversation with the doctor, a "small middle-aged lady" who looked years younger than her seventy-four years. The article stated: "Dr. Carson is well known throughout California, and has had signal honours conferred upon her by the President Theodore Roosevelt administration and the President Wilson administration. She has travelled extensively, and been around the world three times. She has been 'trying to retire' for some years so that she might give her attention more fully to research work."

Dr. Carson told reporters, "I expected to talk with Miss Caisse and go home within 24 hours, but I am going to stay a week or two. Everything in the clinic is absolutely open, excepting for the formula Miss Caisse uses, and I have advised her to keep that her secret for the present."[293]

As she approached the clinic her attention was drawn to "a large assemblage of automobiles, including several ambulances, along both sides of the street."[294] A number of patients comfortably lounged about under shady trees, sociably visiting with each other as they waited for their turn to enter the clinic for treatment. Rene welcomed the doctor into the large, pleasant waiting room where more than fifty people were casually conversing. Dr. Carson later wrote, "I realized that I had never before seen or been in such a remarkably cheerful and sympathetic clinic," and made up her mind to obtain absolute proof of the efficacy of Essiac.

In her distinctive style she recorded that she was amazed at the endurance of patients and those "oppressively afflicted persons, so patiently endeavoring to pleasantly entertain those who were unable to converse owing to the forbidding location and extent of complications.... The prominently manifest absence of moans, groans or grunts were especially emphasized by the fact that not a complaint, criticism or fault of any nature and not the slightest trace of impatience or confusion was evidence anywhere."[295]

CLINIC ROUTINES

The doctor followed the nurse everywhere inside the clinic, writing down Rene's methods of procedure, her answers to questions asked, and personal observations about everything and everyone during the twenty-four days of investigation. The clinic was open from 9:00 a.m. until 7:30 p.m. four consecutive days each week during the summer. In the treatment room, Dr. Carson talked with the patients, heard their stories, and examined some four hundred cancer patients who were willing to be examined by her. One patient declared that, was it not for Miss Caisse's Essiac remedy, he would have departed from this earth! In the evenings, after the clinic closed, Dr. Carson studied the case histories, physicians' signed handwritten diagnoses, and the personal testimonies the patients had given her. She reviewed Rene's "recorded notes of indisputable improvements pertaining to the physical process and progress toward extirpation [destruction] of cancerous substances and involved tissues," and she could hardly "believe that her brain and eyes were not deceiving her."[296] But Dr. Carson noted that Miss Caisse never claimed that her Essiac remedy would cure cancer, but always said, "If it does not cure cancer, it will afford relief, if the patient has sufficient vitality remaining to enable him to respond to treatment."

Rene and Dr. Carson were exceptionally knowledgeable about the subject of cancer and had observed firsthand the damage that X-rays, radium treatments, and surgery could cause. It seemed that they both had a great understanding of the suffering that patients endured from their terrible physical condition and the added assault of the medical treatments.

Dr. Carson recorded that in the Caisse clinic she accumulated data from reports, interviews, statements, and her own personal observations from 150 of the most technical and seriously compli- cated cases, as well as a number of letters from patients whose homes were in other cities. Dr. Carson travelled in the autumn- coloured leaves of Muskoka to visit patients John Vanclieaf of Baysville and James Summerwill of Sunderland. At the end of her extended stay, she concluded in her report, "I am pleased to assure all interested persons that I paid my own expenses and investigat- ed to satisfy my own interest in cancer victims and learn of some remedial agent for cancer that proved superior in every respect to all else, and which I would conscientiously recommend to my friends or interested persons."[297]

"ESSIAC" CANCER TREATMENT ENDORSED BY EMINENT PHYSICIAN

REPORT ON VISIT TO CAISSE CANCER CLINIC, BRACEBRIDGE, ONTARIO, CANADA

BY EMMA CARSON, M.D.
Hayward Hotel,
Los Angeles, Cal., U.S.A.

NOTE: Dr. Carson, well-known lady physician of Los Angeles, Cal., paid a visit during the summer of 1937 to the famous Cancer Clinic of Miss Rene M. Caisse at Bracebridge, and has submitted to Miss Caisse, (now Mrs. McCaughey), the following observations and impressions:

Cordially and courteously extended to all persons, who are and who may be interested:—

"ESSIAC"—Miss Rene M. Caisse's remedy for Cancer has unquestionably established amply adequate evidence, specifically verifying its indisputably efficacious potency for the extirpation of cancer. "Essiac" also includes the extermination or annihilation of the original, primary and "Parent Cause" and the generative progress of cancer.

Cancer has definitely enthroned itself upon a world-famous pedestal, and has appropriated and adjusted a gruesomely significant crown—"Humanity's Arch Enemy Number 1."

Therefore, through mutual interest pertaining to suffering humanity (especially persons attacked by Can-

MISS RENE M. CAISSE
Discoverer of "Essiac" Cancer Treatment.

cer), I am enthusiastically offering this review and commentary by compiling excerpts and extracts from annotations authentically accumulated and carefully recorded during my visits at Bracebridge, Ontario, (including the months of June and July, 1937) for the exclusive purpose of investigating the real merits of "Essiac". The succeeding explanatory narrations should prove an assurance of my explicit confidence in the marvellous efficacy of "Essiac" and its effective results, obtained and demonstrated through the efficiency of Miss Caisse, which was evidenced

when administrating her "Essiac" treatments. A sincerely grateful pa-

Rene's brochure presenting Dr. Carson's report of her visit to her clinic.

Dr. Carson was quoted as saying in the *Huntsville Forester*:

> I am thoroughly convinced Nurse Caisse has cured cancer. I am satisfied of this from the actual results I have seen following a close study of the histories investigated. I am amazed beyond expression. Canada should be proud of her great achievement to medical science and the world should be given the opportunity to acknowledge her discovery as one of the most important in the modern history of medical discovery.... Action by the Government in recognizing the great work Miss Caisse is doing is the first essential and if in view of what I have seen with my own eyes, the Ontario Medical Council remains indifferent it will be a crime against civilization.[298]

She said she would meet with Premier Hepburn and Dr. Bates, head of the Ontario Medical Council, but there is no evidence of such a meeting taking place.

The daily logs created by the California doctor seemed to be the basis for a five-page September report she sent Rene, entitled "Miss Caisses's Successful Work, Cordially and Courteously Extended to All persons who are and who may be interested." It seemed that sometime after July 1938 Rene would arrange the printing of an eight-page pamphlet that contained Dr. Carson's message. (In it, Rene was referred to as "now Mrs. McCaughey [sic]," thereby dating the publication.) It included a portrait of herself, captioned "Discoverer of 'Essiac' Cancer Treatment."[299, 300]

DR. LEONARDO OF BUFFALO

Just as Dr. Carson was winding up her investigation of the Essiac treatment, a second American physician, Dr. Richard A. Leonardo, came into the clinic while on a weekend holiday with State

Attorney General Muscarello at Muskoka's classic Windermere House on Lake Rosseau.[301] The chief coroner of Rochester, New York, was a well-known cancer specialist, reportedly having written several books on the subject, frequently travelling to Europe to study advanced surgical procedures.

On Thursday, August 26, Dr. Leonardo interviewed and examined some patients. Rene regarded his scoffs at her remedy as fair challenge and told him that the only way to prove or disprove the work was to remain in the clinic, see the patients, and watch her work. Which he did. After he spent a day with patients, he told Rene that although he was satisfied that she was getting results, it was her and not her treatments — it was entirely psychological, he insisted.[302]

On the second day, he and Dr. Carson studied case histories and watched Rene administer treatments until the last patient departed at about 7:30 p.m. One of the patients Dr. Leonardo examined was Annie Bonar, whose own doctor could not do any more for her and told her that she had about three weeks to live. She had been diagnosed by biopsy at St. Michael's Hospital by Dr. E.R. Shannon as having cancer of the uterus and bowel, but her cancer spread after radium treatments apparently caused her arm to swell to double its size and turn black. Her weight plunged from 150 pounds to 90 pounds.[303] The American visitor told her that her arm, as far as medical science was concerned, was quite dead and would never move again because of cancer progression.

At the end of his visit, Dr. Leonardo met with Rene. "Young lady," he told her, "I must congratulate you. You have made a wonderful discovery."[304] He'd have to go home and discard his surgical instruments, he said.[305] "He offered to establish and equip a hospital in Rochester, N.Y., if I care to go there and with him," Rene said, but she wanted to prove the merit of Essiac in Canada, she would write years later.[306, 307] Dr. Leonardo left Bracebridge claiming to be firmly convinced of the value of her work, and indicated his intention to return to Bracebridge at a later date. One would wonder how the medical profession received his exciting information. He spoke before a New York medical association on Monday night, August 30, and included in his address references to Miss Caisse's work.[308] Dr. Leonardo said he "was satisfied that she [Miss Caisse] possessed a remedial agent which was far superior to any method of cancer treatment he had ever seen," and suggested that it might change the whole theory on cancer, eventually doing away with surgery, X-ray, and radium treatments.[309, 310]

Following the very demanding visits from the American physicians, Rene spent a few days in Toronto on what was reported as "business."[311]

PROVINCIAL ELECTION LOOMING

With Ontario caught up in the provincial electioneering in September 1937, the usual campaign promises abounded. Expenditures for education, health, and agriculture were increased and voters were reminded that children were spared the ravages of typhoid and tuberculosis now that pasteurization of raw milk was mandatory. And Callander's darling Dionne Quintuplets were now three years old and Crown wards of the Hepburn government, earning hundreds of thousands of dollars as a major tourist attraction.[312]

Frank Kelly was in the midst of campaigning for re-election in his riding of Muskoka-Ontario. Since July 1934, when the Liberal sweep unseated long-time Conservative member George Ecclestone of Bracebridge, the "charming and influential statesman"[313] had continued to handle both his job as mayor of Huntsville and his position as a member of the provincial legislature. Incumbent Kelly, running as the Liberal-Progressive candidate, gave thousands of potential voters handbills displaying Rene's picture. Presumably with her permission, the small convincing poster quoted her as saying she had the premier's positive assurance that legislation would be passed at the very next session of Parliament to permit her to operate her clinic legally.[314]

My Clinic and the Government

I have received many enquiries from my patients all over the Muskoka-Ontario riding, asking for a statement of my position with the Hepburn Government.

While I am not desirous of taking an active part in the present campaign, knowing that my patients must hold divergent views on politics, yet it is but fair to them that I state exactly my position with Mr. Hepburn and his Government.

Through Mr. Kelly, I have, upon several occasions, secured interviews with the Minister of Health and other members of the Government, but no great progress

MISS RENE M. CAISSE

was made until I was able through an appointment arranged by Mr. Kelly, to see the Prime Minister. He was already familiar with my appeals, and had studied the results of my treatment. He received me very courteously and kindly, and finally agreed that obstinacy on the part of the Medical Council could only be met by a special Act of the Legislature, permitting me to legally operate my clinic, and administer my treatment.

He agreed that this would be done, in view of the convincing evidence I had submitted, of the benefits derived by cancer sufferors from my treatment. I have since had his positive assurance that he WILL PASS such legislation at the next session. This is very heartening to me.

I have not seen Mr. Rowe, nor has Mr. Rowe made any attempt to make direct enquiry about my work, or to write or interview me concerning it. Mr. Horner called and expressed personal interest in what I was doing.

RENE M. CAISSE

This rare campaign ad encouraged voters to support the Hepburn government, which promised to create a special act to permit Rene to use her treatment.

However, Kelly's opponent, Mason Horner, who was running for the short-lived Liberal-Conservative Party, wrote open letters to the electors of Muskoka:

> It is regrettable that a private citizen carrying on certain professional and humanitarian functions, Miss Rene Caisse, should be mentioned in the current Political campaign. This has not been done by the Liberal-Conservative Party. It has been done by the Liberal Party. Most of the citizens of Muskoka who have been instrumental in furthering her interests have been Conservatives. They, in particular have been her friends.
>
> I am convinced that Miss Caisse will receive as fair, if not a squarer deal from the Honourable Mr. Rowe and his administration after Oct. 6th than she can ever hope to receive from the Honourable Mr. Hepburn.[315]

Frank Kelly maintained that it was not his purpose to make a political football of the service being rendered so efficiently in the interests of cancer sufferers by Rene Caisse, and he bought newspaper space to tell the voters so. "It transpires, however that my opponents are stealthily, and I think unfairly, dragging the matter into this campaign." But he enforced the government's pledge to invoke the powers of the legislature to permit her to carry on her great work.[316]

Thomas Bengough,[317] the recently retired editor of the federal government's Hansard, the official minutes of the Legislature and House of Commons, urged the public to aid Miss Caisse in her beneficial work in a letter to the editor. In good time for pre-election consideration, the now Muskoka Beach resident wanted to acknowledge the "greatest medical development of modern times." He felt that Muskoka residents didn't fully understand the importance of Rene's remedy and encouraged the newspapers to continue reporting on and promoting her work.[318]

On October 6 the Liberal-Conservatives took just two ridings, while Earl Rowe's Conservatives won twenty-three,[319] and the Liberals swept the province with sixty-three seats, Kelly's among them. Perhaps Kelly's propaganda did assure the generous Muskoka vote, but now, as Horner said, he was faced with Rene's friends in the Conservatives and would have to pick up where he left off, bringing forward government legislation to allow Rene to keep the clinic open.

One of two Liberal ministers to go down in defeat was Dr. Bert Faulkner of West Hastings.[320] Mayor Richard Arnott of Belleville ran on a "vote for one you can trust" slogan and soundly beat him. For the first time, a non-medical man was named health minister. Lawyer Harold Kirby, who had been the outspoken North Toronto alderman with no medical background at all, was the surprise appointment. In fact, the night before the announcements, all the newspapers had presumed he would be made transportation minister.

RENE'S PUBLICITY

All the publicity surrounding Rene Caisse was something she could never have imagined during her rather routine years of nursing. As probably the most unpretentious member of her family, the others having enjoyed more limelight in their younger years, Rene was now herself cast into the public arena, the subject of vocal and published supporters and critics alike.

The hometown newspaper of Drs. McInnis and Minthorn questioned, "Did the Ontario Medical Council tie the hands of doctors who have investigated Miss Caisse and her treatment? Neither medical ethics nor the Ontario Medical Council should be allowed to prevent hope and the chance for cure, or even the alleviation of suffering, from being available to cancer sufferers." The newspapers, in support of Nurse Caisse, were asking that the Department of Health make some fair arrangement to recompense Nurse Caisse and give her freer rein to make the treatment available more generally.[321] Newspapers throughout Ontario, from Toronto to

Temiskaming, echoed their support for the government's positive intervention on behalf of Rene.

Rene received an extraordinary offer in the fall of 1937 from a group of U.S. businessmen through their Buffalo attorney, Ralph Saft, who himself had the usual roster of community service interests. Her lawyer, Charles S. McGaughey of North Bay, Ontario, reviewed it and considered the proposition.[322] In part it read, "It is proposed to organize a Foundation headed by Miss Caisse which will bear the name of Essiac or Miss Caisse; to make $1 million available for buildings and equipment; to pay her $50,000 a year in addition to royalties from the commercialization of Essiac; to make her a gift of $200,000."[323] Another biographer revealed that a few weeks later the businessmen's lawyer sent a letter intending to "sweeten the offer" with a promise of a $1-million "donation" to her work.[324]

The provincial government was settling into its continued activities, while in Toronto on November 13, Rene wrote a note to Hepburn on delicate blue King Edward Hotel letterhead that was probably delivered from the front desk to his suite:

> Could you come to Bracebridge and visit my Cancer Clinic on Sunday afternoon? I treat patients from 1 p.m. to 5 p.m. Sunday. I feel that after one visit you could talk to Sir Frederick Banting not on my behalf but on the behalf of suffering humanity and know that you were right. I would also like you to bring with you Mr. Arthur G. Slaght and George McCullagh[325] if this were possible. I think this would do more good than any personal talk we could have. My work speaks for itself and I do know that you would understand why I am pressing the matter, and forgive my bothering you when I know you are so busy. Respectfully, Rene M. Caisse.[326]

Realizing that she may need special legal assistance over the next while if the government evoked its promises, Rene and

Charles recognized the important role Arthur G. Slaght, KC, was playing in both the provincial and federal governments. He was called a "brilliant counsel for the Liberals,"[327] and although he was a personal pal of Hepburn and prominent in his conclave, he was also Prime Minister Mackenzie King's ally and House of Commons member for Parry Sound. Rene recalled that Slaght, now a wealthy sixty-year-old Toronto criminal lawyer, was a barrister and solicitor in Haileybury while she was in the area, and a Liberal candidate for Temiskaming in 1919. It was there that he made his fortune in Kirkland Lake gold.[328] But not everyone thought highly of Mr. Slaght. The Tory *Muskoka Herald* had noted in 1935 that a "liberal candidate proposed by the Toronto liberal headquarters for the next election in Parry Sound District is none other than the notorious Arthur G. Slaght, K.C. of Toronto."[329]

Arthur Slaght, KC, and Premier Mitch Hepburn. The Globe & Mail *snidely suggested that they may have been discussing Slaght's plans to build a summer home on his large Parry Sound Property.*

The unabashed Rene wrote the premier and asked for Slaght's help and further conference with Dr. Banting. On November 23, Mitch Hepburn wrote Rene, saying, "When a conference is arranged with Sir Frederick Banting and the new Minister of Health, Honourable H.J. Kirby, I shall be glad indeed to invite Mr. Arthur C. Slaght, K.C. to represent you." There is no evidence that the conference ever took place, but records show that Slaght, while he was politically warm towards her, referred Rene's case to one of his partners, Donald Carrick, who was to work with Rene during the next year or so.

The week before Christmas Slaght wrote Rene, telling her he had a letter from Mr. McGaughey describing her recent experiences with Dr. McGhie and Dr. Noble.[330] Slaght had had a long interview with Mr. McGhie, and wrote to Rene on December 20, 1937, that he thought McGhie was "very friendly in the matter." He suggested that they let things stand as they were until his return from Florida in January.

Interestingly, the week before Christmas 1937 Rene was called to meet with the deputy minister of health who "informed her that a check-up of results of her treatment for cancer had been made and assured her that she will not be hindered in her work at her clinic."[331]

CHAPTER 8

LEGISLATION FOR CANCER REMEDIES

RENE A MEDICAL DOCTOR?

In early January 1938, one of Ontario's leading weekly newspapers, the *Alliston Herald*, presented an editorial musing that because the deputy minister of health had assured Rene that she would not be hindered in the activities of her cancer clinic, a further step should be taken.

The *Bracebridge Gazette* reprinted the story January 13, and the editor suggested that Miss Caisse be made a medical doctor, reflecting a precedent established when Sir Oliver Mowat was premier of Ontario. Apparently Mr. Delos R. Davis of Amherstburg, just west of Kingston, was a layman with a "decided flair for law," the story went, and he was regarded by many to be a better lawyer than some graduates of Osgoode Hall. He found himself continually badgered by the Ontario Law Society for practising without credentials. Finally, the Hon. W.D. Balfour, member of South Essex, got enough support to make Mr. Davis a lawyer by an Act of Parliament. His opponents could do nothing further to stop him, and he eventually became an authority on municipal law and KC, the story continued. The editor noted, "With the portfolio of Health in the hands of a non-member of the medical profession [Kirby was a lawyer] it might not be impossible to have Miss Caisse made a doctor by Act of the Legislature."[332]

QUEEN'S PARK MAY DEMAND SECRET CANCER SERUMS

Premier Hepburn determined that at its next meeting, the Ontario cabinet would decide upon the question of procedure in setting up a committee to investigate *purported* cures for cancer. "Surely we can find power somewhere to set up such a committee and bring this difficult, this very serious situation to an end."[333] Premier Hepburn announced that the government intended to set up a committee to test cancer remedies and added that he would consider what authority the legislature possessed to force Dr. Hett and other users of so-called remedies, not only to disclose the nature of their treatments, but to submit them to laboratory and clinical investigation.[334]

THE STAR WEEKLY   3

CANCER CURES?

Dr. J. E. Hett has been reinstated on promise to reveal his serum formula.

Miss R. M. Caisse's herbal treatment has aroused wide interest.

Dr. Hendry Connell, Kingston, discoverer of "ensol." In circle: A patient receiving injection.

Three Ontario residents claim specifics for relief of cancer. Dr. J. E. Hett will shortly reveal his formula; Nurse R. M. Caisse uses herbs, and Dr. Connell's "ensol" is widely used in the U.S.

Bracebridge Public Library, Rene M. Caisse Archive

On April 23, 1938, the Star Weekly *featured Rene with two "cancer cure" physicians, Dr. Hett and Dr. Connell.*

Looking at the larger picture, Hepburn's government had not only Essiac to consider, but also other significant cancer remedies that were very much in evidence. Beside Dr. Hett's serum, Dr. Koch's Glyoxylide was still being fostered after decades, and Dr. Hendry Connell of Kingston was still dispensing his harmless Ensol. Dr. Glover's anti-cancer serum was also well known to the Department of Health. Cancer patients were demanding access to these remedies, so pressure on the government continued to build.

On February 8, 1938, Toronto daily newspapers published such headlines as "Doctors Seek Law to Bare All Cancer 'Cures'" and "Banting to Aid in Cancer Remedies Probe." The *Muskoka Herald* reported, "This week has seen an important development in the question of Government recognition of cancer treatments, and one which may affect Miss Rene Caisse of Bracebridge."[335]

The College of Physicians and Surgeons of Ontario agreed to take action on behalf of the government and demand the revelation of the secret formulae of the cancer "serums" that were appearing in parts of the province. A committee would be formed headed by a layman, and Sir Frederick Banting, who was researching cancer, would be one of the chief members.

Dr. J.E. Hett of Kitchener, Ontario, had defied the college and continued to use his serum treatment for cancer. This complicated situation had seemingly brought the secret cancer serum problem to the forefront of the minds of the college and the government. Like Rene, Dr. Hett had refused Dr. Banting's offer to use his labs, and he felt that the time had not come to reveal his formula. He just wanted to use it for the benefit of humanity. But a committee of his peers erased his name from the medical register and he lost his licence to practise medicine on April 14, 1937.[336]

HEPBURN SCOLDED

Each time Rene took a stand against the Health Department or confronted the medical profession, her confidence increased. In a letter dated February 14, she scolded Hepburn for denying to the *Toronto Star* that he had promised to put a bill through the legislature granting her special licence to practise:

> When I told you that the Medical Association was very powerful, your answer to me was "they are not as strong as our Legislature." Now, if you have found out that the Medical Profession is more powerful than you thought it was, and have

found that your hands are tied and that you cannot keep your promise to me, would it not have
been more manly or more kindly to have admitted that you were unable to keep your promise,
than to publicly deny having made it, making me
out untruthful?[337]

The Tory *Muskoka Herald* too was concerned that the Liberal government had not kept its promise to Miss Caisse and suggested
that the pledge of the legislature enactment on her behalf was
being shelved. They warned the government that the petitions
signed by thousands of people and the highly placed medical men
who had visited and been impressed with her work showed strong
public support of the Bracebridge nurse and her remedy. She stated that she "had pathological proof of cure by her methods." The
story continued, "She does not claim to cure all who come to her,
because some come after they have tried everything else, often
with deep-seated radium burns, which she has to heal as well as to
cure the disease. The percentage of improvements is, however,
astounding."[338]

The college asked for her co-operation, but Rene complained
that it was ridiculous for the government to ask a person who had
worked for years with inadequate means on a discovery to work
with those who "had everything, every opportunity to make discoveries and who have found nothing. I have indisputable proof, which
the medical authorities have accepted and do accept, why should I
have to go back to treating mice?"[339]

Miss Caisse felt that Premier Hepburn, who had promised to
act on her behalf, would keep his pledge to her. The public, she
declared, is with her, and already thousands have signed the petition now being circulated by her patients. Even the Toronto
branch of the National Labour Council representing thousands of
workers pledged its support and promised to dispatch a protest to
Queen's Park deploring the government's attitude toward cancer
treatments. They asked that legislation be passed to permit Miss
Rene Caisse to distribute her cancer serum widely.[340] CNR engine

watchman Tony Baziuk of Capreol, a grateful patient who felt that his lip was healed, and Mrs. R. Whitmore of Toronto, who claimed that her cancer was cured, were collecting signatures in Burk's Falls for Rene's latest petition. Mr. Baziuk had already collected three hundred signatures in his hometown after neighbours saw his progress.[341]

Rene threatened to close her clinic if the government passed the bill Mr. Hepburn was proposing. She warned that she'd leave Ontario and consider the two splendid offers she recently received from Buffalo and Chicago, but she didn't want to leave her patients. "At the same time, I have been assured that the Government of Alberta is interested, and that I could be given freedom to practise there."[342]

An editorial in the *Muskoka Herald* explained:

> Mr. Hepburn is understood to have agreed to pass an act of the Legislature at the session this year to give Miss Caisse a license to practise medicine, and it is stated the Hon. Harry Nixon, Provincial Secretary, confirmed Mr. Hepburn's pledge.... There have been changes made in the Department of Health since the elections, for the former Minister went down to defeat in his own riding. The new Minister cannot have been said to be entirely familiar with the argument presented in Miss Caisse's behalf.[343]

Also awaiting the outcome of the government's decision to approve her treatment was a colleague of Buffalo attorney Ralph Saft, James C. Kennedy, who followed up on Saft's earlier proposal to establish a foundation that would feature Rene's cancer remedy and place him in charge. On February 18 he sent Rene a letter to reflect on her concerns about the probable failure of the private bill that would allow her to practise freely with cancer patients and tried to set up a rush meeting with her. "I hope, regardless of whatever opposition crops up, your legislative connections do not weaken on their promises to secure provincial recognition for you." Kennedy, also president of the *Buffalo Courier Express*, wanted the meeting to precede the arrival of Saft and two of his clients, who were on a "mission which concerns the raising of money." Presumably their ability to raise money to finance their project depended on whether or not the government would grant Rene a licence to treat cancer, but Rene's records do not list any concluding details to this account. (In 1939, James Kennedy would write a column in his newspaper about Rene Caisse and her Essiac phenomenon.)

Commercialization and exploitation of Essiac: the very terror that was to haunt Rene all her life.

The application for Rene to practise medicine in the treatment of cancer "in all its forms and of human ailments and conditions resulting therefrom" from Charles McGaughey's North Bay office began a chain of events.[344] In preparation for her fight, Rene sent off a typeset letter to the premier on February 22, 1938, along with a list of some 210 patients from all walks of life who had benefited from her treatment. Most of them had cancer and many were terminally ill. There were farmers, gentlemen, housewives, labourers, ladies, and great number who were elderly and retired. Others included a baker, a captain, a lawyer, a cashier, a chauffeur, a fire ranger, a janitor, a hotel keeper, a mason, a mechanic, a notary/conveyancer, a stenographer, a teacher, and a truck driver. At that time, the petition had been signed by approximately twenty-eight thousand voters in the province asking that Rene be given a licence to carry on her "humantarian [sic] work." Had the weather not been so harsh, the list of names could have been double in length, she claimed.

Her opening statement may have upset a number of her colleagues, particularly Dr. Fisher, who had worked closely with her during the experimentation of the Essiac herbs and their response to the patient's condition: "I have discovered and developed unaided 'Essiac,' a beneficial treatment, and in some cases a cure, for the most dreaded of diseases, Cancer."

During the last days of February, Frank Kelly announced that he would "speak for her on the floor of Legislature, whether or not his leader agreed."

"The definiteness of the promises given by Premier Hepburn and later echoed by Frank Kelly cannot be treated lightly," Bob Boyer of the *Muskoka Herald* wrote. "It was by means of such pledges that many of Miss Caisse's supporters were led to support the Government in the general elections. It cannot be said that they 'were only promises made in the heat of an election campaign' for they were made before the election was decided upon."[345]

THE PRIVATE BILLS

The Ontario legislature had three contentious issues in the form of private bills coming before them when they reconvened in March 1938. One was prepared to enable osteopaths and chiropractors to use the title "doctor." Another regarded Dr. J.E. Hett's licence reinstatement, and the third issue was, of course, Nurse Rene Caisse.

It would seem that in late February, in an attempt to head off the government's consideration of alternative cancer remedies with "secret" ingredients, professor of pathology Dr. William Boyd from the University of Toronto warned members of the Royal Canadian Institute in Convocation Hall that these "cures" for cancer were nearly all without value. Dr. Boyd stated that supposed discovers of secret remedies refuse to disclose their composition "for the good reason that were the ingredients known the worthlessness of the claim would be at once apparent." He insisted, "There is a tide in the affairs of cancer which, taken at the flood, leads on to cure, but if we allow it to pass without using the tried means which science has placed in our possession, the blood of the patient is on our hands."[346, 347]

Re-elected government backbencher Frank Kelly made good on his promise to table a bill to allow Rene to practise medicine in Ontario, using her treatment for cancer. But not without some problems. On Rene's behalf, Charles McGaughey delivered a draft copy of the bill and the petition to the legislative assembly supporting the bill to the clerk's office on February 23. The petition revealed that Rene had been actively engaged in developing a remedial and curative treatment for cancer during the past fourteen years and, with permission of the Department of Health during the past three years, conducting a cancer clinic in Bracebridge. Her effective formula had been successfully treating many cancer patients. In two days, a severe letter arrived at McGaughey's North Bay law office advising that his client was too late in entering her application in order to have it considered during the present session of the legislature. She had failed to advertise her application once a week for six weeks, and certainly there wouldn't be time to get any more than three copies of the advertising in before the specified time, the letter chastened. Enclosed were the draft copy and her cheque for $240.[348]

However, on March 2, Premier Hepburn and Opposition Leader Leopold Macaulay, a Peterborough-born lawyer, agreed to permit the nurse's bill to be introduced in the legislature. In a rare action, the rules of the House were suspended on March 2 to allow it to be presented without customary notice.[349] With neighbourly legal advice from Arthur Slaght, his federal colleague in Parry Sound, Liberal Kelly tabled the bill requesting that Rule No. 63 be suspended. Conservative Macaulay seconded it, and with unanimous approval the bill was carried and qualified to begin its process. According to press reports, the bill put in by Miss Caisse was presented too late and she had to pay a penalty for the late entry.[350]

Rene Caisse took a moment of relaxation that week in Bracebridge when she attended a card and games party at St. Joseph's Parish Hall to honour the Very Reverend Dean Michael O'Leary for twenty-seven years of ministry in their parish. The dean mentioned Rene's work and asked her to address the guests. Then Rene's niece Valeen Slater came forward, made a speech, and presented Father O'Leary with a handsome Gladstone bag.[351]

Robert Boyer, editor of the *Muskoka Herald*, reminded readers that the legislature had no lawful right to demand Rene's formula, "since patents and discoveries are really the jurisdiction of the Dominion government."[352]

CANCER COMMISSION TO BE FORMED

Days after the Caisse Bill was tabled, the Hon. Harold J. Kirby stunned Rene and countless other Ontarians by announcing his intention to introduce legislation creating a commission to investigate cancer treatments.[353] The local press kept up its barrage, and Rene again threatened to leave the province.[354] Picked up by the local press, the news of the proposed legislation sent shock waves through Bracebridge. It would give a committee power to force anyone treating cancer to hand over his or her formula, as well as to make a finding as to the value and merit of any remedy it investigated. But at least the new law had been notably modified from the original drafts that had been in development since at least late 1936.

National Archives and Library of Canda 10531

Premier Hepburn and Lt-Gov. Dr. Herbert Bruce discussed the proposed Cancer Remedy Act.

When Ontario's lieutenant-governor, Dr. Herbert A. Bruce, received his review copy of the proposed Cancer Remedy Act back in January 1937, he did so with personal interest and expertise. Dr. Bruce was formerly a professor of clinical surgery at the University of Toronto and wrote several professional papers on cancer from the early 1920s to the late 1930s. As a surgeon in 1922 he wrote, "I personally cannot see any advantages, in delaying an operation for cancer for the purposes of preliminary radiation. After the growth is removed radiation is always employed and seems of value."[355] During 1931 he took a three-month trip to cancer centres in Europe and wrote about it to share what he had learned with others.[356] In 1932 Dr. Bruce gave a gleaming $500 operating table with all the up-to-date attachments and electric heating to the new two-storey brick veneer hospital wing in Bracebridge.[357]

Regarding the planned cancer act, Dr. Bruce wrote the deputy minister of pensions and national health, Dr. R.E.Wodehouse, to say that he was assured Mr. Hepburn would "put this through as a Government measure if the expense of setting up the Commission for the Control of Cancer Remedies is borne by the King George V Jubilee Cancer Fund. It seems to me that there is no purpose to which this fund could be so well employed as in this way."[358]

Provincial bureaucrats Drs. J.G. Cunningham and B.T. McGhie felt that the concept of control would be very unpopular with patients and the public.[359] Another edition of the draft added the word "investigation" along with the dreaded word "control," likely to soften the blow. Now the 1938 legislation dropped the word "control" and limited the powers of the Act to investigate and demand the formulas, but not to ban or restrict the remedies, presumably making it much more politically acceptable. Interestingly, one major newspaper used the offending word in the title of a short item about the proposed the legislation: "Act Planned to Control Cancer Cures."[360] The sweeping powers to inquire into any treatment for cancer included penalties for violation of not less than $100 and not more than $500, or a prison sentence of thirty days. A second offence had more severe penalties.

Rene's supporters were horrified by the demands of the proposed new legislation, and Rene was concerned that if committee members protected under this act left the commission, they could then reveal any formulas learned during their tenure and use them for personal profit. She figured that the doctors on the commission were political appointments and would be ousted in a change of government. "The people of Ontario would be paying a group of men to develop something that was developed and discovered 15 years ago," Rene was reported to say. "I have developed and proven a cure right here in Bracebridge and I am running a clinic where hundreds of cancer sufferers are being treated and helped." And she was not about to give her formula "to a group of doctors who never did anything to earn it."[361, 362]

Rene threatened to close her cancer clinic and take up one of many offers to practise in the United States if her private bill seeking the authority to practise in Ontario failed.[363] One report claimed that if she could gain the right to practise, American interests promised that they would finance a $1.5-million sanitorium somewhere in the Muskoka district, where the majority of her patients live.[364] She was understandably bewildered by the crossfire of support and dissension suddenly rocking her world. It was coming from all directions: from patients, physicians, and politicians. Wilbert Richards was the Bracebridge member of the recently formed Muskoka Tourist Development Association, and on March 14 he promoted the preparation of a petition of support for Rene.

Bracebridge council passed the same resolution. It was estimated that the presence of the clinic in town meant a financial benefit to the community of $1,000 per week, helping to pay for the cost of maintaining the building for the clinic.[365] But neither the prime minister nor the minister of health would receive the deputation with the twenty-eight-thousand-signature petition.[366]

Selection of the members of the proposed cancer commission was underway. The Health Department was swamped with recommendations for membership, and the *Globe & Mail* reported that "great care will be exercised in making the selections."[367] Locally, a search was launched for a Muskoka man to ensure a balance of representation on the committee.[368]

DEBATE OF PRIVATE BILL

March winds and a numbing cold of −32° C challenged those trudging the open spaces of Toronto's Queen's Park, while activities inside the government buildings created plenty of heat. On March 15, MPP Kelly gave the first reading to Rene's private bill asking for a licence to practise the treatment of cancer patients. The next step would place it before the Private Bills Committee in a few days. Rene's life was now a wrapped up in two sets of proposed government legislation: one that would set up the dreaded cancer commission and one that would allow her to treat cancer with Essiac.

The debate before the Private Bills Committee on March 24, 1938, in the Ontario legislature buildings was lively. Someone lugged several heavy fourteen-inch binders of petitions from citizens in support of Rene's bill. It was a who's who of residents, patients, doctors, and others who had signed their names, addresses, and professions on the hundreds of pages over the past three years.

Rene claimed at various times that some fifty-five thousand signatures[369] from Washago to Rosseau, from Vankoughnet to Gravenhurst, and north to Huntsville and beyond — arguably an inordinately large number — had been collected to support her.[370]

Rene is proud of the petitions to be presented to the Private Bills Committee.

To augment the numbers during the campaign, Bracebridge patients and friends sent petition sheets to other people across Canada and the U.S. who either used or believed in Essiac. Former Conservative premier George S. Henry and members of his party signed it as well.[371]

Parkdale's Conservative Member Fred McBrien invited Rene to address the committee chaired by Minister of Public Welfare David Croll. "The reason I asked for this Bill is that I cannot diagnose cancer," she explained. "I asked for it [so] that it would put me on a different standard with the medical profession and would allow me to treat patients in an ethical way. I refuse to submit my formula," Rene stated, "until the medical profession admit[s] from the cases they see, not the material I use, that there is some merit in my treatment. If and when they do that, I will be willing to give my treatment to the world."[372]

When a committee member suggested that the bill did not require disclosure of the formulas, Minister of Health Harold Kirby argued, "There is a clause in the Bill that provides that if in the wisdom of the commission they think the formula is required, they can command it."

Frank Kelly then spoke on Rene's behalf to the members on the committee and acknowledged the reluctance of the medical profession to recognize cancer "cures," even if the cancer did not recur for years. He said that opposition was to be expected from doctors, and that they would argue that Miss Caisse was unwilling to reveal her formula. The Muskoka MPP did not claim that she had a cancer cure, but firmly declared the following: [373]

> I know people who were sick and now are well. Their cases were diagnosed by doctors as cancer, and I know that up to a time at least, Miss Caisse would not take an case unless it was diagnosed as cancer. I know that doctors will say these people did not have cancer. Well, I say it is a crime for doctors to tell you that you have cancer if you haven't. I know that I would pass out if a doctor told me that. I

know scores and scores of people who have been helped by this treatment.

I think she's perfectly right in not submitting her treatment to the medical profession till she finds out if she is recognized or not.... Even if she prolongs life, I think she should be allowed to continue.... This is a Bill which if turned down today will deprive thousands and thousands of suffering people![374]

Many patients who were anxiously watching the discussion cried, "No! No!" The minister of health again protested. "This was an absolute misstatement," he said. "There had been nothing done by the department of health to prevent her from practising." Barrister Leslie M. Frost, recently elected Conservative MPP for Victoria-Haliburton, Ontario, asked, "Is there anything to prevent her carrying on?" Mr. Kelly replied that there was nothing to prevent her treating patients now, provided she didn't charge a fee. And he added, "There had been persecution and police interference for 15 years."

Rene's counsel, Don Carrick, the young lawyer sent by Arthur Slaght, who could not be present, read aloud James Summerwill's letter about going to Miss Caisse in November 1935, and now being pronounced by physicians as without any growth. Then he announced, "I have many patients here willing to speak to the committee, if asked." Chairman David Croll suggested that there would be no questions for Rene in that the committee members were all laymen (presumably they would not understand her medical language). "The Government is setting up a board to deal with these reported 'cures'," Croll continued. "Since it can be proved so far beyond doubt that this treatment is a valid one, and has proved so effective many times, I suggest this Bill be reported favourably and sent back to be held for approval of the Lieutenant-Governor."

"The Bill was not to allow Miss Caisse to practise medicine," Mr. Carrick emphasized, "only the treatment of cancer." He went on to say, "Miss Caisse cannot treat cases unless a diagnosis has been made by a doctor and sent by him asking her to treat the patient.

There have been many refusals by doctors lately, I leave it to the committee to draw any inference."

A woman from a back seat in the audience called, "My mother is a cancer patient yet three doctors refused to give a written diagnosis, though they gave it verbally. We finally had to get it by a falsehood."[375]

Frank Kelly suggested that there appeared to be a cabal of doctors against Miss Caisse lately, and loudly maintained, "Every case used to be diagnosed and recommended by the doctor. She got many cases sent to her, but none are coming now. There seems to be some nigger in the woodpile."[376]

Daniel Lang, on behalf of the College of Physicians and Surgeons and the Ontario Medical Association, urged the committee not to pass the bill, but to leave the matter to the investigating committee. "If the committee passes the Bill, it will go all over the country that there is a cure for cancer."

"Is it true," asked Mr. Kelly as he turned toward Mr. Lang, "that doctors are forbidden to send patients to Miss Caisse or diagnose for her?"

"Certainly not!" he replied. "The Medical Council has no such right."

"I believe that there is some underground way in which doctors are told they must not do it," Mr. Kelly persisted, "but I will take your word for it. While patients still flock to Miss Caisse's place at Bracebridge, like patients do to Dr. Locke at Williamsburg," he continued, "they no longer go with their doctors' approval."[377]

Liberal Dr. M.T. Armstrong, a dentist from Parry Sound, proclaimed, "I back up everything Frank Kelly has said. I don't know whether it is a cure or not, but I certainly have seen people who have been helped by her. I've been talking to practically every medical doctor in the legislature and there isn't one who is against Miss Caisse."

When Conservative W. Duckworth (Dovercourt) contended "every court had to take the evidence of the people" and the committee should hear the witnesses present, there was supporting applause from the large audience. Then another

Conservative, W.A. Summerville (Riverdale) cited two cases he knew in which a patient had been given up by the medical profession. Both went to Miss Caisse and benefited greatly. He explained to the committee members, "We want to help suffering humanity. What Miss Caisse wants is protection. This committee should do something to protect her."

About fifty patients applauded so loudly that the Speaker threatened to expel them from the House. "She should be helped," Summerville continued. "The Minister says that the health department has not interfered with Miss Caisse. Well, I say that heads of the department change. They may be gone in two or three years."

Rene was beginning to feel encouraged by the positive responses from the members who were vocally supporting her. Liberal Dr. A.S. Duncan of London said the medical profession would "be tickled" if it is proved by the committee that she has a "cure." If so, the nurse should be financially rewarded and the government should put up $1 million.

"She should not be asked to give up her formula unless she is protected," he asserted. "But I don't think it is the place of this committee to put the stamp of approval on this thing. If we did, we should have people all over North America beating a path to her door. We want to be very sure before we do it."

Mr. Duckworth again referred to the people who were present to give evidence, and his comment was received by prolonged applause.

T. Fred Stevenson made an appeal to the committee on behalf of his wife, whose breast had been removed two years earlier. In spite of X-ray treatment, cancer had recurred in the glands of her neck, and the surgeon told her there was no more hope. Mr. Stevenson pleaded, "Even if Miss Caisse can relieve the pain, she should be allowed to go on."

As the day's debate was about to conclude, Don Carrick[378] again urged the committee to report favourably on the bill, provided that it come into force with the lieutenant-governor's consent, and allow her to continue her practice in the meantime.

SOME BILLS FAIL

The request of Mr. Carrick and some of the committee members to allow more patients to be heard was totally ignored, much to the intense disappointment of Rene and her followers. The petition representing so many voters did not sway the well-lobbied members. About fifty members of the Private Bills Committee cast their votes, but although former premier George Henry and members of his opposition supported her, the bill was defeated by three votes.[379, 380]

The two-star evening edition of the *Toronto Daily Star* published that same day presented a detailed account of the debate that took place under the headline "Hints Cabal of Doctors Against Cancer Treatment: Bill Thrown Out."[381] "The Bill that would have authorized Miss Rene Caisse of Bracebridge to treat cancer and conditions arising therefrom was thrown out today by the private Bills committee," the story read. (One would wonder about the overall accuracy of the coverage of the dramatic meeting when an unidentified *Daily Star* reporter misspelled Rene's name and those of Frank Kelly and James Summerwill.)

The prophesy of the *Globe and Mail* on the morning of the vote, made in a strong editorial in opposition to the bill while admitting the impressiveness of Miss Caisse's claims, came true. "Since The Globe seems to have an inside track in relation to Governmental policy proposals, it was realised what the Government Members would be prepared to do," Boyer editorialized in his paper. "We greatly regretted that Miss Caisse's work should have been made a political football in this manner by any party, and particularly when there seems to have been no intention of doing anything for Miss Caisse."[382]

The fifty or so members of the Private Bills Committee rejected the bill on the grounds that it "would be tantamount to endorsing her treatment as a cure or effective remedy," and would prejudge Miss Caisse's claims before the investigation by the proposed special committee on cancer.[383]

Rene was furious when she learned later that her bill would have passed except that some members of the medical profession had assured the committee that if the bill was not passed they would sponsor the appointment of a cancer commission to hear her case. This, they had implied, would assure her treatment a fair hearing. "It came to light later that the Canadian Medical Association had debated my case with the Legislature before my hearing and had made this false promise," Rene recalled years later.[384]

Not everyone agreed that the formula should be kept secret. Yet Rene was adamant about doing so, despite heavy pressure to make it public. Reverend Canon F.J. Sawers said, "Anyone with a cure is inhuman not to reveal it," and the Department of Welfare minister echoed that thought. Mr. Gibbons, past president of the Toronto Board of Trade, sided with Rene, in the hope that favourable legislation would help generate money from her formulas to further Rene's Essiac research. School trustee Donald M. Fleming[385] and Reverend David MacLennan of Timothy Eaton Memorial Church both spoke out against her.

The osteopaths and chiropractors lost their bill, too; in fact there was nearly a riot in the corridors of the legislative buildings by some of a crowd of about thirty-five disgruntled practitioners and their supporters when former lieutenant-governor Dr. Bruce was insulted and intimidated for speaking against their case.[386] But Dr. Hett, one of the "cure operators" compelled to reveal his formula, was reinstated in the profession.[387]

It would have given no consolation to Rene to know that, in the history of the legislature, very few private bills have ever reached third reading. The committee voted to return her late filing fees of $139.39, which would come late in May.[388]

The debate in the Private Bills Committee must have seemed somewhat academic and unnecessary, considering that plans for a cancer commission were already being quickly developed. And patients, now to be without a clinic, were terribly confused and anxious.

One of the dilemmas faced by the governing body was the fact that Rene's treatment was not the only one believed by its developer to be a cancer cure. Essiac had to be included in the collection of remedies coming forward to the commission.

ONE OF THE GREATEST HUMANITARIANS

As if not recognizing the impact of the outcome of the failed bill, Premier Hepburn wrote the following patronizing letter to Fred Stevenson:

> I have for acknowledgement your letter of March 24th. So far as I am concerned, Miss Caisse may go on and continue treatment of her patients. As soon as the other Bill with respect to cancer cures passes, we shall of course ask the cooperation of Miss Caisse.
>
> If she has, as I hope she has, discovered a cure for cancer, she will go down in history as one of the greatest humanitarians the world has ever produced.[389]

The denial of a licence to Rene to allow her to use her medicine as a treatment for cancer also ended the possibility of funding from a former medical student and Kirkland Lake prospector named Harry Oakes. In a letter arriving at the premier's office on April 5, his representative wrote that Mr. Oakes had heard of her work at Northwestern University in Chicago and would sponsor the establishment of a public clinic on her behalf, if she received a licence to practise. The millionaire did not, however, wish to interfere in public or private affairs in Canada, despite his desire to assist Rene in her fight against cancer.[390] The next year, Oakes would receive a baronetcy from King George, and five years later he would die in a bizarre murder in his Bahamas home.

There was no question that this past month had put a tremendous emotional strain on Rene, her family, and her friends. A long out-of-town rest was much needed, so she closed the clinic on March 29 for a month to regain her strength and plan her future.[391]

KIRBY BILL PASSED

During Rene's absence from the clinic in April, the controversial cancer bill was quickly passed. Its long title identified it as "An act for the Investigation of Remedies for Cancer"; its official short title was "The Cancer Remedy Act, 1938." It was also referred to as the "Kirby Bill." The Act enabled the formation of a governing commission and ruled that anyone with a treatment for cancer would be required to submit samples of the formula, a list of the ingredients used in its preparation, and any information pertaining to the mode of treatment. While other researchers and healers would also be affected by the Act, the law appeared to be aimed directly at Rene. Providing for fines of up to $2,500 and jail sentences of up to six months for refusal to comply, it dashed all remaining hopes of Rene and others aspiring to a future in nonconventional cancer treatments.

A subtle clause in the Cancer Remedy Act would protect members of the scrupulously selected commission and their employees, who had to promise not to divulge any formula entrusted to them by a discoverer. Yet any person even remotely connected with the actual commission appeared not to be penalized for revealing any secret formula. The controlling legislation would be proclaimed law on June 1, 1938.

Provincial health ministry officials continued with the issue of funding the entire investigation of cancer cures, including moneys available from the King George V Silver Jubilee Cancer Fund. Cancer cures were usually expressed within quotation marks as "purported cancer cures," "reputed cancer cures," "so-called cures," or just "cures."

CHAPTER 9

FEDERAL CANCER CURE ISSUES

The Canadian Medical Association proposed in May 1938 that the Medical Research Council should undertake "certain duties in connection with the investigation of reputed cancer cures."[392] But the minister of pensions and national health, Dr. R.E. Wodehouse, was greatly disturbed because this matter had already been carefully considered in Cabinet months before and he felt that the Dominion government had no intention whatever of entering this field.

Back in February, Dr. McGhie, now deputy minister of public health for Ontario, and Drs. J.G. Cunningham and L.M. Leggett met in Ottawa with Dr. Wodehouse. They asked that the federal government make the new Medical Research Committee of the National Research Council (NRC), headed by Sir Frederick Banting, responsible for investigation of reputed cancer cures. At their suggestion, Dr. Wodehouse put in an immediate telephone call to the NRC president, General Andrew McNaughton, and told him that if the task of investigating reputed cancer cures was imposed on the council, it would have to set up a special committee who would be paid, and their findings would only be advisory. Ten minutes later, McGhie and Cunningham arrived at the retired army general's office to put the suggestion directly to him. Among other things, McNaughton asked the Ontario medical men how the province had handled the case of Miss Caisse. Dr. McGhie said, "This had been very simple because all the

Ontario legislation had to do was to refuse her application to operate an hospital."[393]

But Dr. Wodehouse had no intention to take it on. In fact, he suggested, "The National Research Council should adopt a non-committal attitude." By early March, though, Ottawa suggested that Ontario should find a solution to the problem raised by the province,[394] although the Ontario health ministry was still convinced that the Dominion government might undertake the job, and "in that event the Ontario committee would not be appointed." No further move was made to select the committee of inquiry at the time.[395]

Now, on May 5, General McNaughton said in his report that he would have a talk with Chairman Banting, and the matter could probably be "set at rest."[396]

It was reported in the *Globe and Mail* that the minister of pensions and national health, Hon. C.G. Power, told Ontario Health Minister Kirby that they were committed to the King George V Jubilee Fund for Cancer by which the CMA benefits. Kirby was not very hopeful of obtaining Dominion assistance for a cancer investigating committee, he told reporters. The number of people who claim to have cancer cures in Ontario has jumped to seventeen, Mr. Kirby remarked.[397]

The situation would still be under consideration in October when the private secretary to G. Reginald Geary, the federal minister of justice, enquired about funds at the NRC's disposal for the study of cancer and its treatments. General McNaughton told him no funds were available yet, but that some form of conclusion would be reached during the next few months.[398]

CLINIC THREATENED

Rene reopened her clinic on April 30 after returning from a depressing vacation at St. Petersburg, Florida. Distraught over the devastating legislation that was soon to be imposed upon her, Rene had made up her mind to write her patients that she was closing the clinic at the end of May. She wrote: "The Kirby Bill passed though the Legislature of the House becomes law on June 1st. In order not be become subject to this law, I have been obliged to close my clinic because this bill authorizes them to take my discovery from me. The only way I will open my clinic again will be at the request of the Premier. I regret very much leaving you."[399]

The meeting with Dr. Noble on May 19 didn't help much. He was rather brutal in frankness and reiterated that the committee would demand the formula and didn't agree with Rene's contention that the judgement of her treatment should be made on the results achieved rather than upon the method or formula.[400, 401] Rene was convinced her treatment would revolutionize the treatment for cancer, but that the medical profession would toss it out without testing it themselves. Even before the commission had a chance to examine the various cancer remedies, Dr. Noble apparently insisted at his meeting with Rene that none of Drs. Hett of Kitchener, Koch of Detroit, or Connell of Kingston had a cure.

Rene wrote the premier at his King Edward Hotel private suite on May 23 to tell him that she was closing her clinic that day. In a letter typed by her niece Valeen, she charged, "When the medical profession are powerful enough to change the laws of our Province to suit their purpose I feel that there is no use trying to gain recognition here." As well, she said, "I am not going to pay a fine, nor go to jail for doing good to suffering humanity. I am not powerful enough to fight out laws [sic]."[402]

Desperate, Charles McGaughey wrote Kirby, as her solicitor, and advised him that Miss Caisse was entirely in the dark about the developments of the Cancer Remedy Act in relation to her clinic. He asked to meet with Kirby and keep the discussion entirely confidential on any matter he did not want disclosed.[403]

The following day, the *Muskoka Herald* headlined that the Bracebridge clinic was closing and that Miss Caisse was going to the United States. In the article, Rene reviewed the successes of her clinic and thanked the many doctors who had helped her so much along the way. Drs. McInnis, Minthorn, Guyatt, and Arnold were thanked for their generous expressions of approval. Dr. McInnis had called her treatment beneficial and as such the greatest discovery as yet made in medical science.[404] Dr. Minthorn, who had visited the clinic several months in succession, said, "It may not be generally known but it is a fact that several in this part of the North have taken Miss Caisse's treatment and received very marked advantage — to put it mildly."[405]

The Tory newspaper reminded the readers that many of Rene's twenty-eight thousand petitioners "gave their vote and support to the Hepburn Government because of the Premier's promises, echoed in Muskoka by the local member."[406] The Liberal *Bracebridge Gazette* reported, "Sufferers from not only Muskoka, but all Ontario and from Quebec, the three Prairie Provinces, British Columbia and many parts of the United States have come to the clinic for treatment."[407]

Bracebridge Clerk Wilbert Richards revived his writing campaign during the public fiasco and wrote Mr. Kirby on May 28 begging him to let Rene's work continue uninterrupted until it could be given to the medical profession or until the commission had a chance to study her methods. He signed his letter "Ex-mayor."

Letters deluged the offices of the prime minister, minister of health, and other elected officials. Some of the writers begged articulately to be able to continue their treatments. Others had a low level of literacy but laboured over their words with care. They tried to make the government recognize that they were being denied the benefits of Miss Caisse's treatments. Kirby reacted immediately when angry and frustrated people wrote to him. He sent a copy of his statement to Robert Boyer at the *Muskoka Herald*, absolving the government and the college from responsibility of the clinic's closure. In part it read:

> It should be made clear to everyone that nothing in this Act prevents Miss Caisse from carrying on with her clinic as she has been doing in the past. Even if the Commission finds that Miss Caisse's remedy has no merit it has no power to compel Miss Caisse to close her clinic or discontinue the treatment of her patients. There is nothing in the Act to prevent Miss Caisse from proceeding to patent her remedy if she so desires. Miss Caisse

may protect her rights in the remedy by patenting it and using the patent for commercial purposes or she may transfer the patent to some organisation for philanthropic purposes. I desire to emphasise the fact that The Cancer Remedy Act neither prevents Miss Caisse from carrying on with her clinic nor interferes with any patent rights she may have in her remedy.[408]

Hepburn assured Mr. Chas. Naylor in Aurora that, "The Minister of Health and the Deputy Minister have personally interviewed Miss Caisse, and she has been advised that she can carry on her treatment in the meantime the same as she has done in the past." However, the premier noted, "The Commission for investigation of so-called cancer cures has not been set up as yet."[409]

The main headline in the *Evening Telegram* on June 23 read, "Patients Appeal for Reopening of Caisse Cancer Clinic" and presented a front-page story of various patients who presented their situation to the reporter. "Please, please do what you can to get the Caisse clinic reopened — it means my life," reflected the pathetic concern of one patient. The woman who made this plea had an inoperable cancer of the stomach. She had been taking Essiac for two months and was now feeling better and could retain food.

Although Rene now had the sanction of the Ontario government to continue treating patients in her clinic, the law that had the power to create a commission to demand her secret Essiac formula had yet to do so. But she closed the clinic. Under great duress, Rene almost reopened it at the end of the first week in June, and the newspapers could hardly keep up with the confusion. But she reversed her decision and the clinic remained closed.

Leslie Frost, Conservative member of the legislature for Victoria-Haliburton, had taken a keen interest in the Caisse story and was gathering newspapers from the Muskoka district.[410] On his legal firm's letterhead,[411] Frost replied to the husband of one of Rene's patients who was concerned about the closure of her cancer clinic:

My strong recommendation to Miss Caisse was that she should sit tight and go ahead with her work. The undertaking which was given her in April was that she should not be interfered with. The Minister of Health, I understand, has renewed this promise and I do not think the medical people would agree to take any action which would stir up public opinion. I suggested to her that she should rely on these promises and go ahead with her work. She must remember that she has gathered great favour as far as public opinion is concerned and I think she would be making a great mistake to throw this all up at the present time.

I was very much impressed with her attitude and with her obvious desire to help people, and for one I want to say that I do not feel disposed to disregard any possible remedy for this disease. I, of course, do not know what line the Government is going to take nor what Commission they will appoint, but I certainly do know that the public expects any Commission to use a person of this sort with sympathy and consideration and not to close their eyes to any avenue of assistance to sufferers from this trouble.

I think Miss Caisse might well consult her solicitor relative to taking steps to protect her remedy by way of patent to prevent any disclosure adverse to herself. This is a matter of some importance and I think she might be well advised to consult a good patent solicitor in Toronto.[412]

Muskoka's MPP Frank Kelly wrote to the minister of health on June 8 about the "Caisse controversy" in which he lamented, "I am almost sick of the whole thing because you will agree that I exhausted every effort on my part endeavouring to at least stimulate the

Rene takes a moment between patients.

interest of the House in work that she is doing.... I know how the Chief has expressed himself concerning this lady on so many occasions and I feel that he went a long way in asking that she re-open her clinic." After all, the commission was not yet appointed and the Kirby Bill stated only that they *may* require the production formula from the discoverers, he told the *Huntsville Forester*.[413]

Rene's lawyer and friend Charles McGaughey sought a meeting with Mitch Hepburn, and on June 14 the premier wrote that he would be glad to meet with him. Hepburn was called an absentee premier during that summer, so this was an interesting promise, and there is no record of the meeting. According to the *Toronto Daily Star*, Mitch liked to run Ontario from his suite in the King Eddy (King Edward Hotel) and his onion fields and stables at his home in Bannockburn.[414]

ANOTHER DELEGATION TO TORONTO

Toronto's *Evening Telegram* announced on June 16 that the cancer clinic in Bracebridge would reopen. Rene had been advised by her North Bay law firm, McGaughey & Little, that the clinic would not suffer interference from the Kirby Bill legislation. However, the clinic remained closed, and at the end of June, Fred Stevenson led a delegation of some 150 Bracebridge residents to Queen's Park and appealed to Minister Kirby to instruct the commission, still unnamed, not to demand the formula of Miss Caisse's remedy until there had been a thorough investigation of any success she already had in the treatment of cancer.[415, 416] The health minister told the delegation, many of them patients, that by closing her clinic Miss Caisse hopes to "throw the suffering of the poor people she had been treating on the doorstep of the government in the hopes the government would weaken and ask me to open the clinic and meet her views on the situation."[417]

Fred Stevenson wrote Attorney General Arthur Conant requesting a legal opinion on Rene's position under Sections 6 and 10 of the Cancer Remedy Act. Conant advised Health Minister Kirby in a private memo dated June 29 that Miss Caisse is responsible to sub-mit her formula and she would not avoid being prosecuted by clos-ing the clinic because her use of the remedy has become an accom-plished fact. He wrote, "It is the wish of your Department that no consequences would follow and no penalties would be imposed if Miss Caisse were requested to submit her formula and instead of so doing simply closed her Clinic, I think the situation could be met by the practical application of the Act.... Our Department should not institute any proceedings under these circumstances."

House Leader Leo Macaulay sent Charles McGaughey a let-ter on July 14, lawyer to lawyer, telling him that he had had a number of representations made to him by Toronto-area patients of Nurse Caisse:

> It seems to me a serious state of affairs has devel-oped where suffering humanity has to sit and watch the struggle between Nurse Caisse and the Government. I would like to get the real reason why Nurse Caisse has closed her Clinic as it seems to me her proper procedure is to carry on and disregard this interference of Mr. Kirby and put the onus where it belongs on the Department.
>
> How can the Government interfere with Nurse Caisse in view of the promises made personally by Mr. Hepburn, Frank Kelly and others to Nurse Caisse and various deputations that represented her before the last election?

Macaulay also noted that Dr. Hett was continuing to treat patients with his own cancer remedy.

Under this public pressure, Rene finally relented, but not until eleven weeks later. The Rene M. Caisse Cancer Clinic on Dominion Street reopened on Friday, August 5, 1938, although all was not the same.[418] The Essiac formula was still secret, but patients were experiencing increasing difficulty obtaining written diagnoses for Rene's use, which had become a problem as soon as the provincial bill was proposed. Many doctors had stopped sending their patients to Rene, and the reduction in numbers was quite noticeable in her clinic.

RENE MARRIES CHARLES MCGAUGHEY

Another reason for Rene's closure of the clinic surfaced in early September. Returning to the site of her parent's marriage over a half a century ago, Rene and Charles McGaughey were wed in a quiet ceremony in Peterborough on July 28, 1938. They were good friends, and over the difficult months of legislative concerns they had developed a mutual respect for each other, full of trust and companionship. Aunt Mireza, still well after her successful cancer treatments in 1924,[419] and her husband, Norman King, witnessed their vows.

The newlyweds established their home in North Bay's central McIntyre Street with Charles's sixteen-year-old daughter, Jean, and eight-year-old son, Lawrence. It was not easy for the children to accept a new "mother." Their mother had been dead just two years, and their altered lifestyle was a difficult adjustment. Rene felt they didn't really want her around. Charles's other children, twenty-one-year-old Eustace and his younger sister Grace, were away at Queen's University and would serve in the military in 1941. Eustace would be known by his first name, Charles, and distinguish the family by his service as a career diplomat with Canada's External Affairs Department, particularly in Asia. McDuff, as the army dubbed him, retired in 1975 following a three-year appointment as deputy commandant, National Defence College, at Kingston, Ontario. His wife, the former Jessie Porter of North Bay, Ontario, remembers Rene as very pleasant under the trying situation of the family's reluctance to accept their father's new wife.[420] Charles, an Anglican, was two years Rene's senior, and a very respected barrister. He and his brother George had practised law in North Bay for some thirty years, having left behind their boyhood home of Deseronto and their alma mater, nearby Queen's University.

Although Rene was actively operating the Bracebridge cancer clinic, a two-hour train ride south, she and Charles enjoyed a spectacular one-hundred-kilometre view of Lake Nipissing from their summer home on Campbell Street, West Ferris, just southeast of North Bay, when she came "home."

Charles became a commissioner at the Civic Hospital that year, a position he would keep for five years, and looked back on a solid record of community commitment. He had served as magistrate at City Hall from 1923 to 1934 and had been a highly regarded judge of the Juvenile Court. He had willingly contributed his legal advice to the Children's Aid Society and the High School Board, among others over the years, and certainly Rene was proud of Charles's widely recognized deep integrity.

While Rene took her husband's surname, she retained her professional name of Rene M. Caisse, although later she often referred to herself as Rene M. McGaughey.

CANCER COMMISSIONERS APPOINTED

During the summer of 1938 the Commission for the Investigation of Cancer Remedies, as called for in the new Cancer Remedy Act, was being formed under an Order-in-Council dated August 18, 1938.

Six faithful Liberal supporters were appointed that day under the chairmanship of London lawyer Mr. Justice John George Gillanders. Back in February, when he learned that members of the Bracebridge Liberal organization were searching for a Muskoka man to assure a balance of representation on the committee, Kelly insisted that it would be chaired by the head of an insurance company and be composed of individuals chosen from the medical profession only.[421] Instead, the commissioners appointed were Dr. R.C. Wallace, principal of Queens' University, Kingston; Dr. Romuald E. Valin, an Ottawa surgeon whose daughter was a prominent member of the Ottawa-based Hepburn provincial election in 1934; Dr. W.J. Deadman, a pathologist from Hamilton; Drs. T.H. Callahan and George S. Young, both of Toronto; and E.A. Collins, the assistant to the general manager of International Nickel in Copper Cliff. Of interest to Collins was probably the cancer concerns of miners in various mining industries, and the amendment to the Damage by Fumes Arbitration Act, which was passed on the same date as the Cancer Remedy Act, probably accounting for his being selected to represent the Northern Ontario city of Sudbury.

The commisioners were (clockwise from top left) Gillanders, Wallace, Deadman, Callahan, Collins, and Young. Valin is not pictured.

One of their first duties was to scan the cancer remedy situation and gather information from the College of Physicians and Surgeons. Case histories of Rene's patients were placed on file at the college at the request of the minister of health. For instance, records from the department of radiology of the Toronto General Hospital had been there for over a year.[422]

On September 3, lawyer Arthur Slaght requested in a letter to Justice Gillanders that an appointment be arranged for Miss Caisse as early as possible so that the nurse and her counsel, Messrs. McGaughey and Little, could present her work to the commission.

A few days later, on September 7, six of the seven commissioners assembled at Harold Kirby's office for their first meeting. Only Dr. Valin was absent. They discussed with members of the government the procedure of collecting necessary written information to submit to the commission's "experts" for their study and reports.

On behalf of the college, Dr. Noble introduced the question of cancer in a letter to Chairman Gillanders, stressing its vital interest, particularly in the protection of the public in the use of "so-called cancer remedies."[423] He confided that the college had important information that was at his disposal, and he offered to be of assistance in any way.

The second meeting of the commissioners took place on October 3 at the Speaker's office, where the questionnaire drawn by the medical members headed by Dr. Deadman was discussed. Secretary Fred T. Egener (Jr.)[424] was instructed to send each of the applicants a copy of it along with a request for a sample of the substances in question and supporting documentation. Egener, the young solicitor for the province's Department of Health, was officially appointed secretary to the commission on November 1, 1938, at a salary of $75 each month. He was instructed to place an advertisement in newspapers throughout the province, as follows: "THE CANCER REMEDY ACT, 1938. All persons desiring to have any substance or method of treatment investigated under the Cancer Remedy Act, 1938, are requested to communicate with the Secretary, The Commission for the Investigation of Cancer Remedies, Parliament Buildings, Toronto."

The third meeting was set for October 26, when Dr. Connell of the Hendry-Connell Research Foundation, Inc., with Arthur Slaght, KC, to represent him, would meet at the Speaker's office at 10:00 a.m. It seemed that Mr. Slaght was a busy man, juggling his Ottawa duties as member of Parliament for Parry Sound with legal clients in Toronto and elsewhere. He was also acting on behalf of Dr. Roy

Allan Dafoe, the famous doctor to the Dionne Quintuplets. Rene's nephew Ivan Slater was one of two young Bracebridge men entrusted to rush to Slaght's posh Toronto home a package of documents that were critical in the Chicago case against Dafoe, one of a group being sued for $1 million.[425, 426] And now the lawyer was advising the commission about procedures to be adopted for collecting information and the conduct of the meetings.

Slaght suggested that the applicant's case be made in the same manner as if it were before a court, with evidence taken down by a competent reporter. The commissioners agreed to accept written briefs as though given on oath and adopt the conference method of inquiry. It was also decided that proceedings would be held in camera, supposedly making the private sessions more economical and efficient as well as more fair to the sponsors of the substances or methods of treatment to be investigated and to the commission. It was felt that if the proceedings were held in public, undue weight might be attached to some wholly inconclusive evidence, or a sponsor's case might be damaged by unfounded criticism.[427]

Rene arrived at the commission meeting with her lawyers, Edward Joseph Murphy, KC, and Charles McGaughey, who was also her husband, at two o'clock to meet with the commissioners for the first time. Murphy, a lawyer in private practice, had married Rene's cousin Louise Potvin in 1923 and had been Conservative MLA for St. Patrick, Toronto, from 1929 to 1934.

Murphy proposed that the commissioners go to Bracebridge to observe the treatment given by the nurse and the results she had obtained. Countering, the chairman charged that there be a full revelation of facts by Miss Caisse, pointing out that it would be impractical to make any investigation without first knowing what substance or method of treatment was being dealt with. Rene contended that if the commission was not convinced that her formula was beneficial, then why would it wish to learn about the formula? She urged that the *results* of her remedy be judged, not the formula. When Dr. Wallace insisted that an independent investigation be conducted, Rene's lawyers objected. This inquisition would certainly mean turning over her discovery to another person.

The next day Rene wrote the commission on paper that was headed, "'ESSIAC' Cancer Clinic, Bracebridge." She was furious, and wrote in part:

Dear Honourable Sirs,

After thinking over my interview with you yesterday, it would seem to me that you are taking the attitude of men standing on the shore of a lake who see a man drowning. They see another man throw him a rope and haul him in to safety. They see him safe and well, but they say to the man who saved him, "We saw it but we will not acknowledge that you saved him unless you can show us what the rope was made of."

You told me yesterday that no matter what proof I gave you, even though I could produce all the evidence necessary to show that cancer existed along with the living proof, you would not give your stamp of approval to my work. This looks to me as if you had been persuaded by the Medical Profession to demand this formula. While I sincerely believe in the honesty and integrity of every member of the Council, I cannot feel that this demand is just in view of the living proof I have to produce.

That my treatment is harmless, can be very easily proven, since I have injected it into several doctors who can testify to that effect. Some of them have taken five or six treatments at intervals. I am at present treating a doctor for cancer, a graduate of the University of Toronto, who was given up by the Medical Profession to die. He can testify that he has greatly improved under treatment.[428]

I am sorry but I do not feel that you are justified in asking for the formula before acknowledging the proof of my work.[429]

But Rene did complete and submit Dr. Noble's questionnaire as requested, as did several others. Some twenty-five firms or persons communicated with the commission, including five from people residing outside of the Ontario who were not included in the commission's mandate.

UNWANTED PUBLICITY

As if this year weren't already a nightmare, on September 11 a horrible incident occurred, one that would cause chaos and concern and threaten the future of the Rene's clinic. At the Sunday clinic, a patient named Mrs. Euphemia Gilruth walked into the treatment room where Rene gave her a two cc injection of Essiac for her varicose ulcers, but shortly she became terribly short of breath. Dr. E.G. Ellis[430] was called, and soon he pronounced her dead. A sudden death in a clinic where only terminally ill patients were allowed would seem unavoidable, but Rene was devastated and confused, knowing that she had given nearly fifty patients treatments from the same batch of Essiac that Sunday. According to Mrs. Gilruth's son, David, who had accompanied her on the sixty-five-kilometre drive from Emsdale, her doctors had warned the family she might die of an embolism at any moment; in fact she had fainted earlier that day. But Rene and the clinic came immediately under investigation.

Special scientific investigator Dr. Edgar R. Frankish, provincial pathologist, came from Toronto and conducted an autopsy the next morning. Dr. Ellis opened the inquest, and Ontario's new supervising coroner, Dr. Smirle Lawson, was asked by Attorney General Conant to personally investigate the death.[431] Meanwhile Rene's husband and her cousin Edward Murphy came as her support and legal counsel.

An inquest was held in the District Court right across the street from the clinic. An impressive group of local businessmen who comprised the coroner's jury heard University of Toronto Professor Dr. W.L. Robinson interpret the pathology of diseased tissues and read the pathology report, which indicated that Mrs. Gilruth had certainly died of a clot lodged in the pulmonary artery. She might have died a week earlier, without any injection, the distinguished pathologist said.[432] Interestingly, the publicity surrounding the inquest alerted many other cancer patients to the clinic who would not have otherwise known of its existence.

THE COMMISSIONERS MEET

The next meeting of the commission was held in the chambers of the Honourable Speaker of the Legislative Assembly, Queen's Park, on November 30, 1938, at 11:45 a.m. It was styled as the "First Day"[433] of the commission hearings, and all of the members were in attendance except Commissioner Collins from northern Copper Cliff and F.G. Banting, KBE. Dr. Banting was expected to take a role with the commission, as publicized earlier, but, along with other projects, he was busy testing a cancer remedy on mice in conjunction with the National Research Council submitted by a Nova Scotia man. For several months Banting reported back and forth to J.L. Bowlby of Sydney on his thioglycolic acid injection but told him that he wasn't enthusiastic about his theory.[434]

Following the November meeting of the commission, Chairman Gillanders wrote to Rene in response to her October 26 letter of fury. In fact, the resolute lawyer wrote two letters, one dated December 5 and an edited one on December 12 in which he presented the same message with a little more legalese. He spelled out that the commission and the legislation were quite clear, and suggested that she misunderstood their intent. He told her that the commission was "fully engaged in investigating submissions where full information is given," and he hoped she would reconsider the importance and the necessity in fairness to herself and the commission of having all the facts.

Before the year ended, the commissioners summed up their first four months of operation in what they called an "Interim Report to the Honourable Minister of Health as of December 31st, 1938." The commissioners reported on their policies for procedures for the next year and reported on their progress with the submissions of potential cancer cures.

The Interim Report, which would be the title of all reports for decades, recorded their review of the Rene M. Caisse Cancer Clinic at Bracebridge, sponsor of Essiac, in just over two pages. It pointed out that Miss Caisse was not prepared to disclose the formula of her serum to the commission unless or until they found merit in the treatment. They held to their insistence that without knowledge of the formula, which she refused to reveal, the commission could not conduct desirable clinical investigations. The report also noted that Mr. Murphy had agreed with the commission's position and suggested that an appropriate person may be identified who would satisfactorily investigate for the commission with Miss Caisse's agreement. But still she did not agree to reveal her formula, and had said so in writing.

Five days before Christmas 1938 Fred Egener notified Rene by letter that a subcommittee of the commission had been appointed to go to Bracebridge to visit her clinic sometime before January 14 and obtain whatever helpful information she could give.

Rene had closed her clinic for the holidays and taken a badly needed rest in her new home in North Bay. From there, Rene suggested to Egener that the subcommittee come on the weekend of either January 7 or 14 when the clinic would be open for working patients, but February was finally set to allow her to better prepare information for the commission from patient records and other documents.

Rene's family Christmas was saddened by the death of her brother Joe's forty-five-year-old wife, Minnie, also known as Ella May, who died on November 25. She was his second wife; Jennie, Loretta's mother, had died in 1909.

CHAPTER 10

CLINIC UNDER CLOSE SCRUTINY

HEARING IN BRACEBRIDGE

January 1, 1939, rang in with the first celebrations of the Town of Bracebridge's 50th Jubilee. Since its incorporation as a village sixty-four years ago, the community had enjoyed continued expansion and development of fine homes and paved streets. In keeping with the exciting activities, the Bell Telephone Company introduced the common battery system in Bracebridge. Now residents could lift the receiver of their telephone to reach the operator and no longer had to crank their wall-hung phones.

But there was an insidious feeling of unease building in many parts of the world as Hitler gained frightening power, particularly in Europe. In Ontario another kind of uneasiness was building, as the recently formed cancer commission was preparing to challenge those who were administering new and unapproved cancer therapies to patients. Rene, now fifty-one and married to Charles for nearly six months, had been treating cancer with Essiac for fifteen years, and her mother, who was in fine health, was publicly congratulated as she celebrated her eight-first birthday on January 31.[435]

Finally inspection of Rene's clinic was to take place by provincial authorities. Rene was pleased, although somewhat apprehensive, that two members of the province's cancer commission agreed to come February 3 and 4 to Bracebridge to examine patients and make "personal observation of her claims."[436, 437] The *Globe and Mail* heard about it instantly; Rene told Dr. Callahan in a letter dated January 14 that she had not volunteered the information — the newspaper had called her. She was concerned that this publicity would interfere with the visit.

On February 3, following a record cold night when the temperature sank to –41° C, a subcommittee of the Commission for the Investigation of Cancer Remedies stepped off the morning Northland train in Bracebridge.[438] Drs. W.C. Wallace and Thomas H. Callahan were accompanied by Official Reporter R. Brydie. Dr. Ben Guyatt also came to oversee the proceedings on Rene's behalf. When they arrived at Rene's clinic at 9:45 a.m., twenty-two patients were seated in the reception room.[439]

Some patients had travelled there by car or train, at their own expense, in the terribly harsh winter weather from small rural communities surrounding Bracebridge, and others had come great distances. Sixty-three-year-old George Bruce had come all the way from Deltor, near Bancroft, about 240 kilometres northeast of Bracebridge. Sam Hollingshead came from Huntsville, and S.J. Reynolds from Barrie.

Rene and all three of her assistants in their usual neat white uniforms cordially welcomed the visitors. The clinic had been given an additional polish for the important event. There in Rene's modest clinic Dr. Wallace, the principal of the august Queen's University with his charming Scottish accent of the Orkney Islands, and Dr. Callahan, a prominent Toronto physician of St. Michael's Hospital, held an official hearing.

Rene was the first to be privately interviewed. She outlined her daily routine at the clinic and expressed her appreciation for the Town of Bracebridge, which charged her just twelve dollars per year to bind the contract for the use of the former hotel. She reviewed how important physicians such as Dr. Banting suggested that she reveal the formula of her treatment and apply for facilities to work with. Well, she explained, she feared that if she gave them her formula and they refused her application, they would still have her formula. She thought that was a valid concern, so refused.

About her formula, which was of course of interest to the commissioners, she stated:

I was afraid with all the money spent on radium,
and apex-ray and those sort of things that it being
a simple treatment they would shelve it without a
full enough investigation of its merits. You know
how people are sort of inclined to scoff at anything
simple and the deeper things interest them much
more. I was just afraid that it would not be given a
fair test whether it had merit or not, and I thought
if I cured enough people that it could not be dis-
puted, and I would be sure that when I handed it
over to the medical profession that it would be
made available to the cancer sufferers.

The commissioners were told that in the majority of cases she
had the doctors' written diagnoses with permission to treat
patients. "In some cases, they cannot get it, and the doctor
absolutely refuses, and if the patient has been sent home to die
anyway, I treat them on the off chance that I can help." Some doctors wrote to Rene indicating that the patient wished to take treatment from her. Dr. Wallace, a former professor of geology, inquired
about the length of time she continued such treatments, and the
nurse replied, "Well in a good number of cases three months. Some
breast cases, if they are not too far advanced, will disappear in
about six treatments."

The number of patients varied in bad weather because people from the side roads could not get out to the main highway,
and lately the clinic was open just four days a week, Rene testified. Dr. Wallace complimented her on her fine resume,[440] and
when he asked if she was a graduate nurse she informed him that
she had graduated from Dr. Hyde's Hospital in Greenwich,
Connecticut.

"You have no trained nurses on your staff?" Dr. Callahan
enquired.

"No. Nobody handles this but myself. My sister works in the
office and waits on me." Rene proudly reviewed the procedures in
her clinic, shared some anecdotes, and described her struggles and

successes with the medical fraternity, including the "perfectly sat-isfied" American doctors who visited the clinic.

Rene was upset when told that the subcommittee planned to catch the early afternoon train back to Toronto at one-thirty the next day. She worried that she had asked a good number of patients to come and was unsure of the road conditions. She wanted them to be heard, but, as Dr. Wallace pointed out, "It is not exactly the number of patients, but it is the kind of cases, and a fairly clear idea of such cases as you want us to have, which is important."

"All right, Doctor," Rene responded.

Wallace assured her that they would be glad to give their time to whatever could be accomplished and told her that to save time she should gather together any outside medical information or biopsies for presentation. Rene gave the group many written case histories, including medical diagnoses of the patients. For their records she also gave them complete names of addresses of the doctors involved before she concluded her testimony.

PATIENTS TESTIFY

Twenty-two people testified under oath before the commission on Friday. One patient to speak on his own behalf was former Bracebridge Town Councillor Herbert Rawson, Dr. Bert Bastedo's patient who had been receiving Essiac from Rene even before the clinic opened. It seems that Bert had refused surgery for cancer of the rectum and told the commissioners that a year later he was feel-ing fine and needed no more treatments.[441] John Vanclieaf of Baysville, another of Dr. Bastedo's patients receiving treatments the same year, told his depressing story to the commissioners.

The hearing resumed Saturday morning when the commission-ers returned to Bracebridge from an unidentified out-of-town overnight accommodation. The thirty patients who attended the one-and-a-half-day session suffered painful and disfiguring can-cers in many parts of their bodies. One man was dismissed because he had a benign swelling of the prostate and piles, not cancer. And Alma Rumball, who had a lump in her breast, offered no evidence, such as a biopsy, to prove that it had been malignant. Essiac, she testified, had dissolved it.

After Alma had testified, the commissioners called Rene into the room to be questioned before calling in the next witness. Wallace noted that she had given no direct information in Dr. Noble's questionnaire and asked why cases in which there was definite improvement or recovery, or in which there was no recovery, were not described. The commissioners asked Rene to provide them with a list of patients classified in three categories — improved, cured, and fatal — and she agreed to do so by March 1. But, Rene explained, even the patients who died got relief from pain, and some had from eight months to two years of comfortable life. They didn't have to take narcotics for the pain, she said, and were conscious almost to the last. Do you know of any other treatment outside of narcotics under which a patient may die comfortably, doctor? she asked.

Dr. Callahan had to admit that this was quite true of those fatal cases. Rene told him that she felt she had benefited those patients as well as the patients who are living to testify today.

The two commissioners continued asking repetitious questions that had already been discussed during her first interview on Friday. Soon the demanding session was over. It was reported to be a secret hearing, but Robert Boyer and other unnamed reporters from Bracebridge and Toronto were waiting as patients left the interview room.[442, 443] Boyer unwittingly created indispensable records of the proceedings of the inquiry.[444] Some witnesses willingly gave the reporter resumes of their successful Essiac treatments, which they had sworn before the committee, including Mrs. Guppy, Mrs. J.C. Forsythe, John Vanclieaf, and George Bruce. The commissioners caught the afternoon train to Toronto, and Rene went to her North Bay home for a few days to treat patients.[445]

RENE UNDERGOES SURGERY

Any attempts to rest and prepare for the next moves of the commission were halted when Rene was forced to close the clinic in mid-February and check into St. Michael's Hospital in Toronto. She had to undergo surgery by bone specialist Dr. Frederick G. Lewis for the painful bursitis in her shoulder. For months she had been treating patients, using her right arm extensively, and putting off the surgery until absolutely necessary.[446] On March 11, with her painful right arm in sling, she reopened the clinic to grateful patients and resumed compiling material for the commissioners.[447]

While she was out of Bracebridge, Rene missed the excitement of the sight and roar of the eight- to ten-ton TCA plane as it dumped mail on its new overnight delivery route across Canada.

REPORT OF BRACEBRIDGE ENQUIRY

Meanwhile, Dr. Callahan completed and signed a draft two-page report[448] about the subcommittee enquiry that took place at the Caisse Cancer Clinic the first weekend of that month, but it wasn't yet in Rene's hands. The report noted the cordial reception of Rene and her three neatly uniformed assistants and the clean and orderly clinic. He observed that all the cases submitted were selected and presented by Miss Caisse. "We could not fail to note the feeling of confidence in the Caisse treatments and sense of well-being on the part of the patients. There seemed to be a great deal of fraternizing in the waiting-room, the patients telling one another of their wonderful improvement and the benefits experienced through the Caisse treatments."

The summary also noted that the majority of the patients said they experienced reactions such as chills and fever after receiving an Essiac treatment — fairly common side effects, Rene knew.

There was more analysis of the patient's reports: "A great number of the cases reported a gain in weight following the treatments.

It is our opinion that the gain in weight could be partially accounted for by the mental relief brought about by the assurance of cure that seems to emanate from the Caisse Clinic. It is only fair to mention that a number of patients experienced relief from pain. We have no explanation to offer."

Dr. Callahan noted that the cases presented could be divided into three classes, namely:

> **A.** Cases believing they had had cancer, but without any proof.
>
> **B.** Cases which doctors had reported as having had cancer. In connection with these, upon inquiry, we were informed by those doctors that they had not made any such definite diagnosis, inasmuch as biopsies had not been under taken.
>
> **C.** In connection with a few cases, cancer had been proven to be present. Regarding this last group, it is only fair to state that all of them had had radiation previous to the Caisse treatments. There was no actual proof in connection with any of this group that the radiation had not been a significant factor in the cure previous to the Caisse treatments.

(The word "significant" in the last paragraph was added by Dr. Wallace after his review of the draft in a letter to Dr. Callahan, February 21,1939.)

The report concluded, "On account of the above mentioned facts, we were unable to ascertain any positive evidence in connection with any single case that the Caisse treatments had actually cured the cancer. We cannot help feeling that over confidence in the Caisse treatment before it is a proven cure will only lead to neglect of those cases which might be benefited by recognized procedures. [signed] T.H. Callahan."

COMMISSIONERS FURTHER INVESTIGATE

The commission members continued their correspondence with the doctors associated with the patient cases, soliciting their remarks. For instance, Dr. Herbert Minthorn, who had petitioned the government in 1936 in support of Rene's treatments, wrote to Dr. Callahan about one of his patients, Mrs. J.H. (Elizabeth) Stewart, recalling that he had conferred with Dr. McInnis and examined Mrs. Stewart at Miss Caisse's clinic two years ago this coming March. "I attended the clinic for four months in succession, January to April, one day each month,[449] and saw and examined many interesting cases. The puzzling feature of her treatment is that so many of the cases remain stationary, as it were."[450]

Charles McGaughey dashed off a handwritten letter on February 27 to Minister Kirby from his legal office asking if he could come by on his trip to Toronto and discuss how the Caisse cancer formula could be proven through the Department of Health. But the next day Kirby sent a telegram saying it was "absolutely impossible to discuss any cancer remedies while under review by the Commission set up by the Provincial Government." So there, it could be said.

Rene and Charles were asked to attend the commission's Sixth and Seventh days of hearings held in the handsome Club Room of the Royal York Hotel on Thursday, March 30 and Friday, March 31.[451] Rene agreed to let Dr. Hett, who was also preparing to present his cancer remedy, sit in on her interviews on the Thursday session, but requested that she be free to return to Bracebridge that winter afternoon.

At the in camera meeting, Dr. Noble and Dr. Richards asked Rene about certain patient records and completed questionnaires that had been collected by the college for the past two years. The college had appealed to Ontario doctors for data describing their involvement and experience with patients who had sought Rene's treatments, and now the documents were presented to become a collection of typed transcript exhibits. Rene herself had been obliged to mail off a large number of histories of her cancer patients, some 180 pages, at her own expense. She told the commissioners that she accepted only donations from patients towards the costs of providing treatments and that the cost of corresponding with the committee was unreasonable. Just to obtain a copy of the last meeting cost her a hefty $57.

Rene had been asked by the college to present pathologically proven cases where no other treatment had been used, but she was able to present only two such cured cases, as the majority had tried other remedies before going her for assistance.[452]

Dr. Noble read into the record the petition Rene had presented to the premier on February 22, 1938, and insisted that most of the 210 patients who petitioned that they benefited by her treatment were dead.[453] "There are 32 of these are dead," Rene wrote Premier Hepburn in April. "One of these was killed in an automobile accident, several went back for radium treatment when I closed my Clinic last May, two had amputations after leaving me and died, and 178 are living. I do not think this is a bad percentage."[454]

Among other documents presented that March day was one from Dr. L.A. Weisberger of Capreol who wrote to Dr. E.S. Ryerson, president of the college, and attached a letter from a patient who had written him about Rene's activities. He offered to assist in any way to "eradicate such a hoax."[455]

Rene told the doctors about the late patient Richard Patterson: "Dr. Kenney, Dr. Bastedo's assistant, told me that Richard Patterson would die in two or three days when I undertook the case. A photograph taken after he completed my treatment, and the enclosed statement made by fifteen members of his family will tell you that I benefited this patient greatly, though I could not save him. I have Dr. Bastedo's handwritten diagnosis in this case."

In addition to the family statement, Richard's sister, a practical nurse, wrote the following: "This is my earnest belief that if Richard had gone to Miss Caisse when he first took sick, instead of going to Toronto and taking radium needles, he would have been a living man today."

The testimony that took up thirty-one pages on behalf of the late Mary Curran, a Bracebridge girl living in Toronto, began with the

Dr. Noble, *registrar of the College of Physicians and Surgeons, cut a fine figure in* 1925.

University of Toronto Archives

Toronto General Hospital report to Dr. Faulkner from Dr. W.K. Welsh citing extensive carcinoma of the rectum.[456] There were also letters from Rene describing the physical evidence of her condition following Essiac treatments and a letter to Dr. Noble describing the improved condition of her patient. After her death eight months later, the autopsy analysis of the tissue Rene had collected from her body was described as a blood clot, with no tumour cells present. Further in the autopsy report, although tumour cells were present in her body, there were none noted in her glands, and the cause of her death was recorded as acute general peritonitis secondary to perforation of the wall of the rectum from a carcinoma of rectum. Mary Curran's family had understood her prognosis was about three weeks of life.

Another case was presented at the March 30 hearing in some twenty-seven pages of testimonial evidence.[457] James Summerwill of Sprucedale was diagnosed by the Provincial Health Laboratory as having lymphosarcoma in 1935, and his physician, Dr. A.N. Kitt, gave permission for him to be treated by Rene Caisse. Summerwill's own doctor, Fraser M. Greig of Bracebridge, had received a letter from Dr.G. Lyman Duff of the University of Toronto Department of Pathology and Bacteriology noting that he was interested in hearing about "the Bracebridge prodigy."[458] He confided that he "had a long talk with Dr. Banting about her. He does not believe that there is anything in it, but nevertheless offered her the facilities of his laboratory with a supply of animals with cancer for her to cure. He was not able to give her any financial backing but apparently as much as told her to 'put up or shut up.'"

Dr. Kitt reported that he "would not care to say" that Summerwill had benefited from treatment. "Certainly the mass has disappeared, but as stated above, this is not carcinoma but lymphosarcoma." Kitt agreed later that he could find no evidence of tumour and that he was in perfect health.[459]

Rene was questioned about the withdrawal of insulin injections to diabetic patients while they were undergoing Essiac treatments. She mentioned a diabetic case of Dr. McInnis's who, after she cut the patient off insulin entirely, "got clear of a diabetic condition, as well as the cancerous growth." Rene reported that she felt Essaic works on the pancreas. "Dr. Robert Young brought his father to me in March, 1937. They had operated on him, and did an exploratory, and they found he had cancer of the pancreas, and Dr. Young had him come and take treatments from me, and he is in perfect health at the present time. They did not give him any more than about six months to live after the operation."[460]

The commissioners were interested that the Essiac remedy could be applied externally, injected intermuscularly, and sprayed and always contained the same ingredients and the same strength. "If the case is not very extended, I give less. I give 1 c.c. instead of 2," Rene related.

Once again the commissioners questioned Rene about the formula. The doctors among the commissioners reviewed their positions. Drs. Valin and Callahan did not want to proceed with the hearings without the Caisse formula, but Dr. Young didn't agree:

> Is it not possible the Commission would be able to arrive at the value or otherwise of the treatment by simply reviewing the evidence we have already obtained through the sub-committee, and through what has been put in from time to time, and also by the records which Dr. Noble has submitted? Is it not possible that this Commission may arrive at a definite and final conclusion on that evidence alone, without going any further, and requiring that a certain number of tests cases be dealt with at some time in the future: I may be mistaken, but I feel that the Commission might be able to reach a final conclusion without asking for the formula. If we ask for the formula, it is not helpful at all to us, unless we use the formula in the treatment of new cases under Miss Caisse's direction, perhaps.

"I do not expect you to give a public view, or public opinion of my work before getting the formula, but I feel that I am entitled to your decision on the merits of it, before I give it," Miss Caisse stipulated.

"In other words, you are not prepared now to give the Commission the formula?" the chairman asked.

"No. I am not," Rene affirmed as she completed her testimony.

RENE REELS FROM ATTACKS

Rene implied the harassments of that difficult commission meeting in an extraordinary letter she sent to Premier Mitch Hepburn in April, seemingly without her husband's more genteel and legalistic input, and possibly without his knowledge.[461] In the letter, Rene complained that the commission wanted her to account for every patient she had been unfortunate enough to lose "without taking into consideration the fact that these patients are dying before they ever come to me and are given up by the Medical Profession as hopeless."

At that awful meeting her work was pulled to pieces and she was made to feel like a criminal, she wrote. Rene was still suffering from the bursitis surgery performed eight weeks ago, which instead of helping her had made her condition worse. The surgeons could not account for that, and she worked at the clinic with her right arm in a sling when she wasn't in bed too uncomfortable to work, she informed the premier.

Hepburn, having just faced the new opposition leader, George Drew, in the new session of the legislature,[462] was, among other matters, deep in foreign policy concerns over Germany's aggression into Lithuania and Poland and its potential ramifications. He apparently passed Rene's letter along to the minister of health for reply nine days later. Kirby, who continued his portfolio in the new Ontario government, wrote that he felt she was unnecessarily concerned and she shouldn't be unduly disturbed, as the commission would make an effort to arrive at a decision as to the value of her treatment as expeditiously as possible without embarrassment to anyone.[463]

ESSIAC PATENT PROPOSED

On May 13, Egerton R. Case, registered solicitor of patents in Toronto, responded to a letter from McGaughey & Little acknowledging Mrs. McGaughey's interest in marketing a serum under the name "Essiac." He indicated that "this name would be a trademark and would have to be protected under the Unfair Competition Act, 1932 as a word-mark. The title is now only secured through <u>registration</u>."

Case reminded Rene's lawyers that the description of the cancer treatment in printed form could be protected by copyright merely by printing on the matter issued the words "Copyright 1939." If they wished to record the copyright in Ottawa, he explained, then an application in proper form would have to be made to the government, either before or after publication. He said it was advisable to officially record the copyright, adding, "If you were to apply for a patent, the ingredients would have to be fully disclosed and printed on the label. There is always a considerable amount of uncertainty about the securing of patents on medicines both here and in Gt. Britain. It seems that the antagonism of the medical profession against the protecting of discoveries in medicine has been responsible, to a large extent, for the unfair limitations imposed by the Patent Act."

"When your patents are granted," he warned, "all particulars of the invention are published."

He concluded, "You should weigh carefully all angles bearing on the commercial exploitation of Mrs. McG's remarkable discovery so that when you DO start, your foundation will be as secure as possible."

"Your foundation" referred to the veiled project that had begun back in 1937 when an investor-driven foundation offered to provide Essiac a sure future and Rene a grand income. The legal opinion given to the McGaugheys included the pitfalls that could emerge if a patent were selected to protect the remedy and was wisely understood.

Preparations were being made for a major July cancer commission hearing to take place in Toronto. At great cost to her availability in the clinic — and her personal finances — Rene continued to contact former and current patients and their families, some of whom were living in distant areas of the province, to assure their presence at the Toronto meeting.

Any moments Rene and Charles could spend that summer visiting Caisses Island in Lake Muskoka or enjoying the endless skyline over Lake Nipissing outside of North Bay were savoured.

CHAPTER 11

CANCER COMMISSION HEARINGS

SECRET HEARINGS IN CAMERA

The Tenth and Eleventh days of hearings of the Commission for the Investigation of Cancer Remedies took place July 3 and 4, 1939, at the ten-year-old Royal York Hotel in Toronto. The commissioners were to hear presentations, see exhibits of certificates, letters, and questionnaires, and many of the reports would be read and entered into evidence. As decided by the commission, the hearing was held privately, or in camera. In fact neither the public nor the newspapers were advised of or invited to the event at all. Rene had not been called to attend the previous Eighth or Ninth Day hearings, and she was not scheduled for Monday's Tenth Day. Instead the commissioners had heard presentations from other hopeful cancer remedy proponents.

Dr. John E. Hett of Kitchener described his own successful cancer serum, over which he briefly lost his Ontario medical licence; Dr. David H. Arnott presented "glyoxylide," developed by Detroit physician Dr. William Frederich Koch some two decades ago; and Dr. Hendry Connell of Kingston introduced his harmless Ensol.

Other optimistic exhibitors included: Miss Sarah E. Powers, who offered an ancient, universal medicine that had been given to her written in code; Jacob Vet, who gave his views of why a cancer cure has not been discovered; and Roy Green, who had several cures, but no evidence to support them.

30

Exhibit 29.   (Caisse)

(63 treatments)

Mr. ~~████████████~~, Rosseau.

Dr. Wm. Oakes, Rosseau.

Age 37 years.   Normal wt. 156 lbs.

Dr. Oakes' diagnosis - Pithilioma on both sides
of mouth.

First treatment by "essiac" hypo. April 25, 1937,
wt. 149 lbs.

May 2,   Wt. 151½ lbs.

May 9, pt. feeling better.

May 16, pt. Dr. Oakes says marked improvement.

June 6, Same improvement.

June 19/37.

July 16, Dr. Oakes sees an improvement.

Nov. 1st. Dr. sees wonderful improvement- growth
nearly all disappeared. Gained 5 lbs. in 2 weeks.

Jan. 9, pt. had Dr. see and sees improvement.
Recommends continuing.

Masses of typed transcripts were created during the hearings.

Florence N. Farwell described a nutritional diet with vegetables and fruit juices. John Henry Hill brought forward his crude oil remedy, and Mrs. Allen Peterson read several remedies copied from a book. An electric short-wave machine cure was described by William Edward Holder, and Dr. George Francis Watson told about a remedy made from calves' spleens. Three people recommended medicinal plasters: Dr. Donald MacKenzie advocated arsenic plasters; Mrs. Mary Jane Levitt described escharotic plasters that would burn into and slough off cancerous tissue; and Michael J. Hallo supported escharotic plasters and linseed poultices.[464]

Curiously, Toronto's well-known Dr. Thomas J. Glover did not present his anti-cancer serum, which had stirred the local medical authorities for many years. He was busy in New York being investigated by the Surgeon General in the United States. Nor was there any representation from the proponents of other cancer treatments such as X-ray, radium, or surgery.

There wasn't time for some to complete their presentations before the commissioners halted at 7:40 on Monday evening. The testimonies continued in the morning, eating into an hour or more of what was supposed to be Rene's time. Chairman Gillanders dismissed the man with the electric short-wave machine predicted to kill cancer, asked if Miss Caisse was next, and asked what she had "on the programme for today."[465] Commissioner Valin told him that she had "an army of people here." The chairman then invited Rene and her legal representative, Edward J. Murphy, who was her cousin's husband, to come in. Charles McGaughey was there, too. Rene, a nervous wreck, and her loyal supporters had arrived well before the designated time of ten o'clock, and it promised to be a long day.

RENE ON THE STAND

Tuesday's meeting would be an important one for Rene and the others on the agenda. It hadn't been easy assembling her patients to testify on the day following the Dominion Day weekend. Dr. Guyatt told the commissioners during his presentation that some were in Vancouver and others were at the World's Fair in New York City.

Rene had rented the ballroom of the Royal York Hotel, at her own expense, to accommodate the more than 380 patients she expected would be there to support her.[466] To Rene it was clearly to be an event of monstrous proportions, as the fabulous ballroom of the largest hotel in the British Empire could accommodate 855 persons in convention or 650 diners.

"We have about fifty individuals who have come from all over the province at some inconvenience," Edward Murphy declared, "and I think if we could get some expeditious way of handling them —"

"That is what we wanted to discuss. Now, these are patients?" the chairman interrupted.

Murphy assured him that all the individuals who were to be called had been diagnosed as cancer victims. Limited time was available for the fifty or so selected patients, so Murphy suggested that they take ten in an hour, so that in four hours forty of the group could be seen.

"I am not on the Commission," Murphy noted, "but I understood that the Commission was interested in testing out or hearing evidence in connection with these alleged cancer cures, and if doctors throughout the province of Ontario are going to diagnose these matters as cancer, then that is the only basis upon which an individual knows what he is suffering from."[467]

Mr. Rose, who came all the way from Port Arthur to testify, was operated on in 1934, and the condition returned in 1938, Murphy presented. "He claims that this treatment has cured him."

"Since he has come that distance, we will be glad to hear him," the chairman agreed. So began the series of Rene's patients, some who had come a long way in their hot cars and were tired and beginning to complain about the heat in the room they were waiting in.

The people nervously waited for their turn to present their testimonies, and Rene and Charles McGaughey listened to the proceedings, which included testimony from Dr. Guyatt and the presentation of hundreds of letters and documents, both for and against her. Gradually the patients came forward and told their stories as best as they could under what they probably felt were intimidating circumstances. There was confusion as the doctors' documents conflicted with the patients' recollection of the terminology of medical reports that stretched back a few years.

Local Muskoka people including John Vanclieaf and Bert Rawson retold their painful stories and their feelings of much improved health since Miss Caisse's treatments. The medical reports revealed some bewilderment as to actual diagnosis of cancer or detection of growths and discussed the patient's lessening of pain and discomfort. For instance, regarding Mr. Vanclieaf, Dr. Bastedo recorded that the patient had refused to have biopsy taken and that he had never made a diagnosis of cancer in this man.[468] But in an undated report also submitted to the commission, he wrote, "He has what appears to be a carcinoma of the prostate gland, extending into the rectum." After a colonic irrigation and Miss Caisse's treatment he steadily improved.

Herb Rawson was pleased to report that Drs. W.C. Arnold and E.W. Wood of Ottawa had examined him on April 26, 1937, after he had received Essiac treatments, and said they could not find anything wrong. He started to work again and began to feel all right, the Bracebridge man reported.

In another case, Dr. G.O. Dowsley's report was entered into evidence. "There is a distinct mass to be felt to the right of the midline just below the pit of the stomach which is also tender on pressure. X-ray examination shows extensive growth towards the outlet of the stomach which is too extensive for removal. Before long he [Alex MacDougall] will probably require an operation, making a second opening between stomach and bowels to prolong life." The patient refused surgery and took Essiac instead. A later examination yielded the following statement from this doctor: "On comparison, x-ray plates taken recently show very marked improvement on those taken some months ago."[469]

John Tynan had been sent home to die in 1935, but, he certified, after six weeks of treatment at the Caisse Cancer Clinic, the perforations in his bladder were healed. After nine months, Dr. MacDonald could not find a sign of malignancy, he testified. Four years later, he had gained thirty-nine pounds and was in good health. Dr. MacDonald, however, told the commission that Tynan benefited only mentally from the Essiac treatments. He reported that, when he referred Tynan to Caisse, "I was unwise enough to give him a note to see Miss Caisse at the family's request."[470]

The questioning continued, patient after patient. "If it hadn't been for Essiac and Nurse Caisse, I'd have been buried long ago," was a frequent statement. "My doctor had given me up," many assured the commission.

Annie Bonar described her cancer, particularly her enlarged arm. She explained that she had signed in at St. Michael's to have her arm amputated, but on the eve of the operation changed her mind and went to Bracebridge instead. After four months of Essiac treatments her arm had returned to normal and she had gained sixty pounds. She was convinced of Essiac's effectiveness regardless of the terrible radium.

Nellie McVittie was the last patient to appear in the morning session. She explained that her doctor in Wanapitae, just outside of Sudbury, believed that she had cancer of the uterus and neck of the womb. The forty-two-year-old had wasted to a mere ninety-one pounds by the time she was carried, hemorrhaging, into Miss Caisse's clinic. After her first Essiac treatment, on May 29, 1935, her bleeding stopped, and gradually she became stronger and well. "Miss Caisse's treatments certainly put me on my feet," Mrs. McVittie told the commission. "I could barely get around at all when I went to her."[471]

Charles McGaughey recommended that the proceedings be adjourned for lunch at noon, and the chairman agreed to reconvene at two o'clock.

At the afternoon session, Mrs. Augusta Douglas testified that she had refused the radium her doctor suggested when a pathologist diagnosed carcinoma of cervix. After examinations by various doctors, she heard about the Caisse Cancer Clinic in August 1938, and the family headed north to Bracebridge. "I went on a bed made in the back of the car on a mattress with a feather tick folded on it, and I could stand no jolting of the car.... As I lay in my bed [in the boarding house where she was living for six weeks], I could see the clinic on the hill, and it reminded me of the Cross on the Hill of Calvary. I know you men do not care anything about this but just the same, it was the only ray of hope I had in the whole world."

She received only Essiac as a treatment for her condition at the clinic, and she related to the commissioners that her hemorrhages stopped, she gained weight, regained her appetite, and was able to sleep. In fact, she told them, Dr. S. Cosbie was so impressed with her condition after a few treatments that he suggested she should continue to take them. "They are marvellous. They are worth a million," Augusta quoted her doctor. When Chairman Gillanders asked Mrs. Douglas if there had been any subsequent biopsy, she replied that she had gone to be examined by Dr. Cosbie at the Toronto General Hospital just a week earlier and was told, "It doesn't look like there is much wrong with you."[472]

Walter Hampson and Edith Guppy each had a squamous carcinoma diagnosis by Bracebridge Drs. Kenney and Bastedo in late 1937 and insisted on Essiac treatments. Dr. Bastedo warned Hampson that if he didn't have radium treatments on his lip, the lump Dr. Kenney removed would come back and "be all over your lip." Both were in good condition at the hearing.

John McNee[473] of Utterson developed a new cancer on his lip, some eighteen years after one had been surgically removed from the same location by Dr. Peter McGibbon of Bracebridge, his family physician. Commissioner Callahan questioned McNee about Dr. McGibbon.

"He died of cancer himself?"

"Yes."[474]

McNee had asked Dr. McGibbon if he could go to Miss Caisse for Essiac treatments, but he advised him to go to Toronto for radium instead. He went to Nurse Caisse anyway and was given "some medicine to put on — no injections at all," and it cleared up in about six months. He repeated the presentation he made to the February subcommittee hearing in Bracebridge and told the commissioners, "I used an absorbent cotton with some of her medicine, took a bit of sticking plaster to put across it. Day by day there would be a drop of yellow stuff on that cotton every morning for pretty near six months." Finally, nothing came out of the area; the growth had simply healed up.

Richard Wolfenden had also testified before the subcommittee in February and was the final patient to appear before the commissioners that day. X-rays indicated that surgery was recommended for a carcinoma in his rectum, but the patient refused. His friend Dr. W.H. Oaks of Rosseau, Ontario, wrote a letter of diagnosis to Rene asking for her help. After ten months of treatments the pain was nearly gone and was no longer any bother to him.

Mr. Wolfenden's case was the example that Dr. Callahan had been hoping for — a case history diagnosed as cancer, but without taking a biopsy — and Dr. G.E. Richards seemed to concur when he wrote to Dr. Callahan suggesting that "a series of patients be selected who have consulted with Nurse Caisse of their own accord, but none of whom have previously received any acknowledged method of treatment, either surgical or radiological."[475]

During the hearing, many patients spoke of the agony of radium burns and surgery. Almost all testified that their doctors had told them they had only a short time to live, and many went to Rene only after suffering a recurrence following radium or surgery. For most patients the hearing was a terrifying and embarrassing experience. Some just broke down and cried and didn't testify. The cancers they described attacked every site in the human body.

DR. GUYATT ON THE STAND

Dr. Benjamin Leslie Guyatt was the final witness to testify early that evening, and the commissioners were interested in what he had to say.[476] Murphy asked him how he came to hear about the Bracebridge nurse.

Dr. Guyatt replied that a prominent doctor had told him about the clinic in early 1936. It was usually open three days each week, and when he visited there on weekends, about thirty to fifty people would come in for treatment. On his first visit, he observed patients arriving in very bad shape, but as he dropped by from time to time, he found definite improvement in a number of cases. He was so impressed that he brought the matter to the attention of Dr. Routley of the Canadian Medical Association and asked that some investigation be made into that form of treatment.

Some patients who were experiencing a great deal of pain had been taking morphia when he first examined them and later had ceased to use it because the Essiac treatments had eased their suffering. "The relief lasted from one week to another," he said. "It impressed me."

Since that time he had been following a number of cases believed to be cancer, and they were certainly improving. The doctor said he based his observations largely on the clinical diagnoses of patients. When Dr. Young asked Dr. Guyatt if a case of carcinoma of the rectum would improve after a few Essiac treatments, he replied, "If it was an advanced carcinoma with an abscess, yes. I have treated a good many cases of abscess of the rectum. I saw a number of these. I was interested in the last man you had, Mr. Wolfenden, because I had seen him before [at the subcommittee hearing]. He has evidently made a distinct improvement. There's no doubt of the diagnosis in his case. Three doctors passed on him and said he had carcinoma. That was the impression of Dr. Callahan too."

Dr. Valin continued the long and intense examination of Dr. Guyatt by the medical members of the commission: "But a case like that would have to be examined every month to see whether or not there was a regression of the tumour," Dr. Valin stated.

"I would not have been satisfied unless I had visualized this tumour," Dr. Guyatt concurred. "I was impressed sufficiently to feel that some closer observations should be made."

Commissioner Valin reflected, "A lot of these patients have had radium, these cancers of the lip, and when they are in reaction from the radium, they go to Miss Caisse."

Dr. Guyatt responded, "I only know of one case where that occurred. Those I took an interest in were those which occurred in two, three or four years after they had radium, which we consider a definite recurrence of the growth, and over which radium has no influence. Anything that happens after six months, those who are authorities feel that if you get a growth persisting or increasing after that time, you had better … do something about it because you cannot rely on what they have already had to cure the case."

"I suppose, Dr. Guyatt," Murphy said, "like others, you have observed some cremations done by radium before the individual died?"

"There have been accidents, yes," the doctor admitted. "You cannot destroy a tumour without destroying some of the other tissues." The witness retired.

REFUSAL TO DIVULGE FORMULA

After Dr. Guyatt departed, Chairman Gillanders complained to the commissioners, "We have heard more about Miss Caisse's case histories than from any other sponsor. She is the only one who has not been willing to disclose her formula. What she is asking us to do is to pass on the case histories, without the Board having any knowledge what the substance contains, or the theory of its operation or administration."

Dr. Valin again stressed the need for obtaining the formula in order to carry out such an investigation, because it was certainly worthy of being examined. He spoke to Ed Murphy, saying Miss Caisse "is in a peculiar position. She is not a graduate in medicine, and she is practicing medicine —"

"Oh, I don't think so," Murphy interjected.

Valin continued, "The treatment of cancer is the practice of medicine. She really is privileged. I do not think there is anywhere else in any other province in this country where she would be allowed to have a clinic and treat patients."

"And," said Commissioner Callahan, "give medicine by mouth."

The chairman questioned the future of the commission's report considering the requirements of the Cancer Remedy Act, as the commission had yet to investigate the substance and determine its content. "I am not sure that we are in a position to make a determination under the Act until that is done. I am not curious about the formula in any way. I am thinking of our position in dealing with the matter, when she gives us part of it, and keeps the rest of it back."

"Of course," Murphy argued, "the position is, I presume once you turn in the formula — the formula might be just as you say; it might be perfectly good, or it might be found by somebody in the Toronto University to be of no use whatever. They will treat guinea pigs, and mice with it for a while, as they have in the past, and then they may say, 'It is no good.' And then there you are at the end of the road, when apparently a great number of people are satisfied with the results that they have obtained."

Commissioner Young said that he would like to be perfectly clear on his understanding of the point. At the present time Miss Caisse refuses to allow anybody else to use her treatment, and she proposes to hold that position in the future. Mr. Murphy agreed that she would. Young continued, "Supposing she has a cure for cancer and she should die tomorrow; what happens to the people who have cancer?"

"I understand that," Murphy agreed. "I mentioned that to her and I understand she has protected that by placing it somewhere where it can be had upon her death."

Young: "So people up to the time she dies will be dying of cancer, because there are thousands who cannot be treated by her."

"I would not go that far," Murphy cautioned.

Valin said, "There is the problem; she has a cure, or she has not. If she has a cure, and is sincere when she says she has, why should she deprive the whole population of that cure?"

"Insulin is in use all over the world," Dr. Deadman offered.

Further, Young said, "If it is found that Miss Caisse really [is] the possessor of a cure for cancer, her name will be known throughout the world, and she will go down in history as another example of a non-medical person finding something which all the medical men and scientists could not find."

Valin continued, "We want to continue this investigation with some control in the future of cases which she will treat, whether she controls these cases from a diagnostic standpoint, biopsies, x-rays, and so forth, and follow them up and examine these patients. That is the way we feel we should conduct an investigation, if we want to do it thoroughly, before we can make an intelligent report in regard to the cure."

"Suppose," Murphy questioned, "we said, 'here, now, here is the formula,' what would be done with it, Mr. Chairman?"

The chairman replied, "At the moment, I cannot say. I am not a doctor. But Dr. Valin has given you some idea of what his thought on it is. That is, that there should be further treatment under controlled conditions, supervised by somebody who has knowledge of what is being done, and can appreciate the results.

"There may be something in it, as Dr. Guyett says. He thinks it is something which should be investigated further. That is why he suggested to have some independent investigator go ahead, and he appeals to the Ontario Medical Society |sic| to have it investigated. That is his impressions, and he is a disinterested party. He is not biased. We feel we should like to pursue our observations further, and that is the reason why we want the for-mula — that is the main reason."

"The only difficulty," Murphy pleaded, "is she says that these cases which have come there have to have a proper medical cer-tificate as to their —"

"A lot of them have had improper diagnosis by the doctor," Valin interrupted.

"That is pathetic," Murphy chided.

"Yes," Valin answered, "but there have been diagnoses which have been inaccurate."

"That throws her job to the winds," Murphy groaned.

"It does not," Dr. Valin rejoined. "On the other hand there were proper diagnosis in a few cases, but the majority of them have been seen by medical men, and which from our knowledge of it have been improperly diagnosed."

"Yes," Dr. Deadman agreed, "and you know how frequently the right method of diagnosis has been recommended by a physician, and not accepted by the patient."[477]

The meeting was adjourned at 7:22 with no further meeting planned.[478]

INTIMIDATION

A review of the transcripts over a half a century later raises a variety of concerns. It questions the intimidation of members of the medical profession by the College of Physicians and Surgeons and the obvious threat to their future in the fraternity. Again and again, the commissioners questioned the accuracy of the diagnoses the patients offered, and some doctors denied their own diagnoses in letters to Dr. Noble. Doctors appeared to reverse their medical opinions, and indeed their diagnoses of wretched patients, possibly to protect their reputations and not admit that an herbal remedy in many cases did make a difference.

Some, such as Dr. Charles Hair, who had co-signed the 1926 petition to the minister of health, now spoke about her cure for cancer as being "much the same as many of the other hum-bug remedies that from time to time make their appearances." He admitted keeping in touch with Dr. McInnis, who was interested in Essiac, as well as Dr. Wallace.[479]

In a December 1937 letter, addressed "to whom it may concern," Dr. Hair wrote:

> I feel the advice I gave her when she first started out was the one she should have followed. She should have gone directly to Dr. Banting and submitted a report of all her cases and remedies to the Banting Institute for investigation. I am of the

opinion that the claimants for alleged cancer cures should be forced by law to submit their remedies to a competent board who will tell the public whether these cures have any value or not and more than that I would make it a punishable offence for any doctor to accept a fee from these unfortunate victims, as well as cancelling his license. I feel that to-day, in view of the prevalence of cancer every effort should be made to investigate every cure, no matter what source it comes from and we as a profession must take a definite stand along those lines....

Personally, I do not believe that Miss Caisse's remedy has any value other than there may be some tonic effects from its use internally and certainly local cancerous ulcers may improve under her treatments. [Author's note: Some would say that even those attributes were worthy of further investigation.]

Some doctors wrote degrading personal insults about patients. Others arrogantly demeaned Rene with ridicule and unprofessional references, using phrases such as: "faith healer type," "cancer cure woman," and "Bracebridge prodigy."

The patients who had been referred to Rene were considered terminal — persons the medical doctors were unable to heal — and most were elderly. Essiac, she always insisted, was a complementary treatment that assisted in centralizing cells for surgery. In reading the transcripts, one almost feels a sneer and curled lip of some physicians who ridiculed her on the pages.

Some doctors had no record of patients. Most were reluctant to answer the question, "In your opinion was the patient benefited by Miss Caisse's treatment?" "No" was regularly the answer, even after pages of testimonials suggesting the contrary. Some avoided answering the question. And worse, many physicians who originally supported Rene's treatment appeared to turn against her when they filled out and signed Dr. Noble's questionnaires. It will be recalled the success Dr. Smith reported on Maxwell in 1932. But in October 1937, his description of the clinical and pathological findings in this case was: "He was a sclerotic-generalized sclerosis of arteries." According to the information Dr. Smith submitted on the questionnaire, the patient did not benefit from Miss Caisse's treatment. Dr. Smith did, however, remark, "A tentative diagnosis of a new growth in his pancreas was made early in this man's case but was subsequently found to be missing."[480]

Implying that there had been pressure on doctors to renounce their early findings, Edward Murphy said, "If this matter [of diagnosing] is done so sloppily, there should probably be a commission to investigate that." Patients who are told they have cancer must assume that they do, Mr. Murphy contended. "Some doctors through fear of the provincial licensing body had declined to stand by their original diagnosis," he charged.

The commissioners themselves showed concern about some cases of misdiagnosis by doctors. On the Tenth Day, before Rene and her patients presented their testimonies, they discussed the problem, most of which was not reported by direction of Chairman Gillanders. It was noted that Miss Caisse might say, "Cases which came to her — many of them could not be cured. They now draw back from what they have said themselves."

The chairman, a lawyer, said, "We found that in one or two cases in London."

Commissioner Valin, a physician, responded, "They what?"

Commissioner Wallace, the university principal, said, "They now draw back and are much more conservative."

"The doctors?" the chairman questioned.

"Yes," Commissioner Wallace continued, "I think she may indicate that. In other words, saying there is hostility among the medical profession to prevent any kind of evidence which would be advantageous to her. I am not sure; it may not come out. That again is not for the record."[481] And indeed additional discussion did not become part of the proceedings.[482]

THE LONG SUMMER WAIT

It was a long summer as the commissioners and medical fraternity sorted out the complex hearings that had taken place over that hot Dominion Day weekend in Toronto. Meanwhile Rene's life continued to be divided between conducting clinics in Bracebridge and North Bay and keeping in touch with her family. Her father would have been amazed to know that the little barbershop he began in Bracebridge would celebrate fifty years under the continuing ownership of his son and grandson.

As summer cottagers and holidaymakers trekked south following their summer vacations, an insidious tension was invading the country. Citizens and employers were encouraged to give their young men time off work to train with the nearest army militia unit, and ex-servicemen were sworn in August 29 by Magistrate Thomas to guard the South Falls power plant at Muskoka Falls. Six men took the Oath of Allegiance and were sworn for guard duty at Bracebridge's CNR bridges and the South Branch bridge, equipped with army issue and bayonets.

On September 7, Governor General Lord Tweedsmuir described the irrevocable commitment that a formal declaration of war can bring, and announced to the frightened country that a state of war existed. The Red Cross Society, one of the most important means whereby citizens of the town could aid in the war against Hitlerism and repression, was already in action. There was an urgent need for size eleven handmade socks for the servicemen, and Friselda Caisse joined the women's auxiliary and produced many dozens of warm socks with Henry Bird's wool from Muskoka's own lambs. On September 10, 1939, Canada was at war.

CHAPTER 12

COMMISSION ADMITS ESSIAC SUCCESS

AWAITING REPORT

Time weighed heavily on Rene and those who wanted results from the July 1939 hearing of the commission. Rene wrote to the minister of health on November 2 to ask if there were some way he could speed up the report from the cancer commission: "The doctors have in a body refused to give any diagnosis of a case coming to me. I have people visiting my clinic begging for treatment and as you know I cannot take them without their Doctor's diagnosis. Would it be possible for you to give me permission to treat any patient who came to me stating that his or her doctor told them that they had cancer, and to have them sign a statement to that effect?"[483] Her frustration must have been intolerable, as no reply is recorded.

However, Chairman Gillanders sent a two-page report to Commissioner Wallace and enclosed a copy of Rene's letter to the minister of health, who immediately acknowledged receiving it, promising to get in touch with her again as soon as he received "a report relative to her cure." He said:

> I think we should be particularly careful in reporting on the Caisse matter because, if I understand it correctly, it is the unanimous opinion of the Commission that the evidence does not warrant proceedings to obtain the formula.... I anticipate that when the report is furnished to the Minister

and a copy sent to Miss Caisse, as it is required by the Act [Section 8] she will have objections thereto which she will make known in as forceful a way as possible. I am, therefore, anxious that our report be accurately founded on the evidence, and be as carefully considered as possible.[484]

On November 27, Dr. Wallace wrote to Judge Gillanders, thanking him for his report and stating how impressed he was with the way the mass of evidence presented before the commission was dealt with. He was concerned about one particular matter in the report that may need some further consideration. It read, "But from a careful examination of all the evidence submitted, and as analysed herein, the Commission is unanimously of the opinion that the evidence does not establish any merit or value on the part of 'Essiac' as a remedy or treatment for cancer, and would so report." Dr. Wallace noted, "I am doubtful whether that statement can be borne out by the analysis of the cases submitted which had been given in the report. There are some, though very few cases, where the recovery is attributable to 'Essiac' or improvement claimed from 'Essiac'. There is a discrepancy which would need to be looked at somewhat further. I would hesitate to go quite so far as the statement quoted would indicate."

On December 6, Gillanders dropped a brief note to Dr. Wallace in Kingston, saying, "I think the points you mention are well taken. As a matter of fact in the Caisse matter I felt the paragraph you mention was too definite and an invitation for comment, and would appreciate you submitting a suggested draft of the conclusion which we should express. I think it important that we should be particularly careful in this matter on this point."

Finally, on December 27, 1939, Fred T. Egener[485] sent a copy of the Interim Report to "Miss Renee [sic] Caisse," but just the pages referring to the "remedy sponsored by yourself." The summary, in which her name was misspelled, this time as Reine, stated that in cases where a diagnosis had been by biopsy, one recovery and two improvements were attributable to Essiac; in cases diagnosed by

X-ray, one recovery and two improvements were attributable to Essiac; in clinically diagnosed cases, two recoveries and four improvements were attributable to Essiac.

- 22 -

MISS REINE CAISSE, Bracebridge, Ontario.

In the Commission's report of December 31st, 1938, the Commission reported in effect that Miss Caisse who operates what she calls a "Cancer Clinic" at the town of Bracebridge, Ontario, is the sponsor of a substance called "Essiac", which she claims to be a cure for cancer.

Without repeating in full what has been said before she claims to have been treating cancer for some 15 years, but has kept no records except during the pat three years, during which time she has treated from 1200 to 1500 cases.

She definitely declined to reveal her formula to the Commission, but was desirous of submitting certain evidence, for the most part that of patints whom she had treated and patients' case histories, and in order to make some progress in the matter, and with a view to forming whatever appraisal was possible on the evidence submitted, the Commission appointed a sub-committee, consisting of two members of the Commission, who went to Bracebridge, where her clinic is located, made an inspection there,

The analysis of Rene's remedy appears in the Interim Report with her name spelled incorrectly.

The commission believed that three of the diagnoses were wrong, ten were questionable, and four were not positive. Eleven were accepted. Five cures were attributed to previous radium treatments. Mrs. Annie Bonar, who was faced with amputation of her arm after a year of radium and X-ray treatments, was livid that her cure was attributed to radium and not Essiac.[486]

"It is the opinion that the evidence adduced does not justify any favourable conclusion as to the merit of Essiac as a remedy for cancer," the commission decided. "If, however, Miss Caisse is desirous of having her treatment further investigated, and wishes to submit further evidence and is prepared to furnish the formula of Essiac, together with samples thereof, the Commission would be glad to make an investigation in such manner as is deemed desirable and warranted."[F87]

The commission offered the following plan of compromise if the government would accept its advice:

> The public to be fully informed of the results of the Commission's investigation, special stress being laid on the lack of positive diagnosis of cancer in the selected cases presented by Miss Caisse in support of her claim.
>
> Miss Caisse to be allowed to continue her clinic for the treatment only of cancer cases which have been positively diagnosed. The diagnosis in every case to be made by doctors or hospitals designated by the Commission, if it is willing to continue its clinical investigations; otherwise by the government. The fewer the diagnosticians the better, and each should have available all the diagnostic aids necessary.
>
> Such a plan should allow the patient to choose Essiac in preference to surgery or radiotherapy, although the diagnostician would be free to advise the plan of treatment he thought best.
>
> Such a course would mean that Miss Caisse would carry on her clinic in a very limited way and

for one specific purpose — to show whether she can cure cancer or not. [Signed] George S. Young, T.H. Callahan.

Unaware that Rene had received her copy of the Interim Report just before the New Year, the *Muskoka Herald* published a major article in its first 1940 issue asking, "When will Cancer Commission Report be Given?"[488] It pointed out that Rene as well as her patients and supporters are wondering why the commission's findings had not been issued after the nurse placed a great deal of evidence before it earlier in 1939. "Over fifty patients appeared before the Commission at the Royal York Hotel on July 4th, and testified as to the efficacy of this treatment." The article highlighted Mrs. Charles Guppy's battle with skin cancer and her successful recovery with Essiac treatments.

The *Muskoka Herald* obtained a copy of the testimonial Dr. Ben Guyatt presented to the commission, and Bracebridge readers were given the entire presentation. The curator of the University of Toronto's anatomy department wrote the following in support of the Caisse treatment:

> During many years it has been my privilege to follow and dispel the ravages of disease. Some of these seem almost to vanish as the morning mist under the magic spell of the physician; others defy in a most adamant manner the almost exhaustless efforts of the dauntless medico.
>
> During the past three years it has been my privilege to observe in the Caisse clinic at Bracebridge, Ontario, the work of Nurse Caisse whose enthusiasm, endurance and optimism has been an inspiration to me. Miss Caisse has worked chiefly unaided, but has received much encouragement from those who have observed results, and been greatly inspired by those patients who have responded to treatment.

The first most noticeable response observed in this Caisse Clinic is the cheerfulness and optimism of treated patients. This fascinated me; the treatment received appeared to be attacking the disability from the angle which had greatly interested me. In most cases distorted countenances became normal and pain reduced as treatment proceeded. The relief from pain is a notable feature as pain in these cases is very difficult to control. On checking authentic cancer cases it was found that haemorrhage was readily brought under control in many difficult cases, open lesions of lip and breast responded to treatment, cancers of the cervix, rectum and bladder have been caused to disappear, and patients with cancer of the stomach diagnosed by reputable physicians and surgeons have returned to normal activity.

The number of patients treated in this clinic are many hundreds and the number responding wholly or in part I do not know, but I DO KNOW that I have witnessed in this clinic a treatment which brings about restoration through destroying the tumour tissue, and supplying that something which improves the mental outlook on life, and facilitates reestablishment of physiological function.

Dr. Emma Carson's report of her 1937 visit to the clinic was also presented in this remarkable newspaper coverage.

INTERIM REPORT NOW PUBLIC

At long last, the report of the Commission for the Investigation of Cancer Remedies, to be forever known as the 1939 Interim Report, was tabled in the legislature on January 10, and the *Globe and Mail* revealed much of it in a front page story the next day.[489, 490] It was the first public indication of the undated "inquiry at Toronto." The report told readers that only four of the forty-nine cases placed before the commission apparently recovered from cancer as a result of Miss Caisse's treatment, the only presenter who could claim any recoveries. Remedies considered worthy for further examination were Ensol, presented by the Hendry-Connell Foundation of Kingston; Dr. Hett's serum; and Glyoxylide, formulated by Dr. Arnott of London.

Dr. Noble continued to track physicians who had experienced the Caisse Cancer Clinic, and Dr. Richard A. Leonardo of Rochester, New York, responded to the cancer commission early in January 1940.[491] He recalled his 1936 visit to Rene's clinic (it was actually in 1937) and stated that "at first I thought her essiac injections were of value in treatment of Cancer — but on returning that Fall I found many of her Cancer cases had died in spite of her treatment." These, of course, were patients already given up by the medical profession as terminally ill. He continued, "Whatever she does use to make essiac she knows not what it really contains."

RENE CAISSE ON CANCER

Rene read everything she could find on the subject of cancer and spent many hours writing her own paper, entitled "Cancer," which was published in the midst of the publicity over the commission's report. In it, she showed her knowledge of current writings in the press and told about her work as a graduate nurse, particularly in regards to cancer. She wrote:

> It has been found in post mortems that individuals have had cancer during their lives without knowledge of its existence and the cancer had ceased to exist and all that remained was the evidence that destructive work had at one time been done and stopped. Nature had either supplied the body with

resistant, or more probably, the human system ceased to supply the malignant cells with the material vital to its existence.

With this idea in mind, some 18 years ago I attempted to supply the living healthy cells in the system with a substance which would resist the demands made upon them by the malignant cells and take away what was necessary to supply the malignant cell with life growth.

I can also truthfully say that I have in many cases been able to stay the disease and in many really bad cases prolong life, and in practically all cases alleviate the pain and suffering so that the patient is not compelled to resort to opiates or narcotics in increasing doses as is usually the case. If I had not accomplished more than this, I think I deserve the recognition of the medical world as a distinct step ahead in the treatment of cancer.[492]

LOCAL PRESS LAUDS RENE

The local papers proudly published the cancer commission's determination that Miss Caisse's method was the only treatment investigated to which recovery could be attributed. Although the commission failed to recommend her work to the government for support, they noted that the commissioners requested her to bring them the complete formula and method of treatment.[493, 494] *Bracebridge Gazette* publisher and lawyer Redmond Thomas, KC, wrote:

Up here in Muskoka we know and respect Miss Rene M. Caisse, now Mrs. C.S. McGaughey. We know that usually she has had only those patients whose condition doctors have considered hopeless. We know that good, respectable Muskoka people honestly believe that Miss Caisse has cured them of cancer and they gratefully proclaim the fact nor do they worry about the formula she used. When those good Muskokans board a train they are satisfied to be taken to their destination and they do not care a rap whether steam, electricity or diesel power makes the train go.[495]

Robert Boyer of the *Muskoka Herald* pointed out in his editorial:

The Commission feels the evidence brought before them "does not justify any favourable conclusion as to the merits of 'Essiac' as a remedy for cancer". In stating their opinion in this manner, the Commissioners were careful to refrain from including that they felt that no "unfavourable conclusion" was likewise justified. Indeed they did not feel that way, for they appended a suggestion that Miss Caisse bring to them now her complete formula and method of treatment.[496]

He also made very sure that Rene was interviewed. She said:

The investigation was indeed a difficult one, because the Commission would not consider any recovery by Essiac unless there had been no other treatment previous to the taking of Essiac. I have been obliged to treat so many cases sent to me by doctors after everything in medical science had been used ineffectively. I have not been allowed to take a cancer case without a doctor's diagnosis. The patients who tried neither surgery, radium or x-ray before coming to me for treatment were few and far between because in the majority of cases the doctors will not give me a diagnosis of a patient for cancer unless he considers the patient beyond the help of medical science.

There were doctors who, though they had given me their written diagnosis of cancer, in cases where they were called upon to confirm their findings, sent written denials of their own diagnosis or even denied they made one.

There is no way of combating this situation. That I was able to prove success in any degree was something little less than a miracle. The only thing I can depend on is the diagnosis of the doctor and the living proof of my success.

There are healthy people all over the country who can testify that they were ill, and that their individual doctors told them they had cancer and advised operation, radium or deep X-ray and that they came to me and were made well. After all, one can only depend on his or her medical adviser's professional opinion.

If at any later date those opinions were denied, the patient has at any rate become free of his or her growth, and living in health due to Essiac treatments. Everyone knows that the weight of evidence is that most cases of cancer are generally diagnosed as such at too late a stage for the doctor to be of much, if any, assistance, and no doctor would tell a patient the awful fact if he was not thoroughly convinced that he had it.

Case after case was presented by me to the Commission which showed increase in weight and mental and physical upbuild, freedom from pain and cessation of hemorrhages, but no mention of these benefits were made by the commission.

I was treated most kindly by the Board and am thankful for their patient attention to me, but I must say that the rigidity of the rules set for me in this investigation, unprepared as I was for the method of elimination, made it a most difficult task for me as I thought that the chief aim of the Minister of Health, in appointing the Commission, was to find out if there was any merit in a treatment rather than an attempt to turn the whole investigation into a highly technical inquisition denying everything that did not bear the seal of absolute unqualified proof on its face.

All in all, she felt she had done well in the face of these severe conditions. Hers was the only one of fifteen presentations to be credited with any cures at all.

So, five months after the hearings, the commission decided that only four remedies, those offered by Caisse, Hett, Arnott, and Connell, required any action or investigation. All the others were put aside.

The decision to give Rene an opportunity to present her Essiac formula for investigation did not please her. "Until the medical profession will admit from the cases I have treated that my treatment has merit, I will not give up the formula. When they do that, I will be willing to give my treatment to the world," she said. And certainly she planned to continue operating her clinic "until action by the Government compels me to close it," she told the *Huntsville Forester*. It would serve patients Saturday through Monday, the paper reported.[497]

RENE CAISSE REFUTES COMMISSION REPORT

Rene was greatly troubled during the next few weeks, which she spent in North Bay, and thoroughly analyzed the commission's reports against her records and those of the doctors that were turned over to the commission. She challenged the commission by disputing the findings in their report, in particular in the cases of Mrs. Annie Bonar of Toronto and Walter Hampson of Utterson.[498] Mrs. Bonar had been given about sixty Essiac treatments, and an X-ray examination showed no sign of the growth and she was feeling quite well. But the commission said of her case: "recovery due to radiation." Hampton's lip cancer was recorded as recovery due to surgery, when the only operation he had was removal of a small nodule for analysis. Rene raged.

"What I cannot understand," Rene wrote in her statement to the newspaper editor, "is why in the case of Mrs. Bonar, where radiation and X-ray had failed, and amputation was indicated, the Commission gave radiation credit for the cure, and where Dr. Connell refused the case that I was able to cure, they ignored me, and recommended Dr. Connell for a Government grant of $25,000 dollars."

Rene continued her dispute with the cancer commission in her March letter to the *Muskoka Herald*, this time about E.F. Rose, who suffered stinging black cancerous sores in his nose and face. Refusing radium, he had four Essiac treatments and the stinging stopped. After eight treatments the blackness began to disappear, and when he appeared before the full commission to give evidence, the discoloration had gone and the sore healed. "This was an opportunity for pronouncing it as originally merely an inflammation of the superior ethmoidal concha or some such resounding medical phrase in reference to the nasal anatomy for the benefit of 'the great unwashed.' But no. As the expression goes 'It was as plain as the nose on your face.' The physical evidence was there and could not be refuted," Rene wrote.[499]

Rene also presented the case of Ufford's postmistress, Mrs. Eliza Veitch, who had made up her mind that she was going to die from her second growth, because there was no use going back to her doctor and being tortured again. "The Commission now has a signed statement from the surgeon to the effect that the growth he removed [earlier] was not cancer." Rene's treatments helped Eliza to gain twenty-three pounds, and she stopped hemorraging. Her pains had disappeared except for occasional slight twinges during her busy day.

The commissioners were not pleased with Rene's public letters, and during their continuing March meetings in Committee Room No. I of the parliament buildings in Toronto they discussed the situation. Dr. Valin said, "We cannot get into a controversy with any newspaper or we would never see the end of it." He suggested they write to the minister reiterating the fact that Miss Caisse has not co-operated with the commission, and continued:

> [She] has not furnished us either with the material or the formula and that should be known by him, and then if he wants to give it to the public, he can do so. I think that will settle Miss Caisse with the public. It will not be broadcasted the way that Miss Caisse's report has been broadcasted. However, she is only broadcasting her side of the story, and not ours, and I think if the Minister makes that information public that the public will then know that she has not cooperated with the Commission, and not furnished a sample of her materials, much less the formula. That will discredit her a great deal, I think.[500]

Dr. Callahan was concerned that his name appeared the newspapers over "this man Rose," and insisted that his nose wasn't black. But the man believed it was. "I should like to take exception to that statement in the paper," he complained.[501]

ESSIAC'S IMPACT ON CANCER

Rene formulated her own theory on cancer, and over the years she would gain a great deal of experience.[502] It was her conviction that cancer resulted from a glandular deficiency, and as she observed the symptoms and reactions of patients, she also reasoned how, if not why, Essiac worked. Often patients would report an enlarging and hardening of the tumour after a few treatments. Then the tumour would begin to soften, and if it were located in any body system with a route to the exterior, the patient would report discharging large amounts of pus and fleshy material. After this, the tumour would disappear. Rene believed that Essiac somehow caused the cancerous cells to recede to the site of the original tumour, then to shrink and sometimes discharge — often to vanish altogether.

In some cases, she observed, if the tumour didn't disappear, it could be surgically removed after several Essiac treatments with less risk of metastases arising elsewhere in the body.

Rene concluded that Essiac, a combination of non-toxic herbs, supplied a deficiency of a secretion ordinarily applied to the human body by a gland of undiscovered origin. She called it "Gland XOX." Many of the doctors who had visited her cancer clinic, she recalled, said that they surmised her treatment acted upon the glands of the body. Rene recorded that Dr. Banting had said, "Essiac must actuate the pancreatic gland into normal functioning."

Actually, Rene felt that very few physicians could diagnose cancer, and there were very few symptoms to warn the individual or the doctor in the majority of cases. She pointed out that the disease was often well established or rooted before the doctor, or his patient, even suspected its presence. Sometimes, she reasoned, "Cancer may develop rapidly and make itself felt early, when it can be fairly easily treated. In its rapid growth, however, a few months of progress may make it too late for the surgeon's knife. Then deep x-ray therapy may scatter it to other parts, or radium drive it in or cause further cancer in destroyed tissues."

RENE'S HEALTH SUFFERS

Rene was tired and unwell. In November 1940 she spent some time in the Hagmeier Clinic, where her admirer Dr. Gordon Hagmeier gave her good care. A hometown newspaper reported she had a "serious operation" performed at what was known as Preston Springs, and that Charles and her sister Albina Allen of Toronto were there to support her.[503, 504] Rene, now fifty-two years old, seemingly recovered and returned to her work in Bracebridge and North Bay. But, on December 3, clearly depressed and somewhat confused, Rene wrote to the commission:

> Gentlemen, I noticed in the Globe & Mail paper your recommendation of the work of Dr. Connell of

Kingston as a treatment for cancer. I have just under-
gone a serious operation for gallstones and would
like to know whether or not Essiac is among the fourteen treatments discarded by you in your publication
of that date? If it was there is no use of my carrying
on any further. I produced more evidence of curing
than any other applicant. I thought when I went
before you that you could not help but see the benefits derived from Essiac. However, I found that you
were more interested in trying to prove that it hadn't
any merit than in trying to see the benefits derived
from it. You know, of course, that on the strength of
your statement, the Medical Council closed down on
the doctors, forbidding them to give a diagnosis to
patients coming to me. You are entirely responsible
for this. May God guide your work as He has guided
mine. Trusting to hear from you at your earliest con-
venience, I am, Yours truly, [signed] Rene M. Caisse.

Mr. Justice Gillanders responded on January 9, 1941, most
annoyed. He reminded her, as well she knew, that the commission
does not write press articles, if that is what she meant about "publication," but makes reports from time to time to the minister of
health, the last one being dated December 31, 1939. He thought
her erroneous understanding of the commission's reports must
have been from the newspaper articles.

Rene was making final plans for the clinic, and it didn't seem that
she was going to need further assistance from her sister Permie, who
was anxious to find a new interest. So in time for Christmas sales,
Permelia Caisse opened a lingerie and gift shop in their family building next to the Bank of Nova Scotia where she and her others sisters
had operated a popular millinery shop many years ago.[505]

CHAPTER 13

Clinic Closes — Was It to Be?

THE CLINIC CLOSES

The new provincial law covering cancer remedies cast much ambivalent attention on the community. When the newly elected Bracebridge town council met in January 1941, it discovered that Rene's use of the Bracebridge Inn had exceeded the five-year arrangement, although she hadn't conducted a clinic for many months. One of the first resolutions of the new council decided that Miss Caisse be given the privilege to carry on her clinic at a rate of five dollars a month, but should the property be sold, or the town want it for any other use, she would have to agree to vacate on thirty days' notice.[506]

Rene was crushed and very angry when the hostility and lack of co-operation of the medical profession overwhelmed her. Ailing cancer patients were being refused diagnosis from their doctors — who were apparently following instruction from their medical council — and were unable seek treatments. Turning away these people was too much for Rene. Although the commission did not demand the clinic's closure, Rene still risked government seizure if she did not reveal the Essiac formula, and although she was not charged under the Kirby Bill, she still feared their law. The decision was made; she would close her clinic as of the last week of January.

Rene announced that she could not go on, and the *Muskoka Herald* published Rene's farewell statement on January 23, 1941. Thanking her supporters, the town's officials, former mayor

Richards, and in particular the Bracebridge newspapers for their help and support, she said she was sorry to close her clinic and regretted leaving her patients. "I am proud of my discovery of 'Essiac' and I believe firmly, in heart, that some day, on its merit, 'Essiac' will be recognized and made available to all Cancer sufferers the world over." She offered to "treat anyone who would come to her with a doctor's written diagnosis stating that he or she had cancer or ulcer (ulcers are in the malignant group and therefore will respond to the 'Essiac' treatment as well as cancer does)."[507]

This was the final closure. Totally exhausted, with emotions ranging from frustration to personal pain and in a state bordering on nervous collapse, Rene travelled to her other home in North Bay to be with Charles and his family.

The old hotel that had served so nobly as the Caisse Cancer Clinic for nearly six extraordinary years reverted back to the town and in August was sold for cash to a local man named Leslie Tennant.

WAS IT TO BE?

It was as if the success of the Rene M. Caisse Cancer Clinic was never to be. The fact that it did flourish for so many years, with Essiac alleviating the torment of a great number of cancer victims, was remarkable. As far as the government and the medical fraternity were concerned, Rene's good intentions for suffering humanity were doomed to fail from the very beginning.

A number of caveats had been taking shape from the clinic's conception in April 1935, when Bracebridge Town Clerk Salmon asked the minister of health to examine the Bracebridge Inn and grant permission for a private hospital. That request initiated a number of investigations into government rules and policies. By June, Dr. N. Mosely, inspector of private hospitals, and Dr. J.W.S. McCullough, chief inspector of health, had inspected the site and investigated Rene's nursing qualifications. They discovered that she didn't appear to hold an Ontario nurse's licence. This posed a problem for her to operate a private hospital. It would seem that she wished to exploit a cancer cure, they decided. Her defence to that charge was that she didn't want her American training to stand in the way of declaring her herbal treatment as a Canadian discovery. As far as making money was concerned, she didn't have "one dollar" from her activities. In fact, she indicated that if she was required to travel to meet with them in Toronto, she would have to borrow money from her mother for the trip.[508]

While the 1935 discussions between Rene and Ministry of Health officials were taking place, the establishment of a cancer clinic in the Metropolitan General Hospital in Walkerville to serve the border area of Windsor was announced by the local MPP, who happened to be the minister of public welfare, the Hon. David Croll, who would chair Rene's private bill hearing three years later. The Ontario government would supply $18,000 worth of radium, and the Ontario Cancer Commission promised to appoint a radiologist and to supply more equipment to augment what they already owned. The decision to establish the clinic followed a survey of conditions at the border by Department of Health officials, it was reported.[509]

To further restrict Rene's activities, in 1938 the Hepburn government's lawyers were busy drawing up housekeeping legislation to amend certain acts, the timing and subject of which was quite befitting the immediate events surrounding Rene Caisse. In April, the new amendment to the Private Hospitals Act determined that no person could use the term "hospital" or designate any place as a hospital without a licence under that act, or any other act, and an amendment to the Nurses' Registration Act made sure that no person could conduct a training school for nurses or train or instruct nurses without the consent of the minister of health. (The author is not aware if Rene knew of the amendments to the additional legislation.)

After all these years during which the government, the medical profession, and the commercial purveyors of cancer treatment equipment and chemicals had worked towards the management of cancer, it continued to ravage the population, and the Bracebridge cancer clinic no longer existed.

RMC KIDNEY TABLETS

Along with the demands surrounding Essiac, Rene's little red kidney pills were sought after by those with backaches and urinary problems. In December 1940, Charles McGaughey notarized a number of Rene's patients who obtained relief from kidney-related problems after taking a series of her small compounded herbal pills. Now it was time they applied for both registration of the remedy under the Proprietary or Patent Medicine Act, in order to sell it, and a patent to assure its protection from competition.

Charles handled the legal matters from his office in North Bay, and in August 1941 Rene M. Caisse-McGaughey received a Canadian patent on the product described as "Compositions of matter for Treatment of Diseases of the Urinary Organs and Processes of Compounding Same."[510] The ingredients were to be used in the following proportions: two pounds of powdered prickly ash berries, one pound of powdered juniper berries, one pound of powdered burdock root, two ounces of uva ursi, and half a pound of powdered slippery elm bark.

She called her new venture "R.M.C. Remedies."[511] In September, L.P. Teevens, chief of the Proprietary or Patent Medicine Division, Department of Pensions and National Health, wrote to say that her preparation had been approved for sale by the medical advisers of the department for registration.[512] She had hoped they would accept her wording of the benefits of the R.M.C. Kidney Pills, but they found her claim of assisting "infection in kidneys or inflammation of the kidneys or prostate gland" objectionable and told her not to use it. They accepted instead this description: "The composition gradually assists nature to restore the functional co-ordination of the urinary organs and the bowels so thereby to remove bodily waste accumulated during the lack of functional co-ordination there between."

Next they worked towards obtaining a trademark under the Unfair Competition Act, 1932, which was granted on November 16, 1942.

RENE CONTINUES CANCER TREATMENTS

During 1941, Rene travelled back and forth between her two homes, and while in North Bay she conducted a clinic each Saturday.[513] Judge Gillanders informed the minister of health of Rene's activities with some concern.[514] In an attempt to stop her, and to alert the public to her being subject to the provisions of the Cancer Remedy Act, J.G. Cunningham, as director of the Division of Industrial Hygiene, sent a memo to Dr. J.T. Phair, chief medical officer of health.[515] They discussed putting a statement in all the newspapers, but changed their minds.

One wonders if Rene was aware that Mitch Hepburn's mother, Margaret, had a cancer operation in July. "At the moment it is a question of whether she should undergo a second and more serious operation or let the growth develop again," he wrote Arthur Slaght.[516] "It is very doubtful if she could survive the shock." She did. Mrs. Hepburn would survive until 1946.

Meanwhile, the federal government gained its authority over cancer remedies, and Dr. J.J. Heagerty was now director of public health services. He advised a Chicago physician:

> [The] advertising and sale to the general public of remedies for the treatment of cancer are prohibited in Canada under the Food and Drugs Act and the Proprietary or Patent Medicine Act. Proprietors of so-called cancer remedies have objected and requested that their remedies be investigated. This department, which administers the Food and Drugs Act and the Proprietary or Patent Medicine Act, is not bound by the findings of the [Ontario Cancer] Commission.[517]

On June 26, 1942, the American consul general in Toronto enquired about Rene, and the minister of health wrote and told him that Mrs. Rene Mary McGaughey before her marriage was Miss Rene Caisse and was known to the department for her treatment of cancer. He sent the cancer commission's interim report to him, pointing out the pertinent pages regarding her treatment.

CHARLES DIES

Charles McGaughey had not been well for some time, and at his North Bay home on October 20, 1943, he died of what was reported variously as a heart condition and a rather lengthy illness.[518, 519] He was fifty-seven years old. The war was at its peak, and Charles's funeral was held over for a day while the family made a vain attempt to have his son Eustace, a lieutenant in the army, released from his duties in Newfoundland to travel home. A family funeral was held in their McIntyre Avenue home, and under the auspices of Charles's lodge members in the Independent Order of Odd Fellows, a formal funeral was conducted in St. John's Anglican Church. The cream of the North Bay bar was there for Charles, as were his children, sisters, and his devastated widow, Rene.[520, 521]

Alone, her clinic gone, Rene returned immediately to Bracebridge to live among her remaining family and friends. Soon, both of the McGaugheys' lovely North Bay homes were demolished for local planning "progress," one to allow the continuation of a street, and one to make room for a parking lot. In Bracebridge, some brothers and sisters still lived in the upper apartments on Manitoba Street, but in November Rene bought a little house on Quebec Street. Rene's friend Mary McPherson recalled how Rene valiantly made room for the massive furniture that had been in her North Bay home as well as the animal hunting trophies that Charles had collected on his many trips to far-off lands. A fur mat at the front door sported a gruesome wolf head.

When Mary and countless patients visited Rene to obtain Essiac, they were received in a tiny kitchen with pleasing curtains and a pretty teapot perched on the edge of the stove. The "special tea" was served in a china cup. Often, as reimbursement for the Essiac, Rene received farm fresh eggs or butter, and sometimes freshly killed meat, from grateful patients.[522]

WARTIME PRESSURES

The Second World War raged, and Bracebridge residents responded with responsible rationing and fundraising, and many left to serve their country in Europe and Asia. Registered nurses were required to register with the National Selective Service, and the war effort claimed the attention of many of Rene's friends and those involved in her own personal struggle.

The 1940s saw the demise or withdrawal of several significant figures in Rene's life; it was a terrible time for her. Dr. (Lt. Col.) Ben Guyatt joined in his second great war in 1941 and became commanding officer in military casualty hospitals in Oakville and Hamilton, Ontario, and one near Winnipeg, Manitoba. He would die of a heart attack on November 4, 1953, always much impressed with Rene's contribution to humanity.

On February 21, 1941, Canada grieved when Sir Frederick Banting died of injuries following a plane crash in a snow bank about ninety kilometres northeast of Gander, Newfoundland. Prime Minister Mackenzie King described the purpose of the controversial flight as "a mission of high national and scientific importance."[523] But the flight was doomed; weather warnings from Canada's chief meterorologist, Patrick McTaggart-Cowan,[524] were not heeded.

In Toronto, Rene's earlier research associate, Dr. Robert Fisher, who had watched her clinic conflicts with great interest, died suddenly of a heart attack in his Toronto home on November 10, 1944.[525] Dr. Fisher would never have imagined that in 1977 Rene Caisse would announce her wish to will the Essiac formula to the University of Toronto, in his memory.[526]

Another personal blow came on May 11, 1946, when Dr. John McInnis, Rene's champion from Timmins, died of cancer, the very disease they had fought together. They knew the herbal remedy did not always cure, but presumably, as he witnessed in his patients, it alleviated his discomfort in his last months. "He had a happy cheerfulness that had a healing of its own."[527]

Rene's great source of frustration, the former premier Mitch Hepburn, died in his sleep after a heavy cold at his St. Thomas area farm on January 5, 1953. He was only fifty-six. According to a biographer, he bequeathed more than his liquid assets could provide, and a rigorous review by the federal and provincial governments couldn't find his supposed wealth.[528]

Dr. Herbert Minthorn broke his back in a fall in 1952 and died of pneumonia as a result of his confinement in bed. He never moved from the house he had built when he first moved to Timmins and had been the coroner there for the entire forty-two years.[529, 530] Dr. Charles Hair, who had continued his attention to Rene's activities, retired in 1950 and died after a brief illness in 1953.[531] Colleague Dr. William C. Arnold of Ottawa retired to Blenheim, Ontario, in 1947, and died there in 1960.

Rene and her family grieved over the death of several family members. Aunt Mireza died in 1943, some twenty years after Rene had administered her new herbal treatment. Rene's brother Joseph died of cancer in 1944. "He wouldn't take Essiac," Rene told a nearby resident Vera Goltz, "but I loved him anyway."[532] Joe's barbershop passed on to his son Louis, who was still suffering from war injuries. The eldest sister, Albina (Mrs. George) Allen, Rene's friend and confidante, passed away in early September 1947 at age seventy, and their beloved mother Friselda died of heart disease on February 16, 1948, in her ninety-first year.[533, 534]

RENE ESTABLISHES A NEW HOME

In late 1947, Rene sold her Quebec Street house and moved to Mary Street for a year or so until she became entranced with a splendid house in the north end of town at 29 McDonald Street where it intersected with James. But soon she longed for a home closer to the centre of town. In October 1951 Rene purchased a handsome house with many rooms at 73 Kimberley Avenue, not far from her nephew's barbershop in the family Manitoba Street home, now owned by her sister Permelia. The main floor of her stately three-storey brick house was embellished with unique moulded wood interior ceilings that revealed a Union Jack and other designs.

Soon the basement ceiling was a maze of rows of hanging herbs all drying to exacting standards and draped in clean white sheets.[535] Rene kept her McDonald Street house and leased it to doctors and the Muskoka District Health Unit for investment income.[536]

DEMAND FOR ESSIAC CONTINUES

In September 1950, a Chicago physician, Dr. Nelson F. Fisher, wrote Rene to say that he was interested in Essiac and anxious to give it a thorough trial. Over the next few months, he administered Essiac and encouraged Rene to come to Chicago so that they could "go over some of the ingredients, which might streamline your preparation and be more effective in the treating of certain cases."[537]

Perhaps as a result of the publicity generated over Essiac and Dr. Fisher in Chicago, Rene received several urgent letters in 1952 from a Godfrey A.P.V. Winter Baumgarten from Rome, Italy, requesting that she treat a lady named Evelyn Paro, of Duluth, Michigan. In fact, the cancer patient was Eva Peron, wife of the dictator president of Argentina. Evita, as she was also called, had been wasting away in terrible agony from uterine cancer for about two years. Because her illness was not publicly discussed, Baumgarten disguised her identity, and Rene was advised about how she was to contact her through a U.S. address. The beloved thirty-three-year-old socialist heroine was blackened by burns from radium treatments after undergoing surgery, and yet she continued to deteriorate. Sadly, before Rene could make arrangements to treat her in her Beunos Aires mansion, the lady died and was whisked off to be mummified on July 25, 1952.[538]

Two years later Rene lost another sister, Lily Slater of Bracebridge, who died in May 1954. In November 1957, Rene's unmarried sister Permelia would die at age seventy-two after weary months of illness, and the responsibility of the old family Manitoba property fell to Rene as her executor.[539]

During 1955, Robert J. Boyer, the newspaperman who had given Rene so much support and press coverage over the years, ran for the

Ontario PC party in Muskoka. During one of her many drop-in visits to his office to chat with his mother, Victoria,[540] Rene announced to the surprised Bob Boyer, "I never thought it would happen — I'm voting for you. All of Monsignor's household will vote for you."[541, 542] In fact Boyer topped the polls and would maintain his attention to Rene's activities during his job as MPP until 1971.

The 1950s saw a number of major discoveries and developments in medicine and medical research, including Dr. Hans Selye's important work in Montreal on the effects of stress on the human body. There was the Vitamin E research by Dr. Evan Shute and his brother Dr. Wilfrid Shute in the Toronto area, and Dr. Salk's marvellous polio vaccine in the U.S. Important diabetes and insulin research was being continued by Dr. Banting's successors in Toronto.

While advances continued to be made in various other branches of medicine, the scourge of cancer continued. Rene quietly treated cancer patients with Essiac in her home under the critical eye of Ontario's Health Department and the Ontario College of Physicians and Surgeons. Dr. Noble retired in 1956 as registrar of the latter, but through his dedication to the unyielding codes of the medical profession he maintained a close and relentless watch on Rene's activities.[543] Local residents knew that on least two days per week Rene had a lot of visitors who stayed only a short time.

As it became more difficult for Rene to climb stairs, she set up her bedroom on the main floor to avoid the trip to the upper level. Mr. and Mrs. Frank Henry lived in her house a couple of summers while they let their Muskoka lakeside home to vacationers. They certainly were aware that Rene's house continued to be a healing retreat for many patients.[544] Neighbour Mrs. Nelson Goltz knew Rene worried about her patients and cared that they got regular treatments. Dairyman Tom Ball, Vera Goltz's father, used to say that the cure for cancer would be growing belowground. He had pigs that regularly dug up burdock, left the tops, and ate the roots. He felt the "pigs were smart to only eat what's good for them."[545]

CANCER COMMISSION CONTINUES

The cancer commission continued its activities into the 1940s and 1950s and the Ontario government concluded its ten-year funding commitment to the seven cancer clinics in the Toronto General Hospital, Ottawa Civic, Ottawa General, and hospitals in Hamilton, London, Kingston, and Windsor (Walkerville) in November 1942. But although these clinics were in full operation, 12.8 percent of all the deaths in Ontario, some 4,987 persons each year, were to due to cancer.

Acknowledging its responsibility to improve cancer services, the Ontario government put in place the Ontario Cancer Treatment and Research Foundation Act in 1943, and in the following March the minister of health and public welfare, Durham County's Dr. Percy Vivian, announced the appointment of a seven-man foundation to conduct a program of diagnosis, treatment, and research in cancer.[546] The foundation members were The Consumers' Gas Company president Lt. Col. Arthur L. Bishop, who was a mining engineer; Dr. George S. Young and Robert Brown of Toronto; Arthur Ford, London newspaper editor and president of the Canadian Press; Malcolm Cochrane of Port Arthur; Dr. H.F. Stratford of Sarnia; and son of wealthy investment broker F.H. Deacon, Kenneth Emerson Deacon of Unionville.

The foundation had the authority to establish a hospital with facilities for the diagnosis and active treatment of cancer with control over a number of phases of their cancer program, including work by Dr. Thomas J. Glover. The cancer commission had been impressed with a submission by Dr. Glover, a cancer researcher who worked in Toronto, New York, and Washington, suggesting "some degree of success," they felt.[547] His scientific research on the basis of a parasitic theory of cancer's origin would be encouraged by the commission.

In 1944, the mission of the commission was: "To protect sufferers from the deplorable exploitation of alleged curative treatments, the claims for which had no foundation in fact, and which often delayed cancer patients from taking recognized treatment in time to be of benefit."[548] The activities of Rene Caisse did not go unnoticed. In the late 1940s, the name of the Cancer Remedy Act was altered to pluralize the word "remedy" and reflect the miscellaneous cancer treatments that were brought forward.

The original chairman of the Commission for the Investigation of Cancer Remedies, Justice Gillanders, died in 1945 at a young fifty, and the commission stopped functioning until well into 1946, when Dr. Callahan also died.[549]

Now, in 1958, the commission was under the direction of Hon. Justice R.L. Treleaven, another lawyer with no medical expertise. The only original members remaining on the commission were Drs. Valin and Deadman, Dr. Young having died two years previously. Other members were Dr. J.A. McFarlane, Dr. Wm. B. Phair,[550] and two non-medical persons: Norman F. Meaden, an executive with International Nickel in Coppercliff, and Robert H. Brown of Port Credit, the general representative of a U.S.-based printers' union.

Back in 1938, the annual honorarium had been $1,000 for the chairman and $700 for the members, plus expenses. By 1958, the work was considerably decreased and the honorariums were reduced to $500 for the chairman and $250 per member, plus expenses.

Minister of Health Dr. Mackinnon Phillips assured new member Brown that the task of the commission was not too onerous, as "there are not too many people coming forward with cancer remedies."[551] While the commission was responsible to the minister, Justice Treleaven confided in a letter to Dr. Phillips that year, "All the matters we deal with do not come to your attention and I would like to think that you are rather pleased about that. Some of them are too trivial that though they take a little time it would indeed be unfortunate to have your Department troubled with them."[552]

Two years later, Commissioner Deadman would report to the next health minister, Dr. Matthew B. Dymond, proudly stating, "In the first five years of activity we dealt with more than 60 claimed cancer cures. They are now at a minimum in the province."[553] The commission would receive only six enquiries that year and meet only once to discuss the relation between wheat smut spores and cancer with A.W. Milne.

Certainly the cancer commission heard from Rene Caisse and her supporters. At an unknown date in early 1958, Dr. Harris McPhedran, head of the College of Physicians and Surgeons, "sent his policeman" to arrest her for administering Essiac.[554] At a commission meeting on May 9, a letter Rene had written to the minister of health on February 18 was tabled.[555] As a result, C.J. Telfer, long-time secretary of the commission, wrote to the minister of health reminding him of the nurse who is apparently still using her formula in the treatment of cancer. "The Commission feels that there is no indication that any action should be taken by them," Telfer wrote, "but directed that the matter be brought to your attention in case you might wish to refer this one also to the College."

Leslie M. Frost, who had been prime minister of Ontario for nearly ten years, received many letters from Rene's patients and supporters. She was no stranger to him, but in September 1958 he wrote a formal request to Rene explaining that the commission had her "system" under consideration, but that it hasn't been able to make much progress because of a lack of information. Frost suggested that it would speed matters up greatly if she would get in touch with Deputy Health Minister Dr. W.G. Brown and arrange through him to give the commission the details of her methods, so that the commission could give them a thorough analysis.[556]

Exasperated, Rene sent a blistering and lengthy letter to Dr. Brown, dated October 6. She told him that Dr. McPhedran was under the misapprehension that she was practising medicine and had ordered her to stop treating patients. In part she said, "I am treating, in order to convince the medical world of the benefits that can be derived by Cancer patients with 'ESSIAC' treatment.... I told Dr. Banting, Dr. Noble and Dr. B.T. McGhie twenty years ago, that when the medical world would give me some assurance that this treatment would be used by them in the treatment of Cancer [clinically], that I would be willing to give my formula. They would not give me this assurance, so I decided that if they did not know what I was using, they could not be in a position to condemn it. I have therefore kept my own counsel."

"Now the onus is on the Medical Profession," she warned Dr. Brown after reviewing some of the spectacular history of her Essiac successes.

Dr. Brown sent a memo to the Prime Minister's Office on October 20 and admitted that they had been receiving a number of letters of endorsement of the treatment used by Miss Caisse in the past, but the letters did not require acknowledgement.[557] The medical bureaucrat observed that it was apparent she still was not prepared to provide the commission with any information of her formula that could be studied unless they provided assurance to her in advance that her methods would be adopted.

"It is our considered opinion that with the College of Physicians and Surgeons of Ontario insisting that she does not practice medicine, it will be best to let the matter rest. The only real danger we have to avoid, as much as possible, is that the people spend their money on a useless form of therapy, and that any delusion they may have regarding benefits delays or prevents them from getting early and more effective orthodox treatment."

As the member of the Ontario legislature for Muskoka, newspaperman Bob Boyer asked his colleague Health Minister Matt Dymond in early January 1959 what was going on with Rene and the college. Indeed, Dr. Dymond admitted in a letter to Boyer that Miss Caisse was under the surveillance of the inspector for the college, but that no immediate action in the way of prosecution was being contemplated. "Dr. McPhedran assures me that the College will not prosecute without first getting in touch with my Deputy Minister, or with me. I gathered, however, that it is their hope that Miss Caisse's activities might be controlled by means of surveillance, and that no prosecution would ever be necessary," he wrote.[558]

U.S. PUBLICATIONS PROBE RENE'S ACTIVITIES

A brief reference to the Rene Caisse remedy was noted in a book called *The Cancer Blackout: A History of Denied and Suppressed Remedies*, which was published around this time.[559] Author Maurice

Natenberg, who also published under the name of Nat Morris, disturbed the cancer "industry" by writing, "For centuries there has been an official and dogmatic version of cancer which was dangerous for independent-minded physicians to oppose." Natenburg, in his brief and careless reference to Rene's story, promised that he would meet with her so that errors could be corrected and more information could be included in the next edition. There was never a next edition of that particular book.

True Magazine, a popular mens' magazine published by Fawcett Publications in New York City, seriously considered telling Rene Caisse's amazing story in 1959. Publisher Ralph Daigh and a scientist friend, Paul Murphy, travelled to Bracebridge, interviewed Rene, and sought out three local retired doctors who had practised during Rene's most active period.[560] Dr. Ellis and Dr. Grieg spoke with some hesitation but with fair consideration of Rene, but Dr. Bastedo preferred to not be interviewed at all on such a delicate matter. Fascinated by the results of their somewhat positive conversations that day, Daigh and Murphy asked Rene if she would be interested in participating in a study using human patients and mice inoculated with human carcinoma at an American medical centre run by Dr. Charles Brusch, but Rene was nursing her sick brother Ted and would not commit herself to leave him for a trip to the United States.

U.S. FRATERNITIES PROBE ESSIAC

Nevertheless, in her seventieth year, Rene flew to Cambridge, Massachusetts, in May of 1959 where Ralph Daigh introduced her to Dr. Charles Brusch at the Brusch Medical Center.[561] It had been established by Charles and his brother in 1951 and was now staffed by more than sixty physicians, many of whom were also on the staff of Harvard, Tufts, Boston University, and other leading medical schools. Their hospital affiliations included Boston City, Massachusetts General, St. Elizabeth, and others.[562] Dr. Brusch, who had lost his wife and two sisters to the disease, was very interested in cancer therapy.

Soon Rene began regular trips to Cambridge. From May 22, responsible to the supervisor of research, Dr. Charles W. McClure,[563] she administered a series of treatments on a small number of terminally ill cancer patients as well as laboratory mice implanted with anaplastic carcinoma. Dr. Halsey Loder[564] was observer, and some eighteen physicians were put on the project.[565] Understandably, Dr. McClure wanted to know who of Rene's patients were still living after receiving Essiac treatments during her clinic days and sent out questionnaires to twenty-six of her former patients. Eleven witnessed testimonials were returned, including that of Nellie McVittie, who was treated twenty-three years ago, and Eliza Veitch, who was treated twenty-one years ago.[566]

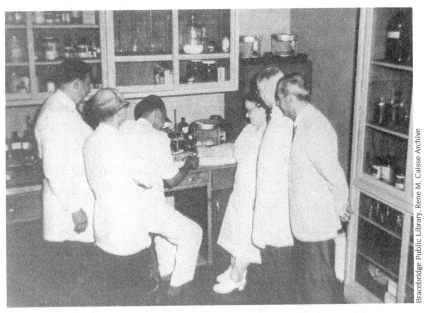

Rene holds a mouse for her colleagues to administer Essiac in the Brusch laboratory.

Dr. Philip Merker, head of the Mouse Host Studies section of the Sloan-Kettering Institute for Cancer Research in Rye, New York, agreed to co-operate with the Brusch project and in June arranged to supply eighteen mice injected with human carcinoma to the Brusch Medical Center. The compromise was that no publicity be attached to the tests and that the mice be returned to Sloan-Kettering for further testing and analysis.[567]

After three months of patient testing, Dr. McClure and Dr. Brusch concluded, "On mice it [Essiac] had been showed to cause a decided recession of the mass and a definite change in cell formation.... On mice it [Essiac] has merit in the treatment of cancer." The report continued, "Clinically, on patients suffering from pathologically proven cancer, it reduces pain and causes a recession in the growth; patients have gained weight and shown an improvement in their general health.... The doctors do not say that Essiac is a cure, but they do say it is of benefit. It is non-toxic, and is administered both orally and by intramuscular injection." Dr. Merker reported physiological change in the cancer growths in the mice, which was "characterized as a tendency of the cancer cells to amalgamate and localize."[568] Rene, of course, had long described this phenomenon as the cancer growth localizing and regressing within itself.[569] But they still did not know the ingredients of the Essiac formula, as Rene continued her standoff.

Now the National Cancer Institute (NCI) at Bethesda, Maryland, was interested in testing Essiac. Dr. Halsey Loder, who had watched the trials, consulted with Dr. Shields Warren, co-founder of NCI,[570] about the favourable reports of the efficacy of the remedy. Dr. Warren recommended collaboration with NCI for further animal tests, but again Rene refused to reveal the formula. Testing with Sloan-Kettering, Brusch Medical Center, and NCI was over and the laboratories would no longer supply mice or process animal autopsies.

Rene felt certain pressure had been exerted on these labs to cause them to cease co-operating with her. Apparently the American Medical Association had forbidden its members to administer "unknown remedies" to patients.[571]

Although Rene could not have imagined that the association with Dr. Brusch was over, she returned to Bracebridge as frustrated as ever. A very tired seventy-year-old, with little energy to keep up her mainland lake cottage property, or even to enjoy its loveliness, Rene sold it for the sum of $7,000. It was, perhaps, a necessary financial decision.

CHAPTER 14

AN ACTIVE RETIREMENT

RENE TRIES RETIREMENT

The days for Rene Caisse during the early 1960s were dragging. She set up her easel, picked up her paintbrush, and wondered if her secret formula and work with suffering humanity would ever be appreciated. Referred by word of mouth, patients continued to come to her, and Essiac was still brewing on the kitchen stove, but the recognition she yearned for was not forthcoming. Once more she tried for royal intervention and sent a package of information to the Duke of Edinburgh in June 1960. As often happens with letters to the royal household, hers was sent on a roundabout route. The prince's office sent the package to Canada's governor general, Roland Michener, and his office sent it to the Department of National Health, which then returned it to Rene. The deputy minister suggested that Rene apply to Canada's National Cancer Institute in Toronto. Rene's records don't include a followup.[572]

Another biographer relates that Rene continued to make and supply Essiac for local patients, and for Dr. Brusch.[573] She communicated with various organizations, such as the Biochemical Institute of the University of Texas and the pharmaceutical firm Merck & Co., in an attempt to interest them in her herbal product. But they required Rene to disclose the formula before they would discuss the matter any further.

Meanwhile at least one medical doctor approved of Essiac, with or without the formula. Dr. Leo V. Roy of Whitney, Ontario, a small village on the southeast fringe of Algonquin Park, was impressed with Essiac's results and wrote an essay on the subject in 1961. As a young doctor in 1953, he became interested in Rene's remedy and referred patients to her for treatment. Recalling his meeting with her, he wrote:

> I was looking for some answers that everybody said did not exist. Her whole stature, then as now, had that quiet assurance of one "who knows". We only had the one day together. But for years after, this meeting, and the ideas that came out of it, were the stimulation and the assurance that a new era of cancer therapy is here — waiting to be made available for the suffering masses.
>
> Each time I referred a patient to Miss Caisse, the results forced the same knowledge deeper into my convictions. The effects of the herbal preparations are rapid and efficient. More and more each year, the simplicity of the therapy shocked the basis of orthodox medical convictions learned in university training.[574]

Complaints about Dr. Roy's work with a purported cancer cure were placed before the College of Physicians and Surgeons in 1963,[575] and allegations of professional misconduct were discussed along with demands that he cease his involvement with Essiac. Dr. Morton Shulman noted in his autobiographical book that he complained to the College of Physicians and Surgeons about Dr. Roy, and on August 21, 1964, his licence to practise was taken away.[576, 577]

Rene was exhausted from nursing her brother Ted for many months in her home, where he died on November 25, 1961. Now she made plans to sell the family home and stores, as the responsibility of owning valuable real estate was becoming an increasing burden. People recall that Rene, now seventy-three years old, was suffering with ailments complicated by her heavy weight, and bit by bit she sold income properties. In early 1962, the Manitoba Street property was sold, thus ending seventy-three years of continuous Caisse ownership.

The formal opening of the beautiful new sixty-five-bed South Muskoka Memorial Hospital took place October 20, 1963, just a few blocks from Rene's McDonald Street house, but Dr. Bert Bastedo, who had helped turn the sod prior to construction, was not there. The community had been shocked when he and his wife were killed by a car on April 10 while walking across a highway in Plainfield, Indiana, at the beginning of their annual holiday to California.

The McDonald Street house was sold in the next few months, with Rene holding the mortgage. This turned out to be advantageous because the mortgagee defaulted and she got the house back two years later, and then sold it for more money than she received the first time.

Her three-storey house at 73 Kimberley Avenue had proved to require an enormous amount of upkeep, with many rooms to care for. She put it up for sale, and it was sold on September 1, 1965. Then she purchased a small bungalow at 293 Hiram Street for a modest $12,000. It was a quiet area on the east side of town where she could continue to brew her decoction for patients and still find time to create the colourful jewellery of pearls and beads she loved to wear. Her friends recalled that she enjoyed an occasional drink of vodka, gin, or a cool rum daiquiri and smoked cigarettes in moderation, always carrying a dainty ashtray with her to use at restaurants.

FIRST BIOGRAPHICAL PUBLICATION

In 1966, Maurine B. Cox of New York City prepared the first biographical publication about the nurse in the form of a privately printed pamphlet, entitled I Was "Canada's Cancer Nurse": The Story of Essiac, with a limited distribution.[578] The piece was a loosely collected series of reminiscences of Rene's life, when at the age of seventy-eight her powers of detailed recollection were being tested.[579] The booklet also included her cancer theory, documents such as petitions by her medical supporters, and part of the celebrated Bill 38. Rene's outspoken disillusionment with the cancer societies was expressed as well. "With cancer therapy, we have to face a financial fact," she stated. "There is more money in cancer than in any other disease ever known to mankind. Millions of dollars, every year, are poured into research grants."[580]

She knew about the terrible effects radiation and deep X-ray therapy had in many of the cases she had treated, and she spoke out: "I believe that radium drives cancer in, instead of out and burns the surrounding tissue. I believe that radium, used in too heavy doses, is a prolific cause of further cancer in burnt tissues." She felt that X-ray therapy may scatter cancer to other parts of the body and radium cause further cancer in destroyed tissues.

The embittered retired nurse wrote:

> I did not then [when her cancer clinic opened in 1935] know of an organized effort to keep a cancer cure from being discovered, especially by an independent researcher not affiliated with any organization supported by private or public funds. Tremendous sums have been raised and appropriated for official cancer research during the last 50 years, with almost nothing new or productive discovered. It would make these foundations and institutions look pretty silly, if an obscure Canadian nurse discovered an effective treatment for cancer![581] ...
>
> What actual progress has been made during the past 50 years in the cancer therapy field? What proportion of patients still die?[582]

A number of brief profiles of recovered cancer patients were noted along with more of Rene's views, such as the following:

> It is my opinion that the hearing of my case before the Cancer Commission was one of the greatest

farces ever perpetrated in the history of medicine. Over 380 patients came to be heard, and the Commission limited the hearing to 49 patients. Then in their report, stated that I had taken only 49 patients to be heard! They stated that X-ray reports were not acceptable as a diagnosis, and that the 49 doctors had made wrong or mistaken diagnoses.... Having spent nearly 30 years trying to get my discovery accepted by the medical profession, I feel that cancer is at present a closed book.

In her last page, Rene reflected:

Once a simple treatment is found, it will revolutionize the entire program and it would lose millions of dollars for the research groups, foundations, societies, doctors, hospitals, equipment manufacturers, drug firm, etc. etc. So why kill the goose that lays the golden eggs?

In my heart I still hope and pray for a miracle — but in my mind I see only closed doors. The disappointment is a tragedy that has made my last years sad and frustrating; I am grateful that God has given me the strength to retain my sanity.

Perhaps some other country will have the courage to find and bring help to suffering humanity, though I had hoped it would be my own beloved Canada, or our neighbour, the United States of America.[583]

The venting of Rene's wrath was probably instinctive because she and her patients, who continued to appear at her door, knew that no matter what the officials said, the special herbal tea gave them relief and many, apparently, cure.

"GRANDMA MOSES"

Rene's retirement did give her opportunities for some relaxation and to pursue some favourite hobbies. She referred to herself as "Grandma Moses."[584] Many of the oil paintings she created are still treasured collectibles by Bracebridge friends, including the author. When she visited her sister in Tacoma, Washington, the two of them would paint mountain scenery, and when she spent winters in Florida, her subjects would be lakes and boats. Rene enjoyed dabbling in various crafts such as painting on velvet, shellwork, and bead design. She liked to wear her beaded creations in abundant strings around her neck, as pictures show. Friends enjoyed the glass bonbon dishes and ashtrays that she decorated with hand-painted flowers. But still, the years in Bracebridge hung heavy as she recalled active times.

Rene had outlived most of her siblings and most of her friends, and her living sisters were a long way away. Some family, Ivan Slater's grandchildren, brightened Rene's days. During their visits they found that Aunt Rene's tummy made a delightful ride as they slid down her sizable girth, much to Rene's enjoyment.[585]

Rene felt that the townspeople had pretty well forgotten her. But letters still came in from former patients and old friends. Some would remember her decades later, such as Manitoba Street merchant Murray Ellis, who as a young man had visited Rene's garage and read the testimonies she had stored in boxes. At the time he called her a grouchy old lady, but now he insists with respect that downtown Bracebridge wouldn't hold all the people who have taken Rene's brew.

Rene was still making and selling her red kidney pills, and each year federal registration No. 20027 was renewed. Back in 1951, the remedy became known as R.M.C. Kidney Tablets. Her patients found that their backaches were eased because the herbal tablets were compounded to increase the flow of urine and relieve bladder discomfort.[586]

In 1968, the Proprietary or Patent Medicine Act required collection of data to determine the annual volume of products registered and manufactured under the Act, and Rene was requested to supply information for the national Health Department. Compounding the tablets and managing the sales were just too much for Rene, so the Everett Drug Store sold them for her for years. It supplied tablets by mail to customers all over Ontario. Even Maurine Cox ordered them from her home in New York City.[587] And Dr. Leo Roy purchased them, certainly in 1973, probably for his patients.

RENE TRIES SLOAN-KETTERING AGAIN

At eighty-five, Rene's heavy weight provoked problems such as swollen and painful limbs, and she was mostly housebound. She loved her chocolates and candies, and although her doctor warned her about the health hazards of eating them, she insisted that she loved her chocolates too much and would take the risks.[588] She ached from arthritis and needed a cane, or sometimes a wheel-chair, to get around.[589]

Rene enjoys visitors Valeen, Elemere, and Victorine at her Florida trailer.

At an age when most people consider that any unfinished business would remain that way, in 1973 Rene decided to write Dr. C. Chester Stock at Sloan-Kettering Institute for Cancer Research in Rye, New York, hoping to reopen the Essiac trials. Rene reminded him of Dr. Merker's earlier interest, and Dr. Stock, now the vice-president and director of the Walker Laboratory, responded. According to the researchers for *Homemaker's Magazine*, he agreed to test her material. Dr. Stock assured her that should they be successful, she would receive due recognition for her contribution. He reminded her that he would have to know what the materials were before Essiac could be tested.

Winter in Bracebridge challenges those who have difficulty navigating the snow and cold, and for the homeowner the responsibility of shovelling safe paths is stressful. Canadian "snowbirds" still take off for Florida, and Rene, whose physical abilities were limited by arthritic pain, spent the winter of 1973–74 in a comfortable trailer in St. Petersburg, Florida, keeping up her correspondence with Dr. Stock.

On a pleasant January day in St. Petersburg, Rene wrote to Dr. Stock, who was probably sloshing around in New York's east coast

Toronto Public Library

Dr. Chester C. Stock was active in the Sloan-Kettering chemotherapy program.

snow, stating that she would give him her formula for Essiac. She wrote that upon her return to Bracebridge in April, she would supply a small amount of ingredients, along with some ampoules that she had saved from the lot she prepared for the trials at the Brusch Medical Center back in 1959 so that Sloan-Kettering could test her remedy. (She stunned investigators in 1977 when she told them that she had thrown some twenty-seven thousand ampoules of Essiac from the 1959 trials in the garbage when she had given up hope of ever having her work recognized.[590]) Rene went on to tell Dr. Stock that "mice inoculated with human carcinoma seemed to get quicker results than any other type of cancer." Others, like sarcoma, took a longer series of treatments to show results, she explained.[591]

Rene, in no condition to travel to the institute on Long Island Sound, southeast of New York City, suggested that she speak on the telephone with the doctor who would be doing the testing.

Rene found a small package of the unidentified dried, unground herb in her luggage, and in a letter Dr. Stock received March 27 told him that she was sending it along so that he could start testing. He was advised to grind the herb to a powder and put it in thirty ounces of pure water, then to boil it at a rolling boil for five minutes. At that point the water would be reduced to twenty-eight ounces. Turn off the heat and let stand over night, she instructed, and then put the clearer part in sterile bottles and use on mice inoculated with cancer, one-half of one cc to the injection. "I know this all sounds crude to you, but I did get results with it! Do this every day for nine days (keeping controls for each mouse) I am sure you would get results."

Rene needed assurance from Dr. Stock that he wouldn't try to have it recognized as a *cure*. "Sir Frederick Banting (of Insulin fame) gave me this advice 'Try to have it accepted as a beneficial treatment, it will eventually prove itself.'"[592]

On April 4, 1974, Rene decided to divulge the crucial ingredient in Essiac to Dr. Stock. It was sheep sorrel.[593, 594] No other herbs or their measurements were revealed. Rene also confided, "You are the only person who knows it. I feel relieved to know I found someone I could trust."

In confidence to you
Dr. S Chester Stock of
Sloan Kettering Institute
for Cancer Research.
From Rene M Caisse McGaughey

Essiac

The herb that will destroy
a cancer (a malignant
growth) is
(Sorrel) the dog eared
Sheep sorrel, sometimes
called (sour grass
(The entire plant) must
be used.
picked in the spring
before the seeds form,
then washed, dried and
powdered. 1 oz of powder
in 1 qt 30 oz water, brought
to a rolling Boil for about
5 minutes. let stand over
night about 8 hrs. pour
off liquid into steril bottles
(or fill one c.c. ampules
to keep. for intermuscular
injections. (one ampule.
should treat 2 mice everyday
inoculated with human cancer

Rene's handwritten instructions for making Essiac divulged only the crucial ingredient.

When Rene returned to Bracebridge from Florida's sun April 13, she awaited a reply from Dr. Stock. However, a Canada-wide postal strike, part of a rash during that period, suspended mail from the U.S., and her frustration was intolerable. Finally, on April 25, Dr. Stock answered her letter, but instead of expressing great appreciation for her secret formula he merely explained that the tests had not yet been started because of problems with the animal tumour system. The news must have dashed Rene significantly.

In a May letter, she asked, "Is it because of the simple Herb I used, and kept secret for all these years, that may be you are not interested? Do not be misled by this because I <u>did</u> get the results I claimed for this, it took years to find out the one Herb that actually worked on the growth itself, the other herbs I used to purify the blood and throw off any infection thrown off by the malignant growth as it regressed."[595]

As time passed and still Rene hadn't heard from Dr. Stock, she began to worry. She sent along some ampoules and in a June letter clarified that she had kept them at room temperature for over twenty years. When she used them, she wrote, she would stand the required number in warm water so they would be about blood temperature.[596]

Dr. Stock had received a series of long handwritten letters from the eight-five-year-old over the period. Her handwriting varied in clarity as her health and strength waxed or waned. It would seem that to her every day seemed endless, as she waited impatiently for a positive response from Sloan-Kettering saying that once and for all her Essiac was proven. Finally, she received the report on the first test in October 1974. It was negative, with no toxicity and no tumour regression.

Recuperating from a fall requiring six weeks in hospital in late 1974 precluded her wintering in Florida that season, but she continued writing to Dr. Stock and sending along herb preparations. Again there was a lengthy silence from Dr. Stock, and on April 28, 1975, he admitted that although he requested tests of Essiac, none had yet been done. Surprisingly, some test results raised her hopes. Dr. Stock announced that two out of six mice showed regressions in sarcoma 180 in the recent experiments.[597] Rene immediately sent more dried herbs to Sloan-Kettering, but the next test, prepared with the latest materials, proved to be negative.

But the Essiac had not been prepared as she had directed. The laboratory's "Immunotherapy Studies" report noted, "Leaves and stems were ground in a mortar, suspended in 60ml sterile water and extracted for 5 days in a refrigerator. Suspension was filtered though a double layer of cheesecloth, diluted to 120ml with water and distributed in vials which were kept in refrigerator."

Rene was furious. On August 4, she steamed:

> I am very shocked at the way your people are using the materials I sent. They might as well inject sterile water. I am sure, I gave you instructions on how to prepare it? They are just using leaves and stems leaving out the roots, they are a part of Essiac, and to strain it through cheesecloth destroys it.
>
> You are the only person in the world that I have trusted completely Dr. Stock, and I had such high hopes that even if I should pass on, it would be made available to suffering humanity (at least as a very beneficial treatment for cancer). I know Dr. Stock that you do not do this testing or preparing yourself, but feel sure you can guide them?[598]

Refrigerating the remedy was against her specific instructions, and that the mice had been injected with animal sarcoma instead of human carcinoma, which she had been under the impression would be used, made her very angry.

Rene spent the winter of 1975–76 in Florida, but she continued to think about only one thing — the testing of Essiac at Sloan-Kettering. Her correspondence with Dr. Stock became repetitious and revealed a tired old lady who may have been considered a pest by the New York research scientist. But it was so important to her. In April 17, 1976, she suggested that he double the strength of each dose administered to mice. "I did this in Boston and got better results."

Rene may have written just one too many letters of complaint regarding the testing procedures involving the sheep sorrel and the tumour system. A final testing in the summer of 1976 was negative. Dr. Stock, now vice-president of academic affairs for the Memorial Sloan-Kettering Cancer Center reached the end of his tether and wrote, "As you apparently wish a type of test we are not in a position to provide, nor would wish to, we will terminate our testing of Essiac. We need the test capacity for materials from others who are satisfied with our testing procedures."[599]

This was a crushing blow to Rene. Dr. Stock had never thanked her for sharing her most precious possession, and they never met.

Nevertheless, she made two more efforts to re-establish testing, and it must have been a very difficult effort. On September 1, 1976, she wrote, "I am sorry you have decided to discontinue Essiac. I was wrong."

Her efforts at apology were disregarded, and Rene was devastated. This terrible outcome was not at all what she had expected after finally revealing, albeit only partly, her long coveted secret. The Sloan-Kettering trials were over. Rene was spent.

CHAPTER 15

ESSIAC STORY SPARKS NATIONAL INTEREST

HOMEMAKER'S MAGAZINE GETS INVOLVED

A Muskoka resident, Sheila Snow Fraser, had interviewed Rene Caisse over a couple of years and compiled an article about the nurse's life that was rejected by *Chatelaine* and *Reader's Digest* as too controversial. In the fall of 1976, Fraser approached Jeffery Shearer, executive vice-president of Comac Communications Limited, publisher of the widely distributed *Homemaker's Magazine*, and he found the subject appealing because one of his staff had just died of cancer.

In early January 1977, Shearer introduced Fraser to Jane Hughes, editor of the magazine, and to Carroll Allen, an investigative reporter on the staff who was asked to present the story in the magazine's successful style and format. It would also be necessary for her to delve into the material provided, meet extensively with Rene Caisse, and carefully verify the evidence to head off any negative questions by the medical fraternity or other readers. Carroll was introduced to the nurse on Friday, January 7, and following her discussions with Hughes the pair determined that Rene's story was an interesting one and wanted to answer questions raised by the situation, such as: Did Essiac work? What was in it? If it did work, they wanted to help her. Cautiously, Hughes and Allen determined that their motive was to tell the story however it turned out. They wouldn't be promoters of Essiac. A March deadline was set so the story could appear in the May issue, and a very tight schedule was struck. Jane urged Rene to provide all the necessary information.

The old lady seemed to enjoy the visits, and as Rene began to reminisce and answer the questions Carroll listened intently, recording what would become a dynamic story. Carroll recalled with a smile the flashy dresses Rene wore with strings of coloured beads, many of which she made.[600] And the wigs! Early in the interviews, Carroll determined that Rene was a champion at wishful thinking. If you didn't join her and support her illusions without any doubt or question, such as requests for proof or information about her formulas, you were part of a "conspiracy" to defeat her.[601]

Rene was not comfortable with the need to verify stories with the doctors, as that was a very sore spot with her, but the writers' plans included meeting the doctors who had conducted clinical trials of her herbal remedy. Rene did show Carroll Dr. Stock's letter dated August 5, 1976, advising her he was terminating Essiac tests on animals. She had boxes of letters, reports, and other documents "stashed under her bed" and could draw out anything on suggestion.[602] Then the discussion moved to the trust that the magazine envisaged and what Rene's thoughts were on the possibility of creating such a thing for her protection. The *Homemaker's* staff hoped that they might speed Essiac through the bureaucratic maze quickly and offered, through a trust, to represent her in any dealings she might have with the government, cancer institutes, or any interested pharmaceutical companies. At the time, she seemed delighted at the idea.

Fraser and Allen flew to Cambridge on January 20 to visit the Brusch Medical Center. When they arrived, Dr. Charles Brusch showed them into his small office where awards, certificates of honour, and family photographs were prominently displayed on its walls. He told them of his co-operation with the Sloan-Kettering Institute (SKI) Essiac study and let them read the 1959 results, and he confirmed Dr. Merker's failed efforts to persuade Rene to reveal her formula. They also read about SKI's supplying mice inoculated with human carcinoma, along with their decision later to halt the mice supply after Rene turned Dr. Merker down.

As it happened, just prior to the Cambridge visit, Dr. Brusch had asked Rene for some herbs to treat a patient with terminal cancer of the oesophagus. She was reluctant to send him any because she had not heard from him in years. Apparently, however, she changed her mind and sent a parcel by registered mail, which had just arrived at the clinic. It turned out that the patient, Patrick McGrail, was the brother of Lena Burcell, who had participated in the 1959 study, and he was to receive his first Essiac treatment the following day.

Having substantiated Rene's story about the Brusch trial and knowing that the doctor would be sending along reports about his patient, the investigators returned to Canada and reported to Rene about the visit with Dr. Brusch. She was angry, although she had been forewarned, and became visibly upset and withdrawn, insisting there was no need to look elsewhere as she had all the evidence in her own house.

A VISIT WITH DR. C. CHESTER STOCK

On Friday, February 11, Carroll and Sheila met C. Chester Stock, PhD, at the Memorial Sloan-Kettering Cancer Center in New York City promptly at 11 a.m. The vice-president and associate director for administrative and academic affairs chatted freely about his work at the centre, leaving his visitors wondering why Rene would label him "untrustworthy." Just minutes into the meeting, a young man in his thirties quietly joined the group and introduced himself as Ralph Moss, PhD, assistant director of public affairs of the centre.[603,604,605] When Carroll asked Dr. Stock why animal tumour systems were used instead of human ones, he explained, "For mice to be implanted with human cancer, they must be so irradiated beforehand that results are inconclusive."[606] He then admitted that the failure of the first Essiac test could have been the result of a possible deterioration of the fifteen-year-old ampoules that Rene had supplied and that had been stored at room temperature.

"I became interested in testing the material because it might be an immuno-stimulant to rouse the host's defences," he said. The researchers were told that over the years Sloan-Kettering had tested thirty thousand compounds and seventy-five to one hundred thousand natural substances. "The tests with Essiac were not encouraging, but Dr. Stock believed there are definite species differences, and doesn't rule out the possibility that Essiac could be effective against human cancer."[607] Dr. Stock believed that plants could vary in medicinal power in different areas of the country, and that freshly prepared herbs might be more potent than dried imported ones. This was the first time the investigators learned about the recently concluded Sloan-Kettering test trials of Essiac. Rene had never told them about the negotiations, even during their recent discussions.

After the doctor hurried off to his next appointment, they were escorted into a small, windowless office where a thick confidential file labelled "Mrs. Rene Caisse McGaughey" was placed on the only table for them to review. It contained three years of correspondence that had been exchanged between the Bracebridge nurse and the head of the Walker Laboratory. As they read some of these letters, the researchers scribbled down notes because they were not allowed to make photocopies. If there were any questions, they knew they could see Dr. Stock again shortly before three o'clock. When they came across the April 1974 letter in Rene's own handwriting that she had sent him from Florida, they were stunned to read that the "herb that will destroy cancer is sorrel, the dog-eared sheep sorrel." This was the herb that Dr. Stock had referred to at the onset of the interview when he slipped them a sheet about Mrs. Johnson of Virginia, who was given permission to use the plant to treat cancer patients in 1740. The women had only assumed the doctor wanted them to read this information and then give him some feedback.

"You are the only person who knows it," Rene had written in May 1974. She had not revealed the three other herbs used in her remedy. Sheila felt that withholding vital information about this could prevent any chance of getting Essiac officially tested again, and Carroll's concern was that a single herb such as sheep sorrel could not be patented.

Who can imagine the burden placed on the two Toronto researchers when they learned the secret cancer-destroying herb in Essiac and were unable tell anyone — particularly Rene? Rene had placed her trust in Dr. Stock, and now they were inadvertently left with an enormous responsibility to maintain that confidence.

When they returned to the head office of *Homemaker's*, they phoned Dr. Stock to ask if he would consider retesting Essiac if provided with more of the dried herb, along with information about the other herbs in the complete remedy. When he tentatively agreed to comply, they persuaded him to submit this in writing to Rene. With respect to SKI's perceived disinterest in Essiac, Carroll told the author that Dr. Stock was "not an impediment" to looking at Essiac or wanting a cure for cancer. He felt that everyone was protecting their own turf, such as those in radiology, chemotherapy, surgery, and especially the pharmaceutical industry.[608]

Allen and Fraser revisited Rene in Bracebridge a few days later, and she was furious that they had met with Dr. Stock. "Why see him when I have proof of everything here?" she protested. Carroll responded simply, "Because we had to hear the other side of this story, because everything has to be checked out."

Rene adamantly refused to send Dr. Stock more of the dried herbs, and said there was no use in discussing it further. If Essiac wasn't tested on humans, or at least on mice injected with human carcinoma, then forget it. She still wasn't sure that they would carry out her instructions. "Last time they froze it," she maintained. "They might as well have been injecting it with distilled water!"

In Carroll Allen's letter of thanks to Dr. Brusch, sent in mid-February, she told him that Rene had been persuaded to send him more Essiac material right away for his other patients. Then she asked him to do the following:

1) Send an immediate report on Patrick McGrail's progress and another update on his condition by early March, just prior to the publication of the magazine article.
2) Send copies of the case to Dr. Stock of Sloan-Kettering as well, because he was particularly interested in such cases as pancreatic cancer.

In a prompt reply to Carroll's letter, Dr. Brusch reported the following: "Patrick McGrail's throat, neck and upper chest were definitely improving. He was also eating and sleeping better. The patient believed this treatment was helping him, whereas others had failed to do so."

An enclosed note under the heading "To Whom This May Concern" read: "This letter is to certify that I have seen the benefits from the treatments of animals and people with 'Essiac' — which is administered by Rene M. Caisse, R.N., at our own clinic." Dr. Brusch may have written this in 1959 while Rene was taking part in her Essiac clinical trials.

Later in February, Sheila Fraser wrote letters on *Homemaker's* letterhead to four of Rene's recovered cancer patients, enclosing forms similar to those used by Dr. McClure at the Brusch Clinic in 1959. Tony Baziuk, Walter Hampson, Nellie McVittie, and Mrs. H.W. Wagner, who had all been treated with Essiac in the mid-1930s, promptly signed and returned them for the *Homemaker's* research files.

RENE REJECTS A TRUST

It was March 3 when Jane Hughes, Carroll Allen, Sheila Fraser, and a company lawyer arrived at Rene's home on a cold, wintry day. Rene greeted them courteously and they sat down over daiquiris to discuss the official wording of the trust. Rene looked it over and raised some questions. She was reassured that an umbrella of protection built into the agreement was specifically designed to guard her interests and those of her heirs. As Rene expressed some anxiety about the possibility of having to reveal her formula, Jane and the lawyer conceded that she might eventually have to, but asked her how else cold she help "suffering humanity" without doing so? Would she trust Dr. Brusch as an advocate? Or his son, a teacher at Harvard's Medical School? But the nurse wanted more time to think it over. The visitors went back to Toronto.

Days later, the magazine staff drew up a draft of the trust, pencilled in Rene's suggestions, and then had it properly drawn up by their legal department with the following conditions:

- that Essiac remain under Rene's control and supervision during her lifetime, and thereafter under the control of the Trust;
- that the Trust do all in its power to get a patent;
- that written and complete disclosure of Essiac be put in a safety deposit box, to be opened only in the presence of Rene or her nominee, and a director of the Trust;
- that the Trust use its best efforts to gain testing and recognition of Essiac under Rene's supervision, and to negotiate contracts for the benefit of Rene Caisse.

Within a few days, Rene phoned Hughes to say that she was turning down the deal, even though her most trusted friend Dr. Brusch had urged her to accept it. She and Carroll tried to reason with Rene, telling her that the trust was to ensure that the Essiac formula and its testing would be placed in the hands of responsible people who would make it available to the public.

But Rene was concerned that she would have to tell six people so she could get a patent. In a telephone conversation Jane told her that a patent lawyer would have to know what he's taking to Ottawa. "Then I won't patent it if he has to know, I won't patent it," she stubbornly responded.

Jane told her, "You have an opportunity to be either an angel of mercy, or an angel of death, and we're going to publish the story one way or the other."

"That's a very wicked thing to say to me. You won't publish the story, I won't let you," Rene shot back.

Jane told her that they believe in her and want to believe in Essiac. Jane felt that problem was Rene. "Every time someone has got it to the point where something could be done with Essiac, you've backed out for one reason or another. The problem is that we're willing to go ahead with this and you're just sitting on it, but this time a lot of people are going to know about it."[609]

Rene also called Sheila to say that she had now decided to drop everything — magazine story, the trust, and further testing, and would not send Dr. Stock any more Essiac. Then presenting the ravages of eighty-nine years of age, Rene phoned Carroll to say that she had changed her mind and wanted everything to proceed again. Everyone breathed a sigh of relief. Especially Carroll Allen, who had been driving around for months with all of her notes and materials regarding the Caisse/Essiac story locked in her car trunk — just so that she could say that she did because of any perceived conflict of interest with her husband H. Fred Dale. He was garden editor of the *Toronto Star* and this was a story the *Star* might have liked to get before *Homemaker's* could publish it. If there was ever a leak, Carroll didn't want her husband to be vulnerable to blame, so she didn't tell him what she was working on.

Rene sent more herbs to Dr. Brusch, and in his April 6 letter to Rene, he thanked her for the "medication" and reported that his favourite patient Patrick McGrail had gained more than six pounds and was feeling very much better. Brusch had also begun to treat a seventy-seven-year-old woman with Essiac for a rectal tumour. The doctor had read over the draft of the trust agreement and mused:

> ...they were very near-sighted about the fact on how they were going to promote the product. Too bad, there wasn't someone that would be favorable to them in the medical field, who could give a bias opinion in the proper direction. I think you should have this story abourt [sic] your life published. I [sic] is of great value to the scientific and non-scientific readers. What I know about your work with Cancer, it would made a great story. I will have your material published here if you wish. In regards to the product, it is by no doubt of great

value, inexpensive, reasonable, sensible, and
shows a lot of merit against those being used on
the market today. It is made up of natural herbs,
and in no way has any accumulative side effects
that would cause a destructive action in the body
with its use.

Dr. Brusch offered to pay Rene for the medication she had sent,
and encouraged her to make a will with provisions for the promotion
of Essiac. He offered to "take any responsibility you want me to."[610]

During April and May, investigative writer/professional journalist Carroll Allen and assistant editor Mebbie Black prepared the
Essiac story for the summer edition of *Homemaker's Magazine* against
a very short deadline. Cub photographer Mike Gluss drove to
Bracebridge and took at least one engaging picture of Rene in all
her jewellery and wildly colourful dress. Rene gave him a couple of
bottles of Essiac to take to his father, who was a cancer patient.[611]

To fill in answers to questions she had raised in her research,
Carroll returned to meet with Dr. Brusch in Cambridge to clarify a few
points.[612] Then Allen digested the information Sheila Fraser had supplied and the enormous data they had gathered during the last few
months, and soon the completed article was ready for print. It had
been several weeks since they had last communicated, but on June
3, Carroll and Sheila arrived at Rene's home with three copies of the
June/July/August 1977 edition of *Homemaker's Magazine*. They sat
together silently reading the article. Unprepared for professional,
candid, personal descriptions, Rene suddenly burst into tears. Far
from being a "hard-boiled" (her word) reporter, Carroll never expected this reaction. Today, a writer may well have described Rene as
being a dynamic "character" and short and plump — almost round.

ADVANCE COPIES OF HOMEMAKER'S MAGAZINE

When advance copies of the June/July/August 1977 edition of
Homemaker's Magazine were hand-delivered to various doctors and top

Rene dazzled photographer Mike Gluss for the cover of Homemaker's Magazine.

government officials as a courtesy, each contained a letter dated June 6 written by Executive Vice-President Jeffrey W. Shearer. It briefly summarized Rene's story and invited anyone interested in the article to personally examine *Homemaker's* research and files, which would be made available to them. Opportunities to contact the nurse would also be expedited, if desired. Shearer concluded his letter with the hope that Rene Caisse's work may be tested by responsible medical authorities to establish its validity and that Rene Caisse's formula would be exposed to wider scrutiny because of their publication. The first response was from H.W. Rowlands, Executive Director, Canadian Cancer Society, Ontario Division, Toronto, Ontario, who wrote to Jane the next day: "The article about Rene Caisse, and her treatment of cancer patients with her own herbal remedy, Essiac, is a most fascinating one. I have brought your letter and a copy of the article to the attention of a number of my associates who are directly involved with research matters.... I am very appreciative of your offer to permit us to examine all the records and case histories that you have in your files with respect to her story."[613] There is no record of Harry Rowlands or any of his people examining the Caisse file.

Dr. K.J.R. Wightman, Medical Director of the Ontario Cancer Treatment and Research Foundation responded with the following:

> Miss Caisse (or Mrs. McGaughey) has been in touch with me and provided some of her newspaper clippings, etctera [sic]. I wrote and told her some time ago that I would be interested to visit her and find out something more about her cancer cure and she has written to say she would be glad to see me.... The position of the Medical profession will undoubtedly be the same as it was before. No one feels that it is justifiable to treat patients with remedies of unknown composition for a variety of reasons, and the people who discovered insulin and penicillin for example, had no hesitation in describing the materials they were using so that they could be purified, standardized and tested under scientif-

ic conditions. Perhaps after all these years she would now be willing to take this approach.[614]

Dr. R.M. Taylor, Executive Director of the National Cancer Institute of Canada, wrote to the *Homemaker's* editor the same day in a less friendly tone:

> As you say, this is a frustrating situation. It is made so by Miss Caisse's absolute refusal to reveal the content of her "cure" even though it was given to her without reservation by her Indian friend.
>
> I know of no acceptable ethical way for testing her compound in the absence of knowledge about the contents and possible toxicity. The evidence supporting her cure is, for the most part, anecdotal and couldn't be used in the study of the efficacy of the compound.
>
> It has been made very clear in this case on a number of occasions that if she will provide information about the contents there are ways of testing its usefulness. I would doubt that she will change her attitude at the age of 88, but maybe her heirs will be willing to listen to reason.[615]

Popular broadcaster/historian Bob Johnston of CBC radio interviewed Rene on Friday, June 10, and asked her a number of questions. One was, "If I drank this stuff and didn't have cancer, would it hurt me?"

"No!" Rene emphatically replied.

Then he mused about what law she might be breaking if she opened a tea room in Bracebridge and served her herbal tea for ten or fifty cents a cup without saying it helped cancer. "With my history," she responded with some humour, "they'd run me out of town." It would have to be run by the medical profession, she furthered.

Former Ontario chief coroner Dr. Morton Shulman wrote to Jeff Shearer on June 25: "By odd coincidence I did a study of the

Legislative Committee Study on cancer cures back in the 30s and 40s. It was their opinion at the time with which I agree, that Mrs. Caisse's herbal remedy was useless. In my opinion you have helped perpetuate a fraud."[616] Curiously, in his book *Coroner*, published just two years earlier, the controversial Dr. Shulman did not include Rene Caisse in the number of "cancer quacks" he had known.[617, 618, 619]

Several Canadian radio stations taped interviews with Rene, although it is not known if all of them were broadcast. Toronto radio station CHUM-FM was so anxious to air the Essiac tale that they didn't mention the source of their story until the omission was brought to their attention by *Homemaker's*. So many listeners wanted more information that they lit up the CHUM switchboard. Jane Hughes chuckled in a staff memo: "Apparently, answering the phone is a lot more work than ripping off a story. Now that the heat's on, they're giving credit where credit is due."[620]

Even *60 Minutes*, the CBS news documentary program in the U.S., seriously considered doing the story. The CP wire service got in on it, and their item appeared in newspapers across Canada. And normal public circulation of the magazine had not yet begun!

HOMEMAKER'S MAGAZINE DISTRIBUTED

During the first week of July, copies of the summer edition of *Homemaker's Magazine* were delivered to the homes of thousands of Canadian across the country. The magazine, published in both English and French, contained the explosive story "Could Essiac Halt Cancer?" The nation now knew Rene's story and reaction to it was immediate. Some readers were sympathetic, with offers of help, and others vitriolic with scathing insults. The article has been reprinted thousands of times, issued under other covers by alternative health interests, and distributed all over North America and elsewhere ever since. The Internet also circulates the article, often without credit. While some information is updated in this book, the question posed by the publication of this story remains the same. "Could Essiac Halt Cancer?"

In the editor's July report to the *Homemaker's* staff, recent events were summarized. Thanks to the Canadian Press wire service, Rene's story had appeared in most newspapers coast to coast. And Canadian cancer patients were being told that Dr. Brusch in Cambridge, Massachusetts, would treat them in his clinic. The most surprising event was when Rene, who had recently told Carroll that the Essiac formula had been willed to "certain people in authority," publicly announced that she was leaving it to the University of Toronto in memory of Dr. R.O. Fisher, with whom she had developed the Essiac serum.[621,622]

When the Bracebridge newspaper learned of *Homemaker's Magazine*'s Essiac story, a reporter/photographer was dispatched to interview Rene in her home. As he got there, a Montreal cancer victim arrived pleading for an Essiac treatment. But Rene told him she was unable to give it and asked him to write to the federal and provincial ministers of health and join "hundred and hundreds of letters" already being sent asking for legalization of her treatment. Indeed many letters were received by members of the Ontario legislature from every corner of the province. Rene issued a veiled promise: "In a few weeks I'll be able to do something, I'm pretty sure now," and offered to contact him about proceeding with treatment. "Now you have hope and you didn't have that before," she said.

While the report about Rene was presented in great detail in the *Herald-Gazette*, unfortunately no credit or recognition was given to the local researcher and her colleague who brought the story to national attention in *Homemaker's Magazine*.[623] As Rene would tell Carroll on the phone in October, Sheila hadn't spoken to her "for I couldn't tell you how long. She got mad about an article that went in the paper and she came here and she just lit into my sister and myself. Blame that reporter, we had nothing to do with it whatever and she just went out like a mad lion. So I never called her or ever contacted her."[624]

The *Homemaker's* office had been overwhelmed with calls and letters from readers volunteering to help with the Essiac campaign. Another phone line had to be installed in Rene's home and three of the staff had to handle hundreds of calls on the switchboard. Callers were told that two petitions already circulating were to be directed to

Marc Lalonde, Canada's Minister of National Health and Welfare and to the Canadian Cancer Society. One petition had nine hundred signatures, and the other had more than one thousand. The Hon. Marc Lalonde thanked *Homemaker's* for the advance copy and the offer to review its records and case histories in his July 6 letter, stating, "While they may be useful, they are still regarded as testimonials."

Eleanor Sniderman,[625] Toronto music publisher of Aquitaine Records, was a well-known mover and shaker of causes she believed in, and the Essiac story in *Homemaker's* caught her attention. On July 5, she arrived in Bracebridge to meet Rene. Mrs. Sniderman had many influential friends, including politicians and important doctors, and asked Rene if she would like to have a doctorate in medicine. Of course Rene was excited about the prospect of such an honour.

Two Ontario physicians were successfully convinced by Mrs. Sniderman to treat some cancer patients with Essiac. One was Dr. David Walde,[626] an oncologist who was instrumental in developing the important oncology program in Sault Ste. Marie. He had already been asked by three of his cancer patients to read the Essiac story and look into the remedy. Dr. Walde, who wanted to be called David, met Rene and obtained a few pounds of powdered herbs and instructions on how to prepare them, and started a trial with twenty patients. He felt it was necessary to establish the effectiveness, or otherwise, of her program, as there were increasing pressures on him and other medical oncologists. Rene informed Dr. Wightman, medical director of the Ontario Cancer Treatment and Research Foundation, that Dr. Walde was taking an interest in her remedy and encouraged her to be frank and open with him. Wightman reminded her that "there are no shortcuts in this work, and it must be done carefully."[627]

Dr. John Barker, director of the Shute Heart Clinic in Port Credit, Ontario, was persuaded in late July to accept a number of Canadian patients formerly treated at the Brusch Center in Cambridge, Massachusetts, and signed Rene's form to assure that he would report only to her. Earlier that month, Brusch's supply of Essiac had been confiscated by the U.S. Federal Drug Administration in Washington, D.C.[628,629] It seemed that Dr. Brusch was experiencing interference to the extent that when frantic cancer patients called his office to seek Essiac treatments, they were told that the Canadian article was not true. The reports were reaching *Homemaker's Magazine*. Taking on a new persona, Carroll Allen phoned the same number and was told, "This is not a cancer clinic, this is a medical clinic and we cannot take any patients under any circumstances whatsoever for cancer."[630] Carroll's next call went direct to Dr. Brusch, who agreed with her that his staff got it mixed up and should have told people that they were not treating patients with Essiac, which was not really true at the time.

SECRET FORMULA IN SAFEKEEPING

Meanwhile, Rene was in her ninetieth year, and she knew her time was running out. And she also knew she must reveal the Essiac formula. Encouraged by her friends, including Eleanor Sniderman, Rene finally agreed to ask a lady of impeccable distinction, Ontario's Lieutenant-Governor Pauline M. McGibbon, to accept the secret formula in a sealed envelope and hold it until after Rene's death. On August 9, Rene wrote to the Lieutenant-Governor to thank her for offering to take care of Essiac. She asked that Dr. Charles Brusch receive honourable recognition from the people of Canada for his outstanding contribution and loyalty in support of Essiac.

In the early morning of August 15, 1977, the Lieutenant-Governor was driven to Bracebridge to accept the envelope, supposedly with no publicity. But to Rene, this was a very special occasion, so she invited a number of her relatives and friends, a few patients, and even Mayor Jim Lang, to a reception that was a surprise to the Lieutenant-Governor. The Queen's representative in Ontario returned to Toronto within the hour to place the envelope and its secret in her personal safety deposit box in a Royal Bank branch on St. Clair Avenue West.[631, 632] Mrs. McGibbon told the *Toronto Star*'s Lotta Dempsey that she was saddened by the calls coming in from hopeful cancer sufferers and their families. "I haven't a clue whether or not the formula is any good. Our staff is talking to people, but there is nothing we can do."[633]

The *Ottawa Journal* broke the story in early September that "two Canadian doctors were defying the medical profession and the government and laying their careers on the line in an effort to test on humans a controversial Indian herbal remedy for cancer."[634] Eleanor Sniderman, quoted in the story, complained that the authorities wanted to use the formula on mice. "Well that's a lot of you know what. I don't care how a mouse reacts to the Essiac. A mouse doesn't have my chemistry or emotions or stress symptoms," she exploded.[635]

TRIALS NOT GOING WELL

It seemed that Dr. Walde's trials were not going well, and Rene could not believe it. She had patients who were definitely improving, she insisted. She did not like hearing about the deterioration of some of Dr. Barker's patients, either. Carroll Allen was so dismayed that she jumped on a plane to Sault Ste. Marie, where Dr. Walde showed her his case records and introduced her to some of his patients involved in Essiac trials. Some were terribly cancer-ravaged, just bursting with disease, she recalled. He told her that his patients felt better after taking Essiac.[636, 637]

But, according to Dr. Walde in a subsequent telephone conversation, Rene was not providing appropriate quantities of Essiac herbs to satisfy the needs of his patients or those of Dr. Barker. When he approached her for more Essiac, she refused to provide him with any. During a conversation with Allen, David Walde lamented that Rene had given him "very very little and if I had had all the other patients on it I would have finished within one day. I wouldn't have had enough to have continued. And you know she has cut John Barker off completely from what I can gather." Dr. Walde examined the material he received and two leaves of what he was sure was sheep sorrel floated out.

Rene told Dr. Walde that she was also providing Essiac mixed herbs to Dr. Rudy Falk of the Toronto General Hospital, enough for two or three patients. But Dr. Falk in fact had enough for twenty or thirty patients, both injectable and oral, and Dr. Walde told Rene that while he didn't care who uses it, he felt it was "a bit ridiculous to start pumping out into more and more exits when already the results are negative."

"She told people," Dr. Walde continued, "that my patients were doing, some of them, were doing very well — which is a load of rubbish."[638]

REACTIONS TO HOMEMAKER'S STORY

The powerful reaction to the Essiac story was even more than expected by the publishers. They knew the decision to publish was a tough one, but their own research had convinced them that Essiac deserved a real break, and if there was a chance for it to be proven successful they would be gratified. The magazine reviewed some of the events in its next issue for the readers' information.[639] A discouraged and disappointed Carroll Allen — because of all the failures evidenced by the limited clinical trials — wished they'd never printed it. But she'd known it was a gamble and had hoped that something good would come of it. Dr. Walde assured her that she had told the story in a responsible way. "You are looking extremely responsible," he told her. "We are all disappointed that it didn't work, but if somebody turns up something I'd be glad to see their data."[640]

ESSIAC FORMULA TO BE REVEALED

Another result of the dramatic story, a more optimistic one, brought a Toronto-based firm of entrepreneurs into the picture, and Rene's life changed forever. On Labour Day weekend, in September 1977, two directors of a firm in the market for a new product in the health care field travelled to Rene's home in Bracebridge to discuss the possibility of sharing the Essiac formula and marketing it. It seemed the time was right and Rene was ready to turn over her treasure to a suave group of business and medical men.

CHAPTER 16

RESPERIN GAINS ESSIAC

FORMULA RELEASED TO RESPERIN CORPORATION

The days leading to October 26 were very difficult for the vulnerable eighty-nine-year-old. Rene was "tired and worried and the rest of it."[641] She had made up her mind to "make a big move" and sign away her Essiac formula. *Homemaker's* Carroll Allen spoke with her on more than a couple of occasions on the phone, and Rene admitted that she was about to "do a big thing, I'm giving it, I'm giving it over to an organization," she stated with firm resolution.

Carroll cautioned Rene, and told her that Dr. Wightman of the Ontario Cancer Treatment Research Foundation was worried. "He has somehow heard, and I don't know how, that you're going to sign up with somebody and he is contemplating coming out with a statement discrediting Essiac," she said.

"Oh, he can't do it with the evidence I had," Rene moaned. "I had these doctors that I'm signing up — top doctors and they're not fools enough to do it if there is anything wrong with it." Rene wouldn't tell Carroll whom she was signing with. "No, I'm not going to," she insisted. "They've asked me to keep it confidential and that's what I'm doing. I am not going to give it out."

Wightman was worried about what he called the "Fingard group" and about Essiac "getting into the wrong hands," Carroll told Rene. Carroll was anxious to get the story straight for *Homemaker's* and perhaps stop the signing from happening.

"You see," Rene said, "I'm at their mercy. It's just been a nightmare." In order to save Rene long distance phone bills, the researcher promised to call her back to talk more. Rene chuckled. "I paid one yesterday — seventeen hundred dollars."

"Gosh," Carroll said incredulously.

Two cancer patients, Julia Cunningham of Edmonton and Nancy Merritt of Toronto, both new patients of Dr. Barker, arrived at Rene's house for Essiac treatments on October 21, 1977. Carroll Allen happened to telephone while they were there, and the patients were delighted to speak to the "lady who wrote the story about Essiac in *Homemaker's Magazine*." They were enthusiastically convinced that Essiac was helping them.[642] Their conversation was interrupted when a person who turned out to be David Fingard, along with Dr. French and a secretary, arrived for an appointment with Rene Caisse. The patients witnessed the beginning of a historic gathering. Before the day was over, the first signatures of an important contract were penned, the transfer of Essiac's secret formula arranged. Probably because one of the principals of the clandestine two-day meeting was Orillia's MP, Dr. P.B. Rynard, the *Orillia Journal* heard about it and moved quickly. Reporter John Kirkvaag and broadcaster Arnis Peterson of CFOR radio arranged an exclusive interview during the remainder of the day and the next.

The *Orillia Journal* broke their story on October 25, announcing that the Resperin Corporation of Toronto would conclude an agreement the next day with Rene Caisse to turn over her long-held secret Essiac formula for testing and production.[643] To assuage the *Herald-Gazette*, which had loyally covered Rene Caisse since she was in elementary school, the Orillia paper arranged for the Bracebridge newspaper to reprint John Kirkvaag's dramatic story.[644]

A delighted Dr. Charles Brusch and his lawyer came from Cambridge to take part in the event and, along with Dr. E. Thomas French, witness the agreement between the Resperin Corporation Limited's M.B. Dymond, MD; P.B. Rynard, MD; David Fingard; and Rene M. Caisse.

And so by October 26, 1977, the old nurse had signed an agreement hoping that her dream would finally be recognized. Resperin would test Essiac on one hundred patients who wished to volunteer for the six-month trials. Following successful testing, Resperin was to seek permission to market it, and at that time, she agreed, the formula would be revealed.[645] The envelope containing the formula would be returned by the Lieutenant-Governor and put in safekeeping with Fingard's friend and Resperin's financier Stephen B. Roman, or another long-time Fingard colleague, Edgar Eaton — but the formula was for David Fingard's eyes only.

Bracebridge Public Library, Rene M. Caisse Archive

David Fingard, ready to take on the ownership of Essiac.

After years of relative quiet, no one could have anticipated the exhilaration that would take place in the Resperin Corporation's borrowed boardroom in Toronto that month when the plans for Essiac were tabled. According to the contract, Rene would receive a weekly stipend of $250 during the trials, and more if the trials proved successful and mass manufacturing could begin. It was said that Brusch had already made an oral agreement with Rene that would give him a 1 percent share when the Essiac formula was marketed.[646] According to a typed statement dated October 20, 1977, and signed by Rene, Dr. Brusch was to receive a 2 percent share should Rene die before Essiac reached market.

"In case the formula is not developed, it is to be returned to Doctor Charles Brusch, Cambridge, Massachusetts 02139, in order that in my name he may continue research with Essiac in the Rene Caisse Cancer Foundation,"[647] the statement continued. "This arrangement is made in appreciation of the work that Doctor Charles A. Brusch has done as my co-worker."

Days, or perhaps only a day, later, the Resperin Corporation issued an undated press release entitled "1977 Report on Essiac" and announced that a "report was submitted in late October to Dr. K.J.R. Wightman, medical director of the Ontario Cancer Treatment Research Foundation, by the two doctors who were clinically testing Essiac on about sixty volunteers terminal cancer patients." They also announced the contract between Rene Caisse and Resperin Corporation.

TERRIBLE TIMING

The timing couldn't have been worse. On November 2, Bracebridge readers were told that a negative statement was scheduled to appear in the next issue of the *Canadian Medical Association Journal*, reported by the medical director of the Ontario Cancer Treatment and Research Foundation, Dr. K.J.R. Wightman.[648] And even more worse, Dr. Wightman would indicate that the recent tests were "conclusive" and he sees "no point" in future tests.[649]

As well, Dr. Walde had sent Jane Hughes a copy of the Wightman statement in advance of publication (which he and Dr. Barker had composed) and advised her of the lack of success they were experiencing.[650] It was presented in the CMA *Journal* as a sidebar regarding Essiac in an explosive feature report about Laetrile by Charlotte Gray, and was pointed out as another "quack cancer cure."[651,652] The inset item referred to two unnamed Ontario doctors who gave Essiac to more than sixty cancer patients and found "no evidence of any alteration in the disease process of any of the patients. However subjective improvements in the sense of wellbeing were noted in a number of the patients, although this could or could not be a placebo effect." But the qualified yet truly crushing final statement read: "These unequivocal negative statistics refute any claims made as to the efficacy of this cancer cure with the materials provided in the suggested dosage schedules."

When Rene learned of this pending negative report, she told a new hometown publisher that she had expected it. "It is not at all surprising that they have tried to discredit me. The medical profession has been trying to do that for the last 40 years."[653]

THE FUTURE OF ESSIAC

The negative results published in the CMA *Journal* and the news media[654] crushed Rene. Had a man named David Fingard not been stimulated by the *Homemaker's* article on Rene Caisse's lifetime fight for Essiac, she would have again sunk into depression and frustration.

The eighty-plus retired chemist was attracted to Rene's plight because, for him, it was déjà vu. Her story took him back about forty years when his own work was being seriously questioned by the College of Physicians and Surgeons at the very time the nurse's remedy was being quashed and she was suffering rejection by that same body.

The similarities of these two powerful entities, Caisse and Fingard, are astonishing. Both had the mastery of gathering movers and shakers around them, and both had dreams of serving humankind crushed by a medical establishment intent on shutting out the remedies each believed had so much merit. How strange that the man who would finally unlock the fifty-five-year-old Essiac secret would be someone who had seemingly "walked in her moccasins" and had come under scrutiny for a remedy of his own during a parallel period.

THE STORY OF DAVID FINGARD

While Rene's remedy was directed to serving mainly cancer sufferers, David Fingard's was designed for patients with respiratory ailments such as asthma, bronchitis, sinusitis, and hay fever.

His story began prior to 1937 in England when chemical researcher Fingard, a native of Winnipeg, and his uncle, Rudolph Duke, were installing their Duke-Fingard Inhalation Treatment equipment in locations all over England, in France, and in other European countries. They claimed to have cured various respiratory conditions in patients of all ages. The method consisted "essentially of the prolonged inhalation of a vapour, sufficiently antiseptic yet in itself non-toxic and non-irritant which slowly reduced the amount of infection on the pathological organisms present."[655] It contained a chemical made from phenol, creosote, garlic, glycerine, olive oil, and other properties.

Duke and Fingard had the support of important medical persons with long collections of degrees and affiliations, and their "hospitals" were serving a great need in polluted European cities. Papers detailing the treatment were published in medical journals and widely circulated as part of their publicity. Even the actor Robert Donat was cured of his bronchitis by the Duke-Fingard treatment. By 1940 there would be some seventeen Duke-Fingard inhalation hospitals in England.

Meanwhile, in late 1937, Premier Mitch Hepburn took some time off to correct his persistent bronchitis during a winter holiday in Arizona. Earlier in the year he nearly missed the opening of legislature due to his severe bronchial condition.[656] The seemingly insignificant newspaper story spawned dozens and dozens of letters from well-wishers who told the premier about their favourite family recipes for curing asthma, etc., and sent clippings of ads in magazines and newspapers for products that were meant to help. Of course, producers of sure products sent their literature and encouraged him to use their medicine, and certainly David Fingard jumped at the opportunity of approaching a premier with serious bronchitis.

It seems that about that time, David Fingard, who had returned to Canada, started up a Duke-Fingard Inhalation Hospital at 923 College Street in Toronto. He had already created one in Winnipeg in March 1938 and, as was his style, he gathered around him high-ranking citizens, including the Manitoba premier.[657] Ontario's premier certainly heard from him, as evidenced by the file of correspondence that exists.[658] In May, the *Globe and Mail* reported that Health Minister Kirby said, "The department is duty bound to inquire into matters of this kind," meaning that Fingard must present his treatment for respiratory diseases to his officials.[659] Fingard sought out medical doctors for support, and one, Dr. Archibald McPhedran, joined the staff by 1941, giving his address as 923 College Street.

An information sheet from the Duke-Fingard Inhalation Hospital instructed patients that the treatment could be given in their Toronto hospital. The charge to patients was per income, or $50 per week for treatment. A machine for use in the home cost $150 (two or three in the family could use it for the same price), a weekly charge of $53 for medication, plus about fifty cents per week for calcium chloride, which was used in the machine to remove moisture from the air. The sheet was signed by A.G. McPhedran, BA, MD, FRCP (Can).[660, 661]

Among the successful users of the treatment was the eight-year-old grandson of Dr. Bert Faulkner, the former minister of health. On Duke-Fingard Inhalation Treatment letterhead, Dr. McPhedran told the Ontario prime minister in a 1941 letter that he could write pages regarding the benefits that had been derived by patients using this treatment in Ontario in the past three years. But he was concerned about the determined efforts of the College of Physicians and Surgeons to prevent the use of this treatment by the doctors in the province, and begged to discuss the matter.[662]

Dr. McPhedran received a letter from the prime minister (ghost-written by Minister of Health Harold Kirby[663]) telling him that no commitment had been made in Ontario by any authoritative body as to the value of this treatment. "The danger of accepting a secret remedy on the basis of public testimonials and the isolated testimony of physicians is generally accepted by the public and the medical profession alike. I feel compelled to leave this matter in the hands of the College as it does not come within the jurisdiction of Government," the letter read.

The hospital operated during the early forties, and, perhaps because of external pressures, Fingard operated as president of the new Asthma Bronchitis Co. Ltd. at the same address between 1946 and 1948. In 1949, he brought in a major investor and the company took a new look. Wood, Fingard, Eaton Co. started up, and Fingard became its first vice-president. Wood was a local investor, and in 1951 Edgar Eaton, the second son of Sir John David and Lady Eaton, became president, and his wife, Mildred, chairman. Edgar Eaton pulled out in March 1955 to run another business for a few years.

David Fingard got hooked on prospecting minerals in the Temiskaming region. Sporting large cigars, he ventured around Elk Lake in the 1950s, meeting the locals and listening for good land tips. He would reward the tipster richly. For instance, he entertained the Venne family at the Royal York Hotel in Toronto, treating them royally.[664]

Stephen Roman was prospecting for uranium during that period, and his major break came when he bought property suggested by three people introduced to him by David Fingard. He started to drill in 1954, went into production in 1957, and history shows his striking success.[665] Roman's young son Stephen Junior took sick, and Fingard's inhalation treatment was called into service. Roman claimed that the remedy saved his son "on his deathbed,"[666] cementing a close business partnership that would last for thirty years.

A new venture seemed to take Fingard out of the inhalation treatment business, and in 1958 he headed the Radio, Electronics and Television Schools of Toronto on Spadina Avenue. A physician named Philip B. Rynard, administrator of his own medical clinic in Orillia, was responsible for Fingard's Northern Ontario operations. Fingard operated the radio school business for a few years and moved to Avenue Road.

RESPERIN CORPORATION FORMED

Fingard never really let his interest in the respiratory treatment enterprise die. A private company called Resperin Corporation Limited was formed in August 1964, its name reflecting respirators and inhalators, some of the products it would promote. The unidentified chemicals used in his preparations were given a marvellous collection of names, all convoluted spellings of the resperin/respirin word root.

Within the next few months, David Fingard gathered an assortment of physicians, politicians, and benefactors to become directors of his new firm, which was to operate a private medical hospital. Stephen Roman, now a millionaire uranium magnate, had a specific financial role to play in the $250,000 share structure and allowed his luxurious Toronto office suites to be the mailing and telephone utilities for the new corporation. Dr. Philip Rynard, now Conservative member of the House of Commons for Simcoe and already a Fingard business partner, stepped into the chairman's job.

Other directors included former Ontario Liberal leader John J. Wintermeyer, QC, and former federal minister of labour Michael Starr of Oshawa. Among the doctors were Dr. Wilfrid Shute of Port Credit, who had been actively working with his brother Dr. Evan Shute on Vitamin E research and operating his heart clinic. He became president.

The product called Respirin was tested on residents of the Huronia Centre for the Mentally Retarded in Orillia during 1967 and 1968,[667] and Dr. Hugh Wilson and others were encouraged with the results, although adverse outside pressures were mounting. The company changed its objectives in 1969 and directed itself to "medical research and medical re-evaluation."

In early 1970, Dr. Matthew Dymond, the recently retired Ontario minister of health, accepted the job as president of the Resperin Corporation, "Suppliers of Respirin, used in the treatment of bronchitis, sinusitis, hay fever and the common cold."[668, 669] However, in May, the federal Health Department issued a cease and desist

Dr. Matthew Dymond joined the Essiac team.

order after the Health Protectorate Branch determined that the terrible smelling treatment was toxic to animals.[670] Now Dr. Dymond was head of a company with no product.

It is sad that Fingard's remedy had not been the non-toxic product Essiac was. One of the elements in the Duke-Fingard treatment was creosote, now understood to be a serious carcinogen. As well, phenol was a poisonous, caustic chemical that at that time was derived from manufactured coal gas. Both chemicals were effective in causing persons with congested lungs to cough up the mucus. In fact, children were routinely taken to the gas plants in Toronto and other cities to breathe in the fumes emanating from the manufacture of coal gas. The children would feel much better after coughing and spitting up the junk from their throats and lungs.[671] For decades, many popular asthma products and soaps contained some parts of creosote.

The long Duke-Fingard saga was over, and Resperin would await a new product to fill the void. The advent of an exciting and potentially lucrative product reputed to cure cancer was just what the failing Resperin Corporation was looking for. It would attempt to prove, develop, and market the herbal cancer remedy.

The medical directors of Resperin at that time still included Dr. Philip Rynard, MP of Orillia; Dr. Dymond; and Dr. Wilfrid Shute, who had a special interest in Essiac. His successor at the Port Credit heart clinic, Dr. Barker, was one of the two doctors who had put Essiac to trial in 1977.

Stephen Roman who was "not considered one who invests in flights of fancy," reportedly invested a quarter of a million dollars into Resperin's $500,000 share structure. An Elliott Lake reporter wrote that this was called "putting a cover of respectability" on the Essiac project.[672] Roman became president, and Dr. Dymond moved into the chairman's seat. The Resperin Corporation was described as a pharmaceutical affiliate of Denison Mines Ltd.,[673] although not defined in their corporate annual reports.

Acccording to Rodaway and Malot, "Resperin reached an agreement in principal with the University of Toronto this past spring to carry out the trials and a detailed proposal of the tests was submitted to Ottawa. The preliminary state of the program would cost Resperin an estimated $50,000 but neither U. of T,'s medical school nor Ottawa could start the ball rolling until chronic quality control problems had been ironed out."[674] But queries to the University of Toronto medical faculty around that time resulted in a surprised response from the researchers. The testing never did take place under their auspices.

The *Elliot Lake Standard* newspaper reflected on Fingard's excitement about Essiac in these words:

> One day an announcement will come that Essiac has the medical profession's seal of approval, and there will be much true rejoicing, an almost holiday atmosphere. I can see full page ads in papers and on T.V. put out by the government telling everyone that cancer has been beaten. And, of course, the treatments will be free, and thousands will crowd the hospitals and will come out cured.... It's a beautiful thought. And, if Mr. Fingard gets his wish, the world will have a mysterious Indian, a fiery nurse, an aging, dreaming chemist, and a conservative Chairman of the Board to thank.[675]

ESSIAC AND LAETRILE IN PUBLIC FORUM

Two controversial alternative cancer remedies, Essiac and Laetrile, were brought to a public forum on April 5, 1978, in hopes of strengthening the push for research funds by the Canadian Cancer Society. Co-sponsored by Toronto Arts Productions, a panel of four cancer specialists was faced with cancer sufferers and their supporters in the modern St. Lawrence Centre on King Street. The site of dramatic theatre and tragic opera made way for the misery of patients who came to hear what the medical profession had to say. Rene Caisse, not strong enough to take the trip to the centre, missed the forum, although it was only a stone's throw from the King Edward Hotel where she had vigorously treated cancer patients with Essiac forty years ago.

Moderator Andy Barry, a local radio personality, handled the emotional evening and gave the doctors opportunity to explain their views on Essiac and Laetrile, the latter being a chemical substance derived from apricot pits that was very sought after in the U.S. and Mexico.

Dr. Ian Henderson, director of the Health Protection Branch of National Health and Welfare gave brief histories of Essiac and Laetrile. Dr. Henderson presented the government regulations that had to be met before the Resperin Corporation could proceed with clinical trials of Essiac on humans. So far only a few anecdotal case histories had been received by his department, Henderson told a surprised audience.

Dr. David Walde, the cancer specialist from Sault Ste. Marie, described the clinical trials of Essiac he conducted last year on forty patients. The audience heard Dr. Walde say that animal tests with ampoules of the main herb, sheep sorrel, which was supposed to regress tumours, failed to show any positive action.[676] But he admitted that a few of his patients had felt better while taking Essiac.

The audience had an opportunity to speak, and many brought concerns of not being able to obtain remedies that had already helped many. An article appeared the next day with the heading "Cancer cures useless? MDs can't convince audience."[677] Certainly Laetrile was considered a quack remedy and Essiac an unknown substance of no proven merit by the panelists. But those who had loved ones suffering from cancer wanted to hear of remedies that at least gave them comfort instead of the sometimes vicious standard approved treatments of chemotherapy, surgery, and radium. As people slowly filed out of the auditorium, many bought cheery daffodils as a contribution to the Canadian Cancer Society campaign.

RESPERIN TO PROCEED

The Resperin Corporation was informed of the filing requirements for Essiac clinical trials in April 1978 by Dr. Ian Henderson in Ottawa fresh from his contribution to the public forum in Toronto. To comply with regulations under the Food and Drugs Act, Fingard was to provide the following information before Essiac could be tested:

1) The objectives of the proposed clinical trial,
2) The formula for Essiac,
3) The methods, equipment, plant and controls used in the manufacture, processing and packaging of Essiac,
4) The tests applied to control the potency, purity, stability and safety of Essiac,
5) The results of investigations made to support the anti-neoplastic activity of Essiac,
6) Any contraindications and precautions known in respect of Essiac, and the suggested treatment of overdosage, and
7) The name and qualifications of all investigators to whom Essiac is to be distributed, and the names of all institutions in which the are to be carried out.[678]

Dr. Dymond wrote Dr. Henderson, presumably to receive more medically orientated requirements for the preclinical submissions, and on June 22, 1978, Dr. Henderson reiterated his instructions and enclosed a quantity of documents that had to be completed by the investigating physicians.[679] So, much against Rene's wishes, the formula, once submitted, would indeed be revealed to all physicians and manufacturers.

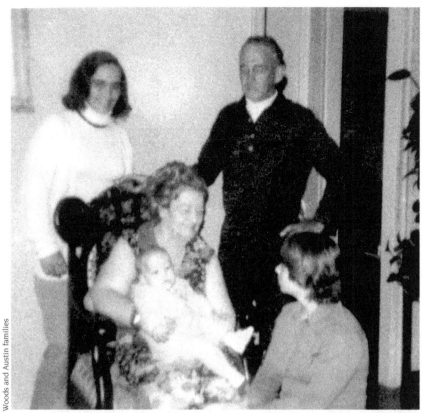

Woods and Austin families

Rene holds her great-nephew Peter Woods, while his mother, Alva Woods, watches. Standing are grandmother Alayne Austin and her father Ivan Slater. Rene's sister Aseline Martin of Tacoma took the photo in 1977 on behalf of her sister Lillian, the baby's great-great grandmother.

CHAPTER 17

ESSIAC IN U.S. COURT AND RENE DIES

FINGARD CONTINUES PROMOTION

In March 1978, David Fingard created an opportunity to meet with Ontario Premier William Davis and was so impressed that in his thank-you letter he addressed him as "The Rt. Honourable" and wished him "deservable [sic] success in leading this country."[680]

The herbal remedy Rene Caisse developed was now being used in many parts of Canada, and the *Homemaker's Magazine* article introduced Essiac to cancer victims further afield. In Detroit, Michigan, Mrs. Pat Judson of the local chapter of the New York–based Foundation for Alternative Cancer Therapies, Ltd. (FACT) wanted to obtain the remedy for their members, including herself, a cancer patient for eight years. While she was able to obtain Essiac in January 1978, a future supply was in jeopardy as the non-toxic herbal tea was not allowed to be imported across the Canada–United States border. The Food and Drug Administration determined that Essiac could not be imported without a "new drug identification number" and seemingly seized it. Mrs. Judson ran a prayer meeting in Detroit, and two thousand souls prayed that Essiac could legally be brought to the United States.[681]

David Fingard brought the Judsons and his colleague of several years, Dr. Hugh D. Wilson of Toronto, to Bracebridge in March 1978 to meet Rene. Eight years ago, Dr. Wilson had co-authored and published a paper on Resperin in a German medical journal;[682] his daughter Libby was the wife of Mrs. Stephen Roman's nephew

John Gardon. But at this meeting, Dr. Wilson, formerly with the Ontario Hospital in Orillia for many years, was apparently introduced as one of the doctors who would take part in the Essiac clinical testing under the Resperin agreement and would work at the P.B. Rynard Clinic in Orillia.

During the visit, Fingard discussed Resperin's plans for holding testing clinics in three unnamed university research laboratories, and Rene gave Judson an Essiac treatment. Fingard told the newspaper reporter in attendance that he would approach MP Stan Darling, Dr. Rynard, and Stephen Roman with the idea of setting up a foundation dedicated to Rene Caisse.[683] Fingard later gave credit for the idea to the reporter.[684]

So aggravated by the U.S. embargo, a group under the FACT umbrella for terminally ill cancer patients filed a class-action suit in the Michigan Eastern District Court, Detroit, against the secretary of the Department of Health, Education and Welfare, Joseph Capilano. President Pat Judson demanded the right for any cancer patient to use Essiac as an alternative cancer treatment. While the plaintiffs somewhat overstated the clause that read "Essiac has been in use for several centuries by Indians on the North American Continent, and particularly the territory incorporated into the United States of America," they did recognize that it reduced tumour size in cancer patients.

The Detroit WXYZ-TV news flew into Bracebridge on June 16 and filmed an interview with Rene Caisse, who was, of course, the centre of the FACT court hearing scheduled for June 26. This was a proud day for the eighty-nine-year old "retired" nurse.[685] Now there would be no doubt about the international fame of Essiac.

During the trial, Mr. James Wells, attorney for the plaintiffs, stated that thirty-nine drugs presently accepted and used for cancer treatment in the United States are known to cause cancer. One person mused, "Since I am free to smoke any number of cancer-causing cigarettes and drink alcohol in copious amounts, endangering the safety of others, why am I denied the freedom to use harmless Essiac?"[686] But the suit was rejected.

RENE, A CONSULTANT

During the months that passed after Rene gave the Essiac formula to the Resperin Corporation she was maintained as a consultant. Mary McPherson recalled that as time went on, Rene felt very disappointed about not being asked to attend board meetings. She had said that if she could not attend, she could have sent a representative of her choice. Even though Resperin called by phone after the meetings, it just wasn't the same as being part of it all.

In an undated letter, probably written in May 1978, President Dymond wrote the aging lady and asked her to continue as a consultant to the corporation for the ensuing year as they undertook further necessary studies in Essiac. Dr. Dymond recognized that her knowledge and experience were very necessary to the undertaking, but hoped it would not be too taxing for her. He also asked her to continue to make Essiac for Resperin "until such time as we can make other arrangements." The letter, copied to Stephen Roman's daughter Helen Roman-Barber, continued, "Your financial compensation will most likely come to you from a source other than Resperin Corporation."[687]

It wasn't until late May that Rene received a response to her complaints to Resperin that she had yet to receive any funds from the firm under the agreement. The secretary-treasurer, Stephen Roman's nephew, named F.G., enclosed "the first of weekly cheques to be forwarded in appreciation of your excellent co-operation to date and in recognition of your arrangements that have and will have to be done to make our mutual endeavour a success."[688] It is unclear whether she received successive cheques.

NINETIETH BIRTHDAY CELEBRATIONS

August 11, 1978, was a day to remember! Members of Rene's family, friends, patients, past and present politicians, and just plain folks turned out to the Centennial Centre to wish Rene a happy ninetieth birthday. Ontario Treasurer Frank Miller[689] was there, and long-time Mayor Jim Lang represented nine previous mayors who had directed Bracebridge since Rene first opened her clinic over forty years ago.[690] Cars and buses lined up in the parking lot, dropping off people from all over the province and beyond.

Framed citations pleased Rene. There was one from Governor-General Jules Léger, Prime Minister Pierre Elliot Trudeau, and Ontario Premier William Davis. Rene's elderly sisters sent best wishes; Aseline Martin, now eighty-five, was still living Tacoma, Washington; Victorine Asher, eight-six years old, was in Florida; and seventy-nine-year-old "Babe," Elemere Chiswell, lived in Guelph, Ontario. Other relatives represented five generations. Rene, sitting amidst the crowd, looked fresh for most of the afternoon, but found the long day tiring. Her sparkling eyes mirrored her enjoyment and her soft skin reflected the years of applying her famous herbal remedy as a refresher.[691]

Mary McPherson collection

Mary McPherson, Rene's nephew Hummie Stortz, niece Valeen Slater Taylor, and great-niece Sandra Askin helped Rene celebrate her ninetieth birthday.

A lot of reminiscing took place, and several humorous stories were told. Such as the day Rene became quite ill with a cold, and her doctor said that if she had a hospital bed and someone to stay with her, she could remain at home. Frank Henry, the administrator of the hospital, loaned her a bed, and Mary, who recalled the story, volunteered her services. The maintenance staff set up the new bed, which had all the gadgets. All was well and Rene lay on the narrow bed. Rene was very large, so the siderails were raised for her protection. By morning, after a fairly good night, a trip to the bathroom was necessary. Her friend tried every way to get the siderails down but could not do it. All this time, Rene was getting more uncomfortable by the minute. As a last resort, she had to call the hospital and ask for a man to come to get the sides down. The laughing that followed did not help Rene at all, but she managed to hold on and all ended well. Rene had a good sense of humour and was able laugh (after she went to the bathroom). Some people said "she laughed with her eyes," while others remembered her really hearty laugh.

Also in attendance was filmmaker John Newton from Minett, just outside of Bracebridge. He had been creating a film about Rene for two years, as he was fascinated by how she fought the male-dominated heavyweights and considered her an inspirational trailblazer. Certainly this birthday party was an important opportunity to film her with her friends. Earlier, John had been allowed to film in her home and especially in her kitchen while she brewed Essiac. In 1997 Newton would assemble much of his revealing footage into a thirty-minute video called "The Rene Caisse Story."[692]

Friends recalled happy times when they examined the beautifully carved teak lotus blossom from India, which had been given to her by a grateful son who worked at a bank in Toronto. Rene had provided him with Essiac to send home to his father in India. Rene had the carving made into a functional living room table lamp.

Of all the unusual situations Rene experienced, one of the most memorable must have been the lady from Michigan who forged a letter to Rene in the spring of 1978 to con Rene into giving her Essiac. Her convincing diagnosis on doctors' letterhead did not reveal that it was really the American's dog who had the cancerous breast. Happily, the dog recovered.[693]

Niece Valeen Slater Taylor, who had worked with her in her clinic, recalled that during that time Rene had a telephone call from a maharajah in Delhi, India, asking her to come to treat his young son, who was dying of cancer and unable to come to her. He promised to give her $1 million and to arrange private transportation for her, but she had to refuse him, explaining that she had at least six hundred patients a week whom she was treating and whom she couldn't possibly leave.[694]

The party was a great tribute from an appreciative audience.

CANADIAN GOVERNMENT APPROVES TESTING

In early October, Rene Caisse of 293 Hiram Street in Bracebridge applied for a trademark registration for Essiac. It was described as a "pharmaceatical [sic] preparation that is of original composition consisting of natural herbs. The formula is private and is derived solely from the applicant's personal research with herbal medicine. The formula is not used in conjunction with any other wares." The trademark application, prepared in Bracebridge on the fourth day of October 1977, was not signed, and it appears that it was not submitted. But a year later there was a notable breakthrough. Resperin Corporation did receive a trademark for Essiac in October 1978, number 248752, and Resperin submitted a Preclinical New Drug Submission to the federal Bureau of Drugs of the Health Protection Branch.

The bureau approved the licence for testing after Dr. Henderson reviewed Rene's files and scrapbooks in her Bracebridge home in the past summer. He found that "between 15 and 20 percent of the cases cited in her anecdotal records had shown improvements that, in his opinion, could be attributed only to Essiac." Dr. Henderson also noted the "possibility that whatever the test results, public and political pressure could lead to its release for personal use."[695] Now Resperin was authorized to test the Essiac formula on humans for one year. This would be the first time that a government had approved such testing.

When Rene received the news that Resperin was given the go-ahead, she was overjoyed and told her friend Mary, "I should be receiving a bouquet of long red roses!" So, with a touch of humour, she phoned a florist and sent roses from Resperin to herself!

Based on Fingard's submission, cancer patients at the Princess Margaret Hospital and the Toronto General Hospital were permitted to take part in the investigation, but the study was never done, as neither of the two centres was willing to treat their cancer patients with Essiac alone.[696]

For a patient to obtain the remedy, the government required that the family physician send Dr. Dymond a brief description of the patient's history, which would then be forwarded with the necessary forms to Health and Welfare Canada. The patient would receive Essiac from Resperin following government approval.[697] But Rene was crushed when she found out that the Health Protection Branch required family practitioners to supervise Essiac treatment for the terminal cancer patients and document the testing. She insisted that would not work because the doctors wouldn't do regular tests and reports that produced accurate figures.

David Fingard told the *Herald-Gazette* in October that two leading universities, one in Quebec (Laval University) and one in Ontario (University of Toronto), had requested permission to use Essiac in a scientifically controlled experiment to test its effects on cancer in human beings.[698] But a year later, the associate dean of medicine at the University of Toronto's medical school, Dr. Keith Dorrington, would concede that the university got involved to "clear the air" and testing could begin only after proven quality control in the drug's manufacture and administration of the trials by an independent medical authority were completed. It is unclear whether either of the two universities ever did any testing.

PATIENTS KEEP COMING

During the already busy year, Rene was still receiving calls from people far and wide who wanted to know how and when Essiac would be available. She also received mountains of mail, which she answered with some help. On January 19, 1978, she received a written diagnosis that stated that a little four-year-old girl named Hope Stanner of Aubrey, Alberta, was suffering from a brain tumour. A biopsy and a partial removal of the tumour had taken place, and she had received several radiation treatments. In spite of those procedures, Hope was given two years at the most to live. Her physician gave permission for Hope to receive Essiac treatments, and her father obtained some of the decoction. By the end of June, Hope could control movements on her right side reasonably well, and her speech had improved with no treatment other than Essiac. With her new strength and mobility she could chase her twin brothers around on the lawn. She was happy and active and had a good colour, her father said in an interview.[699]

Dr. Brusch's patient, Patrick McGrail, continued to do "amazingly well," Dr. Peter N. Oliynyk wrote in October from his Overhold Thoracic Clinic in Boston. "I was just reading over his operative note from February, and he really did have quite an awful looking tumor, and his good progress continues to amaze me, and obviously I'm delighted with his progress. Hopefully, he will continue to have a good long term result."[700] Dr. Brusch obtained the dried Essiac ingredients from Rene, mailed by Mary McPerson.[701]

THE ESSIAC NURSE SLIPS AWAY

Rene was asked to speak at a convention of workers against the suppression of Essiac in Saskatoon, Saskatchewan, and just as the excitement of the government testing approval was made public, her world took a terrible turn. On October 14 she slipped and fell in her home, badly fracturing her hip. She was transferred to Toronto for attention, but she was not able to rally from the complications of being bedridden for weeks. A few days before Christmas, she lay in a lonely hospital room away from home, probably unaware that Fingard was enthusiastically claiming remarkable results from Essiac testing.[702] Rene wanted to go home, and she died quietly the evening of December 26, 1978, back in her hometown hospital, her dream only partly fulfilled.

The funeral of Rene Caisse took place on a snowy morning three days later. The newspapers recorded her variously as the "Medicine Woman,"[703] "Developer of Essiac,"[704] "Cancer herbalist,"[705] "a legendary woman,"[706] and one of Muskoka's "most illustrious citizens."[707] Her death was announced via the Canadian Press in newspapers throughout Canada. Only sisters Aseline, Victorine, and Babe were left of her large family of siblings, but about eighty of Rene's family and friends attended her funeral that holiday week.

With a sense of clairvoyance, Roman Catholic priest Rev. James Greenan said that history might have further to say about her work someday and finally judge the value. The mourners were told that, in nursing, Rene Caisse manifested love and concern for suffering humanity, and in her scientific endeavours she was concerned about the health and well-being of her fellow man.[708, 709] Her laughter, her harassment of and by those who did not support her in her mission, her stubbornness, and her untiring care for others were affectionately remembered. A local newspaper editorialized that in the eighteen months since the *Homemaker's Magazine* article was published, Rene was subjected to incredible pressure, not only from the media, the medical profession, and cancer sufferers, but also from companies that "wanted a piece of the action." It was amazing to watch her handle all the stress, the editor went on. "Of course, she loved the attention and being a celebrity, but she also believed that all the publicity would lead to the acceptance of Essiac."[710]

After Rene's death some of her papers were destroyed in an effort to clear out her belongings. No one would have truly recognized how significant her files and records would become in years to follow. Selectively, Rene's possessions were chosen by or distributed to friends and relatives. With considerable insensitivity to the memory of a remarkable woman, a bold advertisement appeared in a local newspaper offering the final sale of the balance of the estate of Rene Caisse McGaughey, to be held on June 8 and 9, 1979, at her former residence on Hiram Street.[711] Resembling a garage sale, the contents of her house, including some autographed paintings in oil or watercolour, were offered to those who wanted a keepsake of the "Woman of the Year." Charles's law books, which Rene had treasured to the end, were donated to the Ullswater Women's Institute library, friends of Mary McPherson. Rene's little house was sold later that month.

A piece of the Rene Caisse legacy was left in the capable hands of Mary McPherson. A year or so before Rene died, the responsibility of managing the small but active business of her R.M.C. Tablets was being handled by Mary. Federal regulations of the Health Protection Branch now required a Drug Identification Number (DIN), collapsing the patent, which had been held since 1941.[712] There were also the arrangements for manufacture to be made. The complicated documentation, which Mary read, completed, and complied with, would stagger most laymen, so local legal assistance certainly helped her through the mire into the eighties.

CHAPTER 18

ESSIAC CONTINUES

HOPE FOR ESSIAC

The discoverer of Essiac was dead at ninety after an extraordinary life. For more than fifty years she had administered her secret remedy and provided hope to the sick throughout Ontario. Her namesake, Essiac, helped cancer patients in many parts of Canada and the United States, and she allowed her herbal tea to be sent to those who needed it in countries as far away as India.

Rene had agonized over her decision to entrust her Essiac to Resperin. Her most dread fears came to pass. She felt that it was the worst thing she could have done to associate with David Fingard, who was already in the bad books of the medical profession and the government. With a touch of humour, she regularly referred to the briefcase-toting Fingard as "old satchelass."

Fingard referred to her as bright, intelligent, and stubborn as a mule.[713] But everyone warned her against trusting him and his troubled firm. He was a difficult person to work with. "Shut up, I'm talking," he would say. Health and welfare people must have sighed in frustration when Rene signed up with this man who was already too well known to them.

Rene had hoped that eventually the making of Essiac could be moved out of home kitchens and into a sophisticated manufacturing facility with professional equipment and hygienic conditions. Now it was up to Rene's heirs and successors to bring her dream to fruition. Rene didn't have the time or energy to prepare any written instructions or wishes prior to her death. Not too many people are left with so much unfinished business even at age ninety, but in the months before her death her full attention had been taken up with the fallout of the *Homemaker's Magazine* article and the Fingard hubbub.

The excitement surrounding Rene's story was attracting the attention of those responsible for collecting the papers of significant individuals for the Archives of Ontario. Hugh MacMillan, the archives liaison officer, wrote Sugg & Fitton, the legal firm that handled Rene's estate, and asked to examine her papers with a view to acquiring them for permanent preservation and use by future researchers.[714] At Bert Sugg's suggestion, MacMillan contacted Rene's executor, her niece Valeen Taylor, who assured him that the family was also concerned about safe preservation of Rene's papers and that they would be taken care of in the proper fashion.[715, 716]

RENE CAISSE MEMORY KEPT ALIVE

During the winter of 1979, Bracebridge residents were offered a sixteen-part series of articles recounting Rene's lifetime battle, published by the *Bracebridge Examiner*, a weekly newspaper. Editor and publisher Ted Britton, who met her and wanted to "keep her memory alive," assured the readers that the words were all Rene's, derived from her own writings and his private interviews with her during her last year. The series was rerun in the newspaper's sister weekly, *The Weekender*, in 1995.

CHCH-TV's broadcaster and investigator Tom Cherington was enticed into the Essiac drama in August 1981 when he recognized that people were looking for cancer cure alternatives such as Essiac.[717] Cherington came to Bracebridge and spent a fine day filming and talking with Clifford and Mary McPherson, both cancer survivors who had by treated with Essiac. The researchers obtained testimonies from many cancer patients and knowledgeable persons, but the Canadian Cancer Society chose not to take part. Also interviewed for the well-researched film was Rene's niece Valeen, who told of the cars, wheelchairs, and even a horse and carriage that brought patients to Rene's cancer clinic. Ralph Moss, the writer and cancer activist formerly of Sloan-Kettering, spoke by telephone and recalled that Essiac was being discussed at SKI while he was there, but didn't know if it had been given a good testing.

Another of the central figures in the scenario was David Fingard, who continually pronounced Rene's name incorrectly. He spoke out on his hopes for Essiac.

The *Bracebridge Examiner* was pleased that Tom Cherington came to make the film, especially since, as Ted Britton pointed out editorially, the late Rene's birthday (August 11) had passed without any public recognition. In Britton's inimitable style, he decried the handling of the Rene Caisse affair by the medical establishment as "callous and ignorant."[718] "The conventional methods of treatment don't seem to be winning the battle. In fact, cancer is actually on the increase," Cherington told Gravenhurst newspaper writer Lou Specht.[719]

Cherington convincingly told the whole story seemingly from Rene's writings and the *Homemaker's Magazine* text while hosting the program, although inadvertent errors in fact and interpretation crept in. The controversial documentary was aired on September 14, 1981.[720] But it seems that Tom had been asked not to show it, did, and shortly after was looking for work elsewhere.

ESSIAC TRIALS

A story in the *Kitchener-Waterloo Record* in June 1981, probably suggested by Resperin director and local resident John Wintermeyer, anticipated that the results of the two-year government-approved Essiac trials were soon to be released.[721] But it cautioned that the Federal Health Department declined at this point to speculate on whether Essiac could pass the test. "A lot of drugs flunk out," Dr. Ian Henderson was quoted as saying. Actually, in April, the Health Protection Branch had already made its decision to cancel the clearance of the investigational new drug submission for Essiac because of noncompliance to the government's documentation and data submission requirements. In fact, the branch had the available data on Essiac reviewed independantly by medical specialists in cancer treatment and found the clinical studies to be poorly conceived and executed, yielding "uninterpretable results."[722]

Madame Monique Begin, Canada's current minister of health, wrote Dr. Dymond in the summer of 1982 and made it very clear that in 1978 the Health Protection Branch had had no objection to the distribution of Essiac to qualified investigators providing certain conditions were met by Resperin.[723] The conditions included the following:

- attempts would be made to isolate and identify the active antineoplastic substance or substances in Essiac,
- the antineoplastic activity of Essiac or its components would be investigated and adequately established in suitable biological systems or organisms,
- the clinical trials would be monitored by a national agency concerned with therapy of cancer in order to arrive at scientifically valid data to substantiate the effectiveness of this drug in the treatment of malignant disease,
- a description of the quality control procedures used to ensure lot to lot uniformity of the raw materials would be provided, and
- the results of stability studies would be provided.

But, she pointed out, the conditions were not met despite repeated requests. Because of this failure and neglect in complying with certain requirements of the Food and Drug Regulations, the minister notified Resperin that it was in the interest of public health to prohibit further sales of Essiac. The door was left open to resubmission if the conditions were met.

Worse, on December 10, 1982, Madame Begin announced at the conclusion of the Essiac clinical trials that the Health Protection Branch failed to substantiate any objective therapeutic benefit of Rene's herbal remedy, saying that no clinical evidence exists to support the claims that Essiac is an effective treatment for cancer. There had not been scientifically valid data to substantiate, or refute, the effectiveness of Essiac. As well, the drug manufacturer did not fulfil its commitment, and the clinical trial had not been monitored by experts in the field of cancer therapy.

In fact, she reported that over the years her department had received a number of incomplete case reports on Essiac from physicians participating in open clinical trials, and many doctors did not return data. The seventy-four doctors who responded on behalf of eighty-seven already determined terminally ill patients reported that Essiac was of no benefit. The health department recorded that its findings were verified later in 1983 when the National Cancer Institute in Bethesda, Maryland, tested Essiac in their animal screening models (mouse sarcoma) and found no anti-tumour activity.[724,725] As well, the institute had reviewed the 1982 work by Dr. Chester Stock of the Sloan-Kettering Institute and concluded that "he observed no anti-tumor activity."[726] "So," Madame Begin told Parry Sound–Muskoka MP Stan Darling in a February 1984 letter, "my department has no other recourse but to limit distribution of Essiac in Canada."

Meanwhile, in a dramatic letter to Canada's minister of health and welfare, Dr. Bruce Hendrick, chief of neurosurgery at Toronto's Hospital for Sick Children, asked in October 1983 that serious consideration be given to scientific clinical trial of Essiac. He noted that ten young patients with surgically treated tumours of the central nervous system who had been given Essiac only showed significant improvement in their neurological state, although early in their treatment. Dr. Hendrick was most impressed with the effectiveness of the treatment and its lack of side effects.[727] The timing of Dr. Hendricks' letter leads one to think that Mme. Begin may have been hoping for some positive feedback from the medical community to encourage further trials.

EMERGENCY DRUG RELEASE PROGRAM

The Health Protection Branch admitted that Essiac was not harmful to a person's health and that there may be positive psychological effects for some cancer patients.[728] Indeed, on compassionate grounds, in an attempt to quieten the public outcry for Essiac, the federal government made provision under the Emergency Drug Release Program of the Canadian Health Protection Branch so that Essiac could be made available to cancer patients at the request of their physician. These cancer patients could only obtain Essiac on the basis that there was no other appropriate treatment for the patients and that, notwithstanding the lack of objective data demonstrating benefits, the treating physician for psychological reasons wishes to have his/her patient use this herbal preparation.

So, it seemed, if the patient was just about to die, if he had been totally ravaged by cancer and the effects of conventional treatments but needed what was considered a placebo, he would be allowed to secure Essiac with special documentation from his physician. Now Essiac was once again officially permitted. Almost everyone in Bracebridge knew someone who was taking Essiac. Cancer victims wanted to use it because they knew that their friends were outliving their physician's prognoses and suffering a lot less pain. And those who were not obtaining Essiac from their doctors were getting it from friends who made the herbal tea from the "secret" formula.

RESPERIN IN JEOPARDY

Communication between the principals of Resperin had been deteriorating terribly for some time. Fingard wasn't talking to Dymond, the Romans were threatening to pull out their financial support, sheep sorrel was in short supply, and Dymond was objecting to personally paying for the materials he and his wife Jeanne were using to produce Essiac for the flood of orders.[729] Fingard claimed to have had his own cancer, and in 1986 he told a radio audience that he had been "cured."

A doctor from Toronto called and asked for the Essiac formula, but was turned down. Angered, he reported Matthew Dymond to the Health Discipline Board, which called him to appear. That was one of two occasions when Dr. Dymond was "called to court for Rene," as he put it. But he was so concerned about patients on Essiac he would have thrown the whole business up and let Fingard handle it.[730]

The primary business office was within Roman's suite of offices in downtown Toronto, and often the person who wrote letters regarding Essiac would use Resperin letterhead. Fingard never altered the business stationery. The company letterhead did not reflect the acquisition of Essiac, but identified Resperin only as manufacturers of Resperin medication for inhalation treatment.

As of September 1985, the Romans had stopped financing Resperin, and by October 1986[731] they were totally out of the company.[732] Fingard had no authority to sign anything, and he was not sharing in the operating costs. Others said that Fingard continued to sell shares in Resperin, but the shareholders' money went into his lavish personal operating expenses.[733] A very exasperated Dymond felt too old to fight with someone like Fingard, who felt Resperin was his own company and "had not put one cent into the operation of the firm" since at least 1970.[734] Stephen Roman died March 23, 1988.

THE PRODUCTION OF ESSIAC

The production of Essiac has had a varied past. For decades it was made by Rene Caisse from herbs that she cut, ground, and powdered in her kitchen. During the days of her cancer clinic, it was a never-ending process, demanding her attention late into the night so that patients could be assured treatments with carefully brewed decoction every day. Then she allowed Mary and later Dr. Walde to make tea with her prepared dried mixed herbs.

Although the Resperin Corporation would be the first commercial enterprise to brew and bottle Rene's secret formula, for the first months it was still made by Rene in her kitchen. After her death, Dr. Matthew Dymond was obliged to pick up the production in the kitchen of his Port Perry home. He and his wife reportedly wore out two stoves and two grinders preparing the decoction during their dedication to the Essiac remedy. There were other production problems. Resperin was using plastic bottles, and along with some suspect herbs turned out batches that tasted differently. Constant awareness of good herbs was necessary.

In 1984, Fingard hoped that the University of Toronto's Connaught Laboratories, famous for its manufacture of insulin, the Salk polio vaccine, and other important biological substances, would undertake the production of Essiac, along with Sloan-Kettering Institute.[735] But those hopes fell through, and Dr. Dymond continued making Essiac.

Dymond produced nearly 6,500 500 cc bottles of Essiac during 1986,[736] and some 150 patients were receiving Essiac treatments through the emergency supply program when Dr. Dymond finally had had enough. He stopped brewing Essiac in January 1988 and shipped his final 146 bottles, an average weekly production.

In March, Resperin's Dr. Hugh Wilson announced suspension of the manufacture of Essiac "while transfer of production source is taking place. As soon as this transfer is completed, this should be in a couple of weeks, distribution to patients will follow."[737] Patients worried that the four-month supply required by the government would run out. At that time, Albina Bassi, a niece of Rene Caisse who lived near Chatham, Ontario, could not continue to get Essiac for her husband, Richard, who was suffering from lung cancer. The irony was featured in a Bracebridge newspaper article that pointed out the frustrations of patients who were cut off from their supply of the herbal remedy.[738]

Shortly after, Dr. Wilson agreed to take over production — in his kitchen. Dr. Wilson's family and the Dymonds helped out by supplying a few orders. The Health Protection Branch in an Essiac briefing paper claimed that there had been no source of Essiac in Canada for months,[739] although there never was a time that Rene's herbal tea was not being brewed somewhere. Incongruously, there was never a laboratory or company producing it during those many years.

DUKE-FINGARD TREATMENT RESURFACES

During the years that David Fingard's attention to Essiac would have been vital, at least during 1985–1988, he was still actively promoting his Duke-Fingard asthma, emphysema, and tuberculosis treatment, which had lain somewhat dormant. As was his style for decades, he made himself and his product known particularly to public figures who were suffering from any of those conditions. In 1985, the president of the U.S.S.R., Constantine Chernenko, was suffering from emphysema. Fingard appealed to MP Stan Darling, who wrote to the Right Honourable Joe Clark, Secretary of State for External Affairs and former prime minister of Canada, and the minister of regional industrial expansion, Sinclair Stevens, seeking to introduce his treatment Chernenko. Fingard and Dr. Wilson did go to Russia, but there is no record of his purpose or success. Fingard was quoted later as hoping to market Essiac in Russia and other countries.

In June 1988, Rev. Allen Spraggett, a well-known psychic, evangelist, broadcaster, etc., wrote on Resperin letterhead to the Canadian health minister, Jake Epp, promoting the Duke-Fingard inhalation treatment, which he hoped would be accepted by the federal health department. He spoke with conviction about his health as a theological student at Queen's University thirty years ago when he was dubbed "a respiratory cripple." He was told he would never pastor a church, never preach, and never carry on a normal life. After three months of Duke-Fingard treatments he improved to the point that by 1988 he could list numerous accomplishments and bragged that he could out-shout anyone![740]

CHAPTER 19

RENE CAISSE REMEMBERED

PETITIONS SUPPORT ESSIAC

Stan Darling of Burk's Falls, popular MP for Parry Sound–Muskoka, had been receiving poignant letters from constituents for years pleading for his intervention in the Essiac-government standoff. Rene Caisse had, of course, been one of his constituents. The writers spoke of their personal cures and health improvements, and of their family members who used Essiac. More importantly, they agonized over the future availability of Essiac to keep their cancers under control.

At least since 1979 Darling had communicated by writing and in person with every health minister and members of his or her department since Monique Begin.[741] Now in 1988, in an effort to convince the federal health authorities that Essiac was desperately needed by countless cancer patients, Bracebridge residents Darlene Boyes and Patricia Van Heerde spearheaded a drive to petition the government. They obtained 5,558 names requesting the Government of Canada to test Essiac officially in a double-blind study to prove the effectiveness of the herbal remedy and to make Essiac legally available. Enlisting Stan Darling's help, they got the petition tabled in the House of Commons on June 7, 1988, for the public record.

In Minister of Health Epp's prepared response to the presentation, he reiterated, "Essiac can only be made available to individual patients under the guidance of their physicians through provisions of the Emergency Drug Release regulations."[742] The document was undoubtedly deposited in the great petition bin somewhere in the bowels of the National Capital Region. Letters were exchanged with ministers of health Jake Epp and, later, Perrin Beatty for months with the proper political clichés and pessimistic responses the petitioners already knew by heart from previous experience.

The Hon. Perrin Beatty informed the "crusaders"[743,744] in December 1988 that the Resperin Corporation still had not submitted complete documentation as required under the Investigational New Drug Submission rules, so no clinical trials could be conducted with Essiac.

DAVID FINGARD DIES — ESSIAC LIVES

David Fingard was sick. In his mid-80s he experienced, of all things, cancer. He had had surgery and lost much weight, and it is not known if he drank Essiac herbal tea to gain a measure of pain relief. Considering that he lived to a good old age in spite of being exposed to his controversial respiratory medication for most of his adult life, he lived comfortably and apparently well. In July 1989, Fingard died at eighty-five years of age after a blustery but ineffective attempt at making a success of Essiac. In early 1991, with Dr. Rynard and Stephen Roman now also deceased,[745] Fingard's widow, Mildred, and the remaining Resperin directors engaged the services of lawyer Gordon A. Mackay, QC, of Kitchener, Ontario, to handle their corporate matters and take a role as director and shareholder. Mackay was a colleague and friend of Resperin director John J. Wintermeyer, QC, who was becoming increasingly ill from Lou Gehrig's disease and unable to manage Resperin's legal affairs. Wintermeyer, leader of Ontario's Liberals during Leslie Frost's era, was to die two years later.

Essiac continued to be a sought-after potential cancer treatment, and prospective buyers of the formula were willing to pay its increasing price. It took four years after Rene's death in 1978 to execute a new agreement between Resperin and Rene's successors; on May 21, 1982, a new union was documented between Dr. Charles Armao Brusch, Valeen Taylor, and the Resperin Corporation. In a faltering hand, Dr. Brusch signed a document that would finally give him a recognized and financial role in the Essiac business. Rene's niece and executor, in a surprising turn of events, acknowledged, "In 1959 Rene M. Caisse entered into an oral agreement with Dr. Brusch, wherein it was agreed, in part, that Dr. Brusch and Rene M. Caisse would become equal partners in the ownership of the formula for the Essiac treatment and that, in consequence, Dr. Brusch is entitled to one-half of any Royalty Payment paid or payable by Resperin to Rene M. Caisse or the Estate of Rene M. Caisse."

The new agreement stated, "Essiac treatment has not yet been promoted commercially with the result that no Royalty Payments have been paid," nor are any owing to Rene or her estate. Now Dr. Brusch and Valeen would each receive 1 percent of the revenue arising from the promotion of Essiac, payable annually in December.

But there was much unfinished business with Resperin's responsibilities within the agreements. Dr. Matt Dymond, keeping some handle on Resperin from his home in Port Perry, wrote to Dr. Brusch and Valeen in February 1991 and admitted that, as he was once again named president, he was sifting through the files and learned that neither of them had received any royalties since Resperin began earning revenues from the sale of Essiac back in January 1986.[746] The accumulation of royalties amounted to $1,760, and Dr. Dymond saw that each party received a cheque for princely sum of $880. In a benevolent note, which she typed with a healing broken wrist, Valeen told Dymond that she believed Mr. Fingard became "a little vague during [his] last time on earth so it is quite possible that this would be forgotten."[747] Eighty-five-year-old Charles Brusch would die within two years, and Valeen Taylor in October 2002.

In 1993, totally burned out, Matt Dymond, who was always unable to believe that his own colleagues would not sign anything about their success with Essiac patients, resigned from all activity with Resperin Corporation. He died a tired man on February 21, 1996. By then the new proprietor of Essiac, a chemist named David Dobbie, would own Rene's herbal remedy and begin an active marketing and sales program.

PUBLICATIONS ABOUT ESSIAC CONTINUE

Rene Caisse's story continues to charm and fascinate writers and researchers. Most articles are based on the article published in *Homemaker's Magazine* in 1977, which itself has been reprinted thousands of times and distributed all over North America. The information has been reprinted and/or rewritten in endless varieties and styles, each with its own sensationalism. A complete bibliographic record of pieces written about Rene and Essiac would defy most literature researchers. Articles and columns have been published in herbal journals, health association newsletters, government information notices, and a broad collection of small-press magazines and newspapers throughout the world.

Information about Essiac is shared on the Internet, and several publications in book form offer their presentation of this captivating story. Some consider two of the books to be exploitation for their own purposes.

A chiefly anecdotal book by former U.S. chiropractor Gary L. Glum, entitled *Calling of an Angel*,[748] was published privately in 1988 in Los Angeles. It claimed to be the true story of Rene Caisse and Essiac, and indeed much of his information came from recollections of Bracebridge residents who knew Rene and remembered a great deal of the legend.

In the last few pages of the 233-page book, the reader is encouraged to send US$79.95 to obtain a videotape that would reveal the Essiac formula. The eleven-minute video presents the author detailing the recipe and describing the preparation of the decoction. The cost of both the book and video totalled some $150 Canadian, putting it out of each for some readers, but it did spark considerable interest in California and elsewhere. It may have been the Essiac recipe used by Rene Caisse, although at that time the "real" formula was understood to be only in the hands of Resperin Corporation, which was required to submit it to Health and Welfare Canada.

A Bracebridge newspaper reported that Glum complained to Stan Darling that his book had been banned from entry into Canada in 1989, and the Parry Sound–Muskoka MP wrote to the federal health and welfare minister to complain. The Hon. Perrin Beatty responded that Revenue Canada informed him that that book would not fall into the banned category at customs and should have free access.[749]

Later in the nineties, a three-month supply of mixed and dried Essiac herbs could be ordered from Dr. Glum for a cost of US$230. Once a formula was revealed by Dr. Glum, the underground production of Essiac began. As soon as the recipe and the specific herbs became known and available, people with stainless steel or enamel pots, a kitchen stove, access to brown glass bottles, patience, and commitment became producers all over Canada and the United States.

A book entitled *The Essiac Report*,[750] compiled by a person identified as Richard Thomas of Los Angeles, California, contains much information gleaned from *Homemaker's Magazine* and Canadian government archives. It was published in 1993, arguably to promote the Flor.Essence products of British Columbia.

There were other publications about Essiac and Rene Caisse, all claiming to have the most complete story — none Canadian. One U.S.–based author published a slim volume in 1996 based chiefly on long-published works to join the writings about Rene Caisse and Essiac.[751]

THE FIGHT OVER THE FORMULA

Rene's insistence on keeping the Essiac formula secret caused an enormous amount of frustration to the medical community, which wanted to analyze its contents. Rene was called stubborn, selfish, and unhumanitarian, but she continued to withhold the formula from those who might have been helped by its ready accessibility.

Several confusing situations have indicated that Rene's original intent to trust and transfer the secret formula to others went badly awry. The desire to own the cure to cancer was so strong that loyalties and sometimes personal integrity and judgement had to come under scrutiny. Doubt and suspicion, distrust and greed were factors she had had to contend with throughout her embattled years.

Some while after Rene's death, Dr. Brusch phoned Mary McPherson to ask for the recipe, and she gave it to him over the phone. Brusch at that time promised to set up a memorial in honour of Rene — with "every nickel" going into it, presumably from his portion of the royalties from Resperin.[752]

A number of people claim to have obtained the original formula before its known release to Resperin — and they guard it jealously. It was not in her will, and according to Rene it was not given those who worked with her at any time. Gilbert Blondin[753] claimed to have the recipe in Rene's own handwriting; so did others. Did Pat Judson have a version of the secret recipe and sell it to Gary Glum? Stories have circulated that Glum paid someone anywhere from twenty thousand to two hundred thousand dollars for the formula.[754]

If anyone does have an authenticated, handwritten copy of Rene's formula, just where and when they acquired it will always be one the enigmas of Rene's story.

In December 1994, a special ceremony took place in Bracebridge to record the Essiac formula. Town Solicitor Nick Roche witnessed a sworn affidavit signed by Mary McPherson that detailed the names of the herbs and the recipe for making Rene's Essiac. Exhibit "A" to Mary's affidavit gave the following handwritten instructions:

Essiac

6 1/2 cups of burdock root (cut), 1 pound of sheep
sorrel herb powdered
1/4 pound of slippery elm bark powdered, 1 ounce
of turkish rhubarb root powdered
mix these ingredients thoroughly and store in glass
jar in dark dry cupboard
Take a measuring cup use 1 ounce of herb mixture
to 32 ounces of water depending on the amount
you want to make.
I use 1 cup of mixture to 8x32=256 ounces of water.
Boil hard for 10 minutes (covered) then turn off but
leave sitting on warm plate over night (cooling)

In the morning heat steaming hot and let sit a few minutes. Then strain through fine strainer into hot sterilized bottles and sit to cool in dark cool cupboard. Must be refrigerated when opened. When near the last when it's thick pour in a large jar and sit in frig overnight then pour off all you (can) without sediment. This recipe must be followed exactly as written. I use a granite preserving kettle 10-12 qts, 8 ounce measuring cup, small funnel, fine strainer to fill bottles.

Mary was proud that the formula was now safe in the archives of the Town of Bracebridge, its public library, and its historical society.[755]

ESSIAC CLONED

Rene had often said that Essiac would be imitated, and true to her prediction, once the formula became public, clones began to appear. Exaggerated claims of superiority over one another would have had Rene chuckling if she could have seen and heard it all.

In a burst of local pride, in the spring of 1988 MP Stan Darling, along with the mayor of Bracebridge, Jim Lang, and Clerk-Administrator Ken Veitch, rushed to Ottawa to investigate an establishment making an herbal preparation called Easy-Ac, operated by Dr. Pierre Andre Gaulin and his associate Gilbert Blondin.[756] The Easy-Ac producers were baiting the federal government to take them to court to support the fight for Essiac to be considered. After the Bracebridge visitors returned, Darling wrote a letter to the Bureau of Human Prescription Drugs, Ottawa, expressing his displeasure about the Resperin company's being restricted by the Health Protection Branch of the government.[757] The production of Essiac had almost stopped, whereas others were openly making a clone and offering it for sale.

As a result of Stan's letters to his federal colleagues, and following investigations by the Health Protection Branch, in March 1989

Blondin and Dr. Gaulin, a U.S. citizen who practised Chinese medicine, were formally charged in a Quebec provincial court with sixteen violations of the federal Food and Drugs Act.[758] The men, who claimed their product cured cancer, ulcers, and menstrual cramps, had had their homes and offices in the Ottawa-Hull area raided by the Health Protection Branch of the federal government a few months earlier, their records and equipment seized.[759] Not only was the name of the product directly pirated from Essiac, but their bottle label read: "Easy-Ac (from the original Rene Caisse Formula)." They continued to make and market their product as an herbal remedy with no claims to its purpose.

The most public and conspicuous use of Rene's name and product was the herbal preparation named Flor.Essence, promoted since 1984 by former radio broadcaster Elaine Alexander of British Columbia.[760] Using Rene's photo and a brief newspaper-style story of Rene's discovery in (supposedly) 1922, the Flor.Essence advertisement exalted its unique product as the Essiac formula. Alexander was impressed by Rene's work with Dr. Charles Brusch and had in her own way made herself known to him. Exactly what documents, agreements, and understanding were arranged between her and Dr. Charles Brusch cannot be determined.

In Toronto during the early nineties, there was a health drink in the planning stages called Ezziac. There were products called "Canaid Herbal Drink," "Caisse's Herbal Tea," "Native Legend Tea," and an unknown number of others that offered variations of the non-toxic herbal remedy Rene called Essiac.

The four herbs — sheep sorrel, burdock root, Turkish rhubarb root, and slippery elm bark — that comprise Rene's herbal tea are now available for purchase in measured packages in health food stores. Some people seek out brown glass bottles of freshly brewed tea from persons who recreate Rene's days of stirring the musty-smelling brew in her kitchen. Unknown numbers of cancer patients, as well as those who want the benefits the herbs offer other health conditions, can now openly obtain the herbal tea or make it for themselves. Pharmacies and health food stores sell the trademarked herbal medicine still named Essiac.

MEMORIALS TO A NOTABLE NURSE

Rene's hometown offered tangible thanks to her for her lifetime of helping "suffering humanity" and has established a number of tributes. In July 1994, a plaque (that unfortunately contained errors in fact) was unveiled to commemorate the Rene M. Caisse Cancer Clinic at the former Bracebridge Inn on Dominion Street. The ceremony was attended by some surviving members of Rene's family, including niece Margaret Gordon, great-nephew Don McVittie, and great-nieces Jackie Poland and Sandra Askin. Of course, Rene's special friend Mary McPherson was there.[761] Niece Valeen Taylor was unable to make the journey from her home in Barrie but enjoyed hearing about the occasion, which was organized by Bracebridge Mayor Jim Lang and Town Clerk-Administrator Ken Veitch, whose grandmother, Eliza Veitch, was a grateful patient of Rene Caisse.

The Rene M. Caisse Memorial Room officially opened its door June 23, 1996, in Bracebridge's house museum Woodchester Villa, the former home of the Henry J. Bird family. The Bird family in the octagonal house would have known the Caisse family, who somewhat paralleled their period of growing up. Perhaps Henry would have been pleased to offer a room to honour Rene and her accomplishments.

While many pieces of Rene's memorabilia have not survived the years since her death, interesting items are on display in the memorial room. The handsome nameplate that hung over her reception room, reproductions of many of the countless newspaper articles that chronicled her trials and triumphs, and samples of her precious Essiac in tiny ampoules are there. Friends have returned paintings from her "Grandma Moses" retirement days, and other artifacts may yet emerge.

The Town of Bracebridge renamed the lane beside her former home on Kimberley Avenue (the adjacent house was torn down earlier) and in early 1996 placed a new sign in a prominent location off Manitoba Street, the main thoroughfare. It reads, "Rene Caisse Lane."

Tourists to Bracebridge can follow her footsteps with the self-guiding heritage tours entitled "Pastimes," published by the Chamber of Commerce in the spring of 1996. From Rene Caisse's birthplace to her final resting place, her cancer clinic and her homes, visitors can take an informed visit throughout her town.

Probably the most dramatic and visual memorial to Rene is the bronze bust sculpted by Huntsville artist Brenda Wainman-Goulet, which sits on land donated by the Town of Bracebridge overlooking the most spectacular scene in Muskoka. Unveiled on November 15, 2000, the larger than life bust is secured on granite and holds a sheaf of green leaves resembling sheep sorrel, the significant herb in Essiac. Near the former Rene M. Caisse Cancer Clinic and a short walk from the Rene M. Caisse Memorial Room, the donors, Essiac® Canada International of Ottawa, have indeed provided a considerable gift to Rene's birthplace to recognize and commemorate her work. The sculptor also created a duplicate bronze and granite bust of Rene for the Rene M. Caisse Memorial Botanical Garden at the Naturopathic College of Medicine in Toronto in 2003, again funded by Essiac® Canada International.

Rene's humanitarian accomplishments have not been forgotten by a proud community, but her story cannot be completely told.

Norma Kelly photo

Tourist are directed to "Canada's Cancer Nurse" at the Rene M. Caisse Memorial Room as part of the town's Historic Walk.

While the material in this biography is as accurate as research from primary sources can be, it is not complete. Much available information cannot be presented in one volume. This necessarily abbreviated story is offered as a tribute to an amazing lady whose discovery continues to provide a measure of comfort and hope to those who demand it. Cancer patients who sought her help came from all walks of life: farmers, homemakers, doctors, lawyers, and workers in a wide scope of business and industry. Rene's patients could have told more, as could those who have seemed to be her adversaries.

CANCER COMMISSION WITHDRAWS

In October 1997, the Cancer Remedies Act,[762] whose only purpose was to authorize the existence of the Commission for the Investigation of Cancer Remedies for the Ministry of Health, disappeared. It was quietly repealed after a simple evening discussion by members of the legislature on October 8, almost hidden in an unpretentious housekeeping bill of the Mike Harris Conservative government. Aimed at saving health professionals hours of out-of-date paperwork under various health related statutes, Bill 67, called the Government Process Simplification Act (Ministry of Health), had been tabled in June 1996 and had been in committee review ever since. The MP from Niagara South, Tim Hudak, told the legislature that the Regulated Health Professionals Act (1991) was already "protecting citizens from harm from improper approaches to cancer care. This Act was 1938, and perhaps at that time there was some alleged cancer cures that may not have been good medicine. But we have other legislation that governs the health professions to ensure that proper care is taken of patients."[763]

There were no objectors, no public announcements, and no recognition in the press. The commission was gone with no fanfare after nearly sixty years. The legislation that was enacted very much for the purpose of stopping Rene Caisse from administering Essiac to cancer patients in 1938 had vanished.

EPILOGUE

ALTERNATIVE CANCER REMEDIES

One might ask why, if chances of survival with "orthodox" methods are so limited, is there not room for, indeed, requirement for, alternative cancer remedies. Surely after all the claimed cures, and certainly the benefits of pain relief, reduced tumours, and much lengthened lives, it could be acknowledged that some of the therapies had very effective components. Many are from centuries-old botanical sources.

It would take a very large complement of PhD candidates to accurately document the funds, grants, and disbursement for cancer research made during the past century on this continent alone and present a scrupulous record of numbers of patient cures and/or length of human survival as a result of that research.

From indications gathered by Rene Caisse, physicians, and others who have administered their own cancer remedies, the misdiagnosis of true cancer by physicians would appear to be forgiven by their fraternity in order to protect the conventional methods. As Rene Caisse said many years ago, "If the patient given up by the medical profession after its radical cancer treatments got well after taking Essiac treatments, the doctors argued that they never had cancer in the first place, or recovered because of the approved methods given before Essiac."

In 1974, Dr. Edward F. Lewison of the Johns Hopkins University School of Medicine introduced the first conference on spontaneous regression of cancer[764] by saying: "For many years, physicians and surgeons alike have observed the dramatic but rare regression of an occasional case of cancer in the absence of adequate, recognized, or conventional treatment. However, only recently has the concept of spontaneous regression of cancer become respectable." He called it a new audacity in thinking. Perhaps he could have included the thought that alternative therapies offered by sincere researchers may have been part of the healing.

Yes, there have always been snake oil salesmen hawking their wares from the backs of their trucks. But the lack of serious clinical testing of products with known patient improvements is quite reprehensible. One might ask if the cancer business really is dedicated to broadening its search strategy to find a cancer cure. Some say it wants only to continue and protect this major research industry.

SIMPLICITY IS THE SEAL OF TRUTH — A PARALLEL TO RENE CAISSE

Professor Hermann Boerhaave, Holland's greatest physician and Europe's most brilliant teacher of clinical medicine, died in 1737. Medical historians record:

> It is almost paradoxical that, in an age of systems, when every outstanding professor advocated his own medical system, the secret of the most successful and most important physician of all lay in his having no system. Boerhaave declined to set up a complete system. He remained with both feet planted on the ground of facts. He kept in the foreground the clinical signs, which can be observed clearly and explained as physical or chemical reactions. Quite intentionally he did not hold with the theoretical discussion of fundamental conceptions such as life, health and sickness, as these could not be investigated scientifically. His teaching and his

work express the rational spirit of the Age of Enlightenment. Boerhaave's motto read: Simplex veri sigillum (simplicity is the seal of truth).

He emphasized over and over again the value for practical medicine of anatomy and physiology, and also of physics and chemistry. He placed experience at the bedside before all else. The practice of medicine stood at the midpoint of his thought, and in clinical teaching he could unfold his whole personality. Pupils from many lands gathered round this clinician who had so quickly become famous. They received instruction at the side of only twelve beds, six for men and six for women. Boerhaave's two little wards were the foundation-stones of the modern clinic.[765]

Rene said many times, reminding patients in her simply constituted clinic or anyone who would listen, that she was not a physician. In 1966 she wrote:

> I am not a doctor — I am a nurse. I have never claimed that my treatment cures cancer — although many of my patients, and doctors with whom I have worked, claim that it does. My goal has been control of cancer, and alleviation of pain. Diabetes, pernicious anemia and arthritis are not curable: but with insulin, liver extract, and adrenal cortex extracts, these "incurables" live out comfortable controlled life spans.[766]

Rene made the lives of decades of patients easier. The 1977 *Homemaker's* article read:

> There's a tragic and shameful irony in the Essiac tale. In the beginning, a simple herbal recipe was freely shared by an Indian who understood that the blessings of the Creator belong to all. In the hands

of more sophisticated (and allegedly more "civi-lized") healers, it was made the focus of an ugly struggle for ownership and power.

Perhaps our cure for cancer lies back in the past, with our discarded humility and innocence. Perhaps the Indians will some day revive an old man's wisdom, and share it once again. Perhaps this story will be the catalyst; if so our efforts will not have been in vain.[767]

APPENDIX

THE CANCER REMEDIES ACT

The Cancer Remedy Act, 1938, and Subsequent Revisions

1938

The Cancer Remedy Act, 1938
Statutes of Ontario, Chapter 4, 1938.
Assented to April 8, 1938, in effect June 1, (7), 1938.

1940

The Cancer Remedy Act, 1938
Amendment, 1940, c.28, s. 5 (1) and (2) re oath of secrecy and investigation.

1950

The Cancer Remedies Act
Revised Statutes of Ontario, 1950, Chapter 45, which is the consolidation of all legislation during the 1940s. The name of the Act was changed during the production of the R.S.O. 1950 to pluralize "remedy." No bill or statute can be identified to cover this change.

1980

The Cancer Remedies Act
R.S.O. 1980, c. 58 provides administrative streamlining dealing with quorum, investigation, funding, finances, oath of secrecy, reporting, and actions against the commission.

1989

The Cancer Remedies Act
Statutes of Ontario, 1989, c. 72, s. 37, increases the fines for convictions.

1990

The Cancer Remedies Act, 1990
Chapter c. 2, a consolidation of previous legislation.

1997

The Cancer Remedies Act was repealed October 10, 1997, Ontario Statutes, Chapter 15, s. 17. The Government Process Simplication Act (Ministry of Health), 1996 (Bill 67) (see Hansard, October 8, 1997, page 12879), was the final legislative action in October 1997.

The legislation, which was enacted very much to stop Rene Caisse from administering Essiac to cancer patients in 1938, stood throughout the decades. The Cancer Remedies Act in the 1990 Revised Statutes of Ontario is presented here, in part, along with brief interpretations.

"The objects of the Commission (The Commission for the Investigation of Cancer Remedies, which be may only one person) are to investigate, approve, disapprove, encourage or report upon any substance or method of treatment that is believed to be or likely to be, or is advertised, held out to be or used as a remedy for cancer, and the Commission may take such measures as it considers necessary to accomplish its objects." Section 3(1)

"The Commission may enter into agreement with any university, medical association, hospital or other association, corporation or person for the purpose of carrying out its objects, and may hire and pay employees and experts and Commissioners out of its funds." Section 3(2,3,4,5)

"The Commission may require any person who advertises, offers for sale, holds out, distributes, sells or administers either free of charge or for gain, hire or hope of reward, any substance or method of treatment as a remedy for cancer to submit samples of such substance or a description of such treatment and samples of any substance used with such treatment to the Commission together with the formula of such substance and such other information pertaining to such substance or methods of treatment as the Commission may determine." Section 5(1)

The Commission shall not divulge any information and may bind any person who receives information, and the Commission may be only one person and may be required to furnish an audited financial statement, the Act recorded.

"Where a substance or method of treatment is submitted to the Commission under section 5, the Commission shall cause the substance or method of treatment to be investigated and, upon the conclusion of the investigation, shall made a determination or finding as to merit or value as a remedy for cancer of the substance or method of treatment, but the Commission may at any time before concluding its investigation make such determination or finding of a temporary nature as it considers proper, and every determination or finding of the Commission shall be recorded in its minutes." Section 6

The Commission, which is protected from libel and slander actions, must report its findings to the Minister of Health. Contraveners to the act are guilty to a minimum fine of $200 for the first offence and not more than $5,000 for subsequent offences.

ENDNOTES

Chapter 1

1.   A number of spellings of this name were used throughout Mrs. Caisse's life. The spelling most frequently used, and finally in her cemetery record, has been chosen for this biography.

2.   Birthdates of Joseph and Friselda are uncertain. His obituary in the *Muskoka Herald* cites April 23, 1855, while the family bible records April 28, 1956. Friselda, spelled also Frisilde, was recorded as January 31, 185_ (illeg.), and her obituary records her birth as ninety years before 1948.

3.   Obituary of Joseph Caisse, *Muskoka Herald*, July 6, 1916.

4.   Photo quiz regarding Joseph Caisse, *Muskoka Herald*, May 8, 1941.

5.   Obituary of Mrs. Joseph Caisse, *Muskoka Herald*, February 19, 1948, p. 1.

6.   Rene Caisse, "Essiac," in "Formula dominated her life," Ted Britton (ed.), *The Weekender* [Bracebridge], June 2, 1995, p. 21.

7.   Obituary of Joseph L. Caisse, *Bracebridge Gazette*, December 14, 1944.

8.   Robert J. Boyer, *A Good Town Grew Here* (Bracebridge: Herald-Gazette Press, 1975), p. 74.

9.   Boyer, "In and Around the County Town," *Bracebridge Gazette*, June 9, 1904, p. 1.

10.   "Entrance Exams," *Bracebridge Gazette*, July 14, 1904.

11.   "Band Benefit," *Muskoka Herald*, March 22, 1906, p. 8.

12.   Boyer, *A Good Town Grew Here*, p. 34.

13.   "Personal and Social Events," *Muskoka Herald*, August 30, 1906.

14.   "Personal and Social Events," *Muskoka Herald*, September 26, 1907.

15.   "Personal and Social Events," *Muskoka Herald*, November 14, 1907.

16.   Richard Tatley, *The Steamboat Era in the Muskokas, Vol. II, The Golden Years to Present* (Erin: Boston Mills Press, 1984), p. 15; see also *Muskoka Herald*, July 8, 1908.

17.   "Personal and Social Events," *Muskoka Herald*, March 29, 1906.

18.   "Local Items, New Store," *Muskoka Herald*, April 23, 1908.

19.   Advertisement, Joseph Caisse, *Muskoka Herald*, July 16, 1908.

20.   "Personal and Social Events," *Muskoka Herald*, May 31, 1906.

21.   Once a part of the mainland, the island situated at the mouth of the Muskoka River downstream from Bracebridge was created when the construction of three dams at Bala raised the level of Lake Muskoka some four feet. Joseph Caisse and his family would eventually buy the entire

island, and by 1925 it would be known as Caisses Island. Rene and her brother Ted initially bought properties on the mainland at Alport.

22. Ontario Registry data.

23. "Bought Gasoline," *Muskoka Herald*, September 23, 1909, p. 5.

24. "Sudden Death of Dr. W.D. McIlmoyle," *Muskoka Herald*, March 1, 1917.

25. Professional card, *Muskoka Herald*, December 11, 1914, p. 1.

26. "Personal and Social Events," *Muskoka Herald*, February 11, 1909, p. 5.

27. Wallace Fonds, 2002, Queen's University Archives, Proceedings of a Sub-Committee of the Commission for the Investigation of Cancer, February 3–4, 1939, p. 8.

28. Information regarding the nursing schools in Greenwich from: Greenwich Library, March 23, 1996; *American and Canadian Hospitals, a reference...* (Minneapolis: Midwest Publishers, c1933), p. 197–198; Spencer P. Mead, "Ye Historie of Ye Town of Greenwich," 1911; Oral History Project of Friends of the Greenwich Library, Greenwich, Ct, April 19, 1975.

29. Philip A. Kalisch and Beatrice J. Kalisch, *The Advance of American Nursing* (Boston: Little, Brown & Co., 1978), p. 193.

30. Ibid., p. 185.

31. Ibid., p. 156.

32. "Personal and Social Events," *Muskoka Herald*, March 31, 1910, p. 7.

33. Rene M. Caisse, "Cancer," *Muskoka Herald*, January 11, 1940. (This is probably the first time she publicly referred to herself as a "graduate nurse.")

34. "Small Fire," *Muskoka Herald*, October 21, 1909, p. 1.

35. "The Carnival," *Muskoka Herald*, February 15, 1912, p. 8.

36. Boyer, *A Good Town Grew Here*, pp. 162–163.

37. *New Liskeard Speaker*, May 31, 1907.

38. Dorothy Farmiloe, *Elk Lake Lore and Legend* (Little Current, Plowshare Press, 1984), p. 2.

39. Ibid., p. 39.

40. Ibid., p. 46.

41. Dr. John Pollock, "History of Logging in the Lake Temiskaming-Montreal River Watershed," p. 12, in "They Came from All Walks of Life," Proceedings of the History Workshop, Temiskaming Abitibi Heritage Association, April 29, 1995.

42. Haileybury Fire Museum, Haileybury, Ontario.

43. *American and Canadian Hospitals, a reference...*, c1933.

44. His sister Ella May was to marry Rene's brother Joseph in 1917.

45. The narrative developed to describe Rene's life and work in the Temiskaming region from 1912 was created from research in various printed sources, including the two Bracebridge newspapers. Tracing Rene's whereabouts in the microfilmed newspapers for that critical period was hindered by missing and mutilated issues. The dates of her interval in Cobalt have been established from those determined in the notes in the A.E. Saunders photograph collection, Ontario Archives, c1911, and her likeness in the photos. The Elk Lake Hospital photo places her there during Dr. G.L. Cockburn's 1912 period.

46. Mary McPherson recollections. Author's collection.

47. "Doctors Back Nurse Claiming Secret Herb Aids Cancer Victims," *Toronto Daily Star*, January 23, 1932, p. 1.

48. Rene M. Caisse with Maurine B. Cox, I Was "*Canada's Cancer Nurse*": The Story of Essiac (New York: Maurine B. Cox. June 1966), p. 1.

49.   Kalisch and Kalisch, *The Advance of American Nursing*, p. 193.
50.   Leslie McFarlane, *A Kid in Haileybury*, (Cobalt: Highway Book Shop, 1966), p. 55.
51.   In an interview August 19, 1996, Mrs. Walter Clifford Arnold told the author that Cliff used to say that Rene was nice and helped him from time to time.
52.   Ontario Archives, Special Collections, notes in A.E. Saunders photograph collection, c1911.
53.   E.D. McClelland, letter to the author, January 21, 1997.
54.   "Social and Personal Events," *Bracebridge Gazette*, December 4, 1913.
55.   "Social and Personal," *Muskoka Herald*, April 6, 1916.
56.   "Death of Mr. Joseph Caisse," *Muskoka Herald*, July 6, 1916, p. 1.
57.   James McClelland and Dan Lewis (Eds.), *Emerson 1875–1975, A Centennial History* (Emerson [Man.] Chamber of Commerce, 1975), p. 43.
58.   "Bracebridge Agency Deaths," *Muskoka Herald*, January 26, 1922.
59.   Joseph's first wife, Jennie, died in 1909.
60.   "Social and Personal," *Muskoka Herald*, October 25, 1917, p. 4.
61.   "Social and Personal," *Muskoka Herald*, April 4, 1918 p. 4.
62.   Bell Telephone Directory, Toronto, May 1919.
63.   "Social and Personal," *Muskoka Herald*, September 6, 1918.
64.   "Social and Personal," *Muskoka Herald*, October 24, 1918.
65.   Edward's mother was Rene's father's sister, who lived for a time in Bracebridge with Friselda.
66.   "Died of Wounds," *Muskoka Herald*, December 5, 1918.
67.   Unidentified Bracebridge newspaper.
68.   Women's College Hospital wouldn't be completed until 1935.
69.   As was often the case, the spellings of names in the Toronto City Directory were not accurate. The unusual name, Permelia, was recorded by a hurried canvasser as Pamela.
70.   "Social and Personal," *Muskoka Herald*, July 22, 1920, p. 4.

Chapter 2

71.   "Lecture by Nurse Bryan," in Rene's notes, Whitby Hospital, 1921–1922.
72.   See detail in previous chapter and "Doctors Back Nurse Claiming Secret Herb Aids Cancer Victims," *Toronto Daily Star*, January 23, 1932, p. 1.
73.   Dr. Harvey Clare, letter to Dr. J. M. Forster, April 14, 1921.
74.   "Lecture by Nurse Bryan," 1921–1922.
75.   Kathy Ward, librarian, Whitby Mental Health Centre, interview with the author, October 28, 31, 1996. (Rene's notes reflected the topics of Miss Bryan's first-year curriculum.)
76.   Rene's notes, Whitby Hospital, 1921–1922.
77.   Ross Hamilton (ed.), *Prominent Men of Canada*, 1931-32 (Montreal: National Publishing Co. of Canada), p. 514. (The spelling of the name of the medical superintendent of the Ontario Hospital on Queen Street was Dr. Harvey Claire, but he was listed as Clare in Toronto directories. His signature was unclear. The letter from Dr. Forster's office was addressed to Dr. Harvey Clare.)
78.   Dr. J.M. Forster, letter to Dr. Harvey Clare, April 15, 1921.
79.   Rene's notes, Whitby Hospital, 1921–1922.
80.   It is difficult to place the exact time of the previous events. Certainly Rene was taking nursing classes at Whitby a "few months" prior to April 1921

according to Dr. Forester, but Rene's first-year nursing curriculum notes and her poetry place her at Whitby Hospital New Year's Eve, 1921–1922, months later.

81. "Personals," *Bracebridge Gazette*, July 12, 1923.
82. "Personal Mention," *Bracebridge Gazette*, July 27, 1922.
83. "Doctors Back Nurse Claiming Secret Herb Aid Cancer Victims," *Toronto Daily Star*, January 23, 1932, p. 2.
84. "I'm Not Concerned About Money — Miss Caisse," *Huntsville Forester*, July 22, 1937, p. 1.
85. Caisse, I Was *"Canada's Cancer Nurse,"* p. 1.
86. Sheila Snow Fraser and Carroll Allen, "Could Essiac Halt Cancer?" *Homemaker's Magazine*, June/July/August, 1977, p. 12.
87. Chancellor Gisele Roy, CND, Diocese of Timmins, to Donna Ivey, February 5, 1996, and Pierrette Chevrette, s.p., Conseillere-secretaire generale, Soeurs de la Providence, Montreal to Soeurs Roy, January 25, 1996. Also telephone conversation, Ivey-Roy, January 11, 1996. (It is confirmed that no personnel records of the Sisters of Providence Hospital have survived.)
88. "Ten Ex-Muskokans Perish," *Bracebridge Gazette*, October 12, 1922, p. 2.
89. "Many Settlers Lost Their Lives Between Heaslip & Charlton," *Bracebridge Gazette*, October 12, 1922, p. 2.
90. "Bracebridge Barrister Goes through Holocaust," *Bracebridge Gazette*, October 12, 1922, p. 1.
91. "Haileybury Court Forced to Adjourn," *Bracebridge Gazette*, October 12, 1922, p. 2.
92. "Bracebridge Leads Way to Rescue," *Bracebridge Gazette*, October 26, 1922, p. 1.
93. "You May Help," *Muskoka Herald*, October 26, 1922, p. 4.
94. "$1000 and Car Supplied," *Muskoka Herald*, November 2, 1922, p. 1.
95. "Help Burned Ontario Over the Winter," *Bracebridge Gazette* and *Muskoka Herald*, December 7, 1922.
96. Newspaper files on microfilm for 1922 are incomplete. Publication style shows a much reduced reporting of social and personal data.
97. Staff in the office of the Ontario Registered Nurses Association told the author that before the registration law in 1922, hospitals didn't usually hire graduate nurses, only students, and trained them. Graduates worked in other medical settings.
98. "Doctors Back Nurse Claiming Secret Herb Aid Cancer Victims," *Toronto Daily Star*, January 23, 1932.
99. Caisse, I Was *"Canada's Cancer Nurse,"* p. 1.
100. F.E. Speck, *Family Hunting Territories and Social Life of Various Algonkian Bands of the Ottawa Valley, Canada*, Geological Survey, Memoir 70, 1915, p. 11. There were about ninety-five band members.
101. Caisse, I Was *"Canada's Cancer Nurse,"* p. 2.
102. Joseph G. Richardson, *Medicology or Home Encyclopedia of Health* (New York: University Medical Society, 1904), p. 302.
103. Caisse, I Was *"Canada's Cancer Nurse,"* p. 2.
104. "Believes Herb Cured a Cancer Defied Surgery," *Toronto Daily Star*, February 24, 1932, p. 2.
105. Rene related in various interviews that this took place in 1924.
106. Caisse, I Was *"Canada's Cancer Nurse,"* p. 2.
107. "Doctors Back Nurse Claiming Secret Herb Aid Cancer Victims," *Toronto*

Daily Star, January 23, 1932, p. 2.

108. Bell Telephone Directory, Toronto, Summer/Fall 1926.
109. Louise Kent-Boyd, "Sherbourne Street a Grand Old Lady with an Interesting Past," *Cabbagetown Riverdale News*, July 5, 1992, p. 5.
110. Caisse, I Was "*Canada's Cancer Nurse*," p. 5.
111. Ibid., p. 4.
112. "Doctors Back Nurse Claiming Secret Herb Aids Cancer Victims," *Toronto Daily Star*, January 23, 1932, p. 2.
113. Caisse, I Was "*Canada's Cancer Nurse*," p. 4.
114. Fraser and Allen, "Could Essiac Halt Cancer?" p. 14.
115. Wallace Fonds, 2002, Queen's University Archives, *Proceedings of The Commission for the Investigation of Cancer Remedies*, July 4, 1939, Exhibit 46, p. 178.
116. Fraser and Allen, "Could Essiac Halt Cancer?" p. 14.

Chapter 3

117. Because Rene did not to register under the Act, she was not recorded in the Ontario Registered Nurses Association files.
118. As a young doctor, Dr. Ross Blye seemed to have been influenced by the humane work of Rene Caisse. At his death in 1972, it was remembered that he had a reputation of treating everyone, regardless of what they could pay. His prescription pad was always in his pocket, and "Doc" never charged if one of the members of his favourite disabled veteran's club felt unwell and sought his help.
119. Dr. Charles Hair was in Cobalt during 1906–1913 and was the town's first medical officer of health.
120. Bob Johnson, interview with Rene Caisse, CBC Radio, June 10, 1977.
121. Canada Department of Pensions and National Health, *Annual Report*, 1928–29, pp. 82–83.
122. Dr. Frederick G. Banting (1891–1941) was awarded the 1923 Nobel Prize in Physiology and Medicine (for isolating insulin) along with J.R.R. McLeod. Out of respect for the work done by Dr. Charles H. Best, Banting shared his half of the financial prize, and McLeod shared his with James B. Collip. Banting was knighted in 1934.
123. Wallace Fonds, 2002, July 4, 1939, Exhibit 46, pp. 293–295.
124. Doug Hall, interview with Rene Caisse, "Daybeat," CKVR, Barrie, June 29, 1976.
125. No documented evidence has been found to verify Dr. Banting's words published in Rene's I Was "*Canada's Cancer Nurse*," p. 16.
126. Ibid., p. 5.
127. Michael Bliss, *Banting: A Biography* (Toronto: McClelland and Stewart, 1984), p. 157.
128. Peyton Rous would not receive a Nobel Prize until 1966, although William Gye was making major inroads into cancer research all those years — using Rous's research.
129. Caisse, I Was "*Canada's Cancer Nurse*," p. 5.
130. Ibid., p. 6.
131. Ibid., p. 6.
132. Ibid., p. 6.
133. Ibid., p. 4.
134. Bliss, *Banting*, p. 183.

135. "Believes Herb Cured A Cancer Defied Surgery," *Toronto Daily Star*, February 24, 1932, p. 2.

136. Wallace Fonds, 2002, July 4, 1939, p. 175.

137. Author's files.

138. Caisse, I Was "*Canada's Cancer Nurse*," p. 10.

139. Bob Johnston, interview with Rene Caisse, CBC Radio, June 10, 1977.

140. Dr. McGibbon served during 1917–21 and 1925–1935.

141. Caisse, I Was "*Canada's Cancer Nurse*," p. 10.

142. Dr. McGibbon's copy of the *Medical Annual: A year book of treatment and practitioner's index*, 1910, recommended the use of synthetic coal tar derivatives with a wool fat and petroleum base for an antiseptic sedative, and to alleviate eczema and skin troubles, a soap with coal tar, now known to be carcinogenic. Dr. McGibbon would die October 10, 1936, reportedly of pneumonia, but it would be acknowledged at the July 1939 cancer commission hearings that he died of cancer.

143. W.D. Cosbie, *Toronto General Hospital 1819-1965: A Chronicle* (Toronto: MacMillan, 1975), pp. 188–190, 225.

144. Ontario Legislature, Sessional Paper No. 41, 1932.

145. The Royal Commission on the Use of Radium & X-Rays in the Treatment of the Sick. Minutes of meeting, November 23, 1934. Archives of Ontario, RG10-106-11-8.

146. "Doctors Back Nurse Claiming Secret Herb Aids Cancer Victims," *Toronto Daily Star*, January 23, 1932, p. 2.

147. Wallace Fonds, 2002, July 4, 1939, Exhibit 46, pp. 293–295.

148. "Believes Herb Cured A Cancer Defied Surgery," *Toronto Daily Star*, February 24, 1932, pp. 1–2.

149. Roy A. Greenaway, *The News Game* (Toronto: Clarke, Irwin, 1966), pp. 70–71.

150. *The Toronto Star Centennial Magazine*, *The Hundred – A Celebration*, November 1992, p. 35.

151. *The Monitor* [Montreal], December 2, 1932.

152. Dr. Gary L. Glum, *Calling of an Angel* (Los Angeles: Silent Walker Publishing, 1988), p. 29.

153. Wallace Fonds, 2002, July 4, 1939, Exhibit 46, pp. 159–161.

154. Caisse, I Was "*Canada's Cancer Nurse*," p. 5.

155. Personnel records of the hospitals run by Veteran's Affairs Canada have not survived the years. Where she did the "full-time nursing" and just what years she worked in the Christie Street Hospital laboratories cannot be verified for this reason.

156. The actual date when she moved to 387 Sherbourne from Breadalbane Street cannot be verified. A 1932 letter in her files was addressed to Apt. 204, but it was vacant in the 1932 City Directory and another person was recorded in the next year. She was listed as living in the De Los Apartments, Apt. 303, only in the 1933 Toronto City Directory.

157. William Kilbourn, *Toronto Remembered* (Toronto: Stoddard Publishing, 1984), p. 132.

158. Peterborough City Directory, May 1935.

159. Caisse, I Was "*Canada's Cancer Nurse*," p. 7.

160. Fraser and Allen, "Could Essiac Halt Cancer?" p. 16.

161. Rene named Dr. Noble as the chief of the College of Physicians and

Surgeons in both her 1966 autobiography and the *Homemaker's* article in 1977. However, Dr. Noble did not take that job until January 1, 1937.

162. Jack Moranz, "Toronto Personalities" [drawing], *Toronto Daily Star*, August 23, 1932.
163. Canadian Mothercraft Society files, Toronto.

Chapter 4

164. "Deaths by Cancer in Recent Years Show an Increase," *Muskoka Herald*, April 11, 1935.
165. "Tobacco Outlook Reported Bright," *Muskoka Health*, April 4, 1935.
166. *Contrary to Nature*, U.S. Dept. of Health, Education and Welfare Publication (NIH) 79-720, 1979.
167. "Private Hospital," *Muskoka Herald*, January 29, 1891.
168. "Another Cancer Cure," *Muskoka Herald*, March 7, 1907.
169. Dr. Albert Bastedo was a member of council for the years 1929–1941, and mayor during 1946–1949.
170. *Summertimes: In Celebration of One Hundred Years of the Muskoka Lakes Association*, (Erin: Boston Mills Press, 1994), p. 114.
171. Boyer, *A Good Town Grew Here*, several entries.
172. Wallace Fonds, 2002. July 4, 1939, Exhibit 46, pp. 214–219.
173. Wallace Fonds, 2002. July 4, 1939, pp. 1255–1261.
174. Dr. James Albert "Bert" Faulkner, Liberal MPP for West Hastings, was appointed minister of health in the first Hepburn government, July 10, 1934, although it was his first time in the legislature. The Belleville physician was credited with completely changing the definition, admission, and treatment of Ontario's mentally ill. Incidentally, Dr. Faulkner's mother-in-law, Mrs. Vermelyea, was axed to death in front of his office by another of her sons-in-law who came from California to commit the act and return immediately thereafter.
175. Rene M. Caisse, letter to Dr. Faulkner, April 26, 1935.
176. "Bracebridge Council," *Muskoka Herald*, May 16, 1935.
177. Kelly had been posted to Huntsville as a Salvation Army captain and played bass tuba in the popular Anglo-Canadian Leather Company band in Bracebridge.
178. "Petition Circulated," *Muskoka Herald*, May 16, 1935.
179. Wilbert Richards, letter to the Hon. Mitch Hepburn, May 10, 1935.
180. Dr. W. Mosely, letter to Dr. J.W.S. McCullough, June 13, 1935.
181. "Miss Rene Caisse's Cancer Hospital," *Muskoka Herald*, July 11, 1935.
182. Dr. W. Mosely, inspector of private hospitals, memo of visit to Bracebridge, July 8 and July 9, 1935.
183. "Deputation on Behalf of Miss Caisse," *Muskoka Herald*, August 15, 1935.
184. "Deputation on Behalf of Miss Rene Caisse," *Muskoka Herald*, January 16, 1936.
185. "Miss Rene Caisse's Cancer Hospital," *Muskoka Herald*, July 11, 1935.
186. "Card of Thanks," *Muskoka Herald*, August 15, 1935.
187. "Miss Caisse Opens Clinic," *Muskoka Herald*, August 29, 1935.
188. Fraser and Allen, "Could Essiac Halt Cancer?" p. 16.
189. Mary McPherson, interview with the author, March 25, 1996.
190. Fraser and Allen, "Could Essiac Halt Cancer?" p. 16.
191. Wallace Fonds, 2002. Proceedings of a Sub-Committee of the Commission

for the Investigation of Cancer Remedies, February 4, 1939, p. 9.
192. Ibid., p. 7.
193. Ibid., p. 6.
194. Valeen C. Slater, *Rene Caisse McGaughey*, c1979.
195. Mabel Haylett (Wright), RN, "Bracebridge Isolation Hospital, 1937," p. 20, in *Looking at Our Century*, by Patricia Boyer and others. (Bracebridge: Herald-Gazette Press, 1975).
196. "Nurses," *Muskoka Herald*, November 7, 1935.
197. "Annual Report," Red Cross Society, *Muskoka Herald*, October 31, 1935.
198. "Doctors to Probe Cancer Treatment," *Mail and Empire*, September 25, 1935.
199. "Department to Probe Miss Caisse's Treatment," *Muskoka Herald*, September 26, 1935.
200. "Ottawa Civic," *Muskoka Herald*, November 14, 1935.
201. "New Cancer Serum Being Given Trial," *Muskoka Herald*, December 26, 1935.
202. "Quake Rocks Town," *Muskoka Herald*, November 7, 1935.

Chapter 5

203. "Petition on Behalf of Miss Rene Caisse," *Muskoka Herald*, January 16, 1936, p. 1.
204. "Personal and Social," *Muskoka Herald*, May 21, 1936.
205. "A Tribute to Miss Caisse," *Bracebridge Gazette*, May 14, 1936.
206. Wallace Fonds, 2002, July 4, 1939, Exhibit 46, pp. 156, 157.
207. "Was Cancer Patient," *Muskoka Herald*, June 4, 1936.
208. Ibid.
209. John T. Saywell, *Just Call Me Mitch* (Toronto: University of Toronto Press, 1991), p. 208.
210. "Court Refuses to Condemn Sunday Ice Men in This Heat," *Evening Telegram*, July 11, 1936, p. 3.
211. "Nurse is Promised Aid for Research," *Toronto Daily Star*, July 11, 1936, p. 16.
212. "Cancer Cure Claimed for Bracebridge Nurse," *The Globe*, July 11, 1936, p. 11.
213. "Assure Bracebridge Nurse Aid in Her Cancer 'Cure'," *Evening Telegram*, July 11, 1936, p. 3.
214. "Sir Frederick Banting to Test Cancer Treatment," *Muskoka Herald*, July 16, 1936, p. 1.
215. "To the Editor," *Evening Telegram*, July 17, 1936, p. 6.
216. "Need for Cancer Clinics to Assure Early Diagnosis," *Muskoka Herald*, July 11, 1936, p. 12.
217. Bliss, *Banting*, p. 215.
218. Caisse, I Was "Canada's Cancer Nurse," p. 5.
219. Sir Frederick Banting, letter to Rene Caisse, July 23, 1936.
220. Bliss, *Banting*, various pages.
221. An unidentified newspaper clipping, probably from the *Toronto Star*, 1934 or 1935, Archives of Ontario, RG10-106-11.2.
222. Bliss, *Banting*, p. 184.
223. J. Frank Kelly, M.L.A., letter to Rene M. Caisse, July 29, 1936.
224. Fraser and Allen, "Could Essiac Halt Cancer?" p. 18.
225. "Miss Caisse to Prove Treatments Value," *Muskoka Herald*, August 6, 1936, p. 1.
226. Edward was never crowned; he abdicated in December 1936 and his brother George VI ascended to the throne.
227. Rene would try to reach the king again three years later, and in an almost

identical letter from the secretary to the governor general was told that her petition was referred to the Department of Pensions and National Health. Her next try, in the summer of 1960, was to the Duke of Edinburgh, whose response regarding her "highly technical medical matters" once again was routed to the governor general.

228. Wallace Fonds, 2002, July 4, 1939, Exhibit 48, pp. 293–294.
229. Caisse, I Was "Canada's Cancer Nurse," p. 16.
230. "Cheery Chatter," Bracebridge Gazette, December 16, 1937.
231. Wallace Fonds, 2002, July 4, 1939, Exhibit 46, p. 82.
232. The controversial use of radium continues to the present time. Historically, the devastating effects of further damage to the patient and the injury and death of hundreds of health professionals exposed to the toxic and burning radiation during its administration have been widely documented in scientific literature and by enraged investigative researchers. In recent years radium damage has been reduced by new protective technology.
233. Mary McPherson's reminiscences, c1994. Author's files.
234. Fraser and Allen, "Could Essiac Halt Cancer?" p. 19.

Chapter 6

235. "American Offer to Miss Rene Caisse," Muskoka Herald, August 20, 1936.
236. "Miss Rene Caisse Has Attractive U.S. Offer," Muskoka Herald, October 15, 1936.
237. "Cancer 'Remedy' Claimed in Bracebridge Goes to U.S.A.," The Globe, October 19, 1936.
238. "Nurse Spurned in Ontario Claims U.S. Clinic Satisfied Cancer Treatment Helpful," Evening Telegram, January 5, 1937, p. 2.
239. The Globe's story further confuses the date of Rene's discovery.
240. "Cancer 'Remedy' Claimed in Bracebridge Goes to U.S.A.," The Globe, October 19, 1936.
241. Dr. Wolfer, letter to Dr. Noble, August 31, 1937. In Wallace Fonds, 2002, July 4, 1939, Exhibit 46, p. 88.
242. "Personals," Muskoka Herald, November 26, 1936.
243. "Miss Caisse Going to U.S.," Muskoka Herald, October 29, 1936, p. 1.
244. Ibid.
245. Wallace Fonds, 2002, July 4, 1939, pp. 90–93.
246. "Nurse Spurned in Ontario Claims U.S. Clinic Satisfied Cancer Treatment Helpful," Evening Telegram, January 5, 1937.
247. Dr. John A. Wolfer, letter to "To Whom it May Concern," January 7, 1937.
248. "Local Items," Muskoka Herald, January 21, 1937.
249. Glum, "Calling of An Angel," p. 42.
250. Ibid., p. 42.
251. Ibid., pp. 42–43.
252. Dr. John A. Wolfer, letter to Dr. Noble, January 14, 1938. Wallace Fonds, 2002, July 4, 1939, Exhibit 46, p. 96.
253. Rene spelled the word "ampules."
254. Dr. John A. Wolfer, letter to Dr. A. Moir, August 12, 1937. Wallace Fonds, 2002, July 4, 1939, Exhibit 46, p. 87.
255. Dr. Wilberforce Aikens had retired from his twenty-two-year association with the college on January 1, 1937, when Dr. Noble took over.
256. The cases were presented in detail to the Commission for the Investigation

of Cancer Remedies, July 4, 1939.

257. Dr. John A. Wolfer, letter to Dr. Noble, August 31, 1937. Wallace Fonds, 2002, July 4, 1939, Exhibit 46, pp. 88, 89.

258. Ibid., pp. 90+. Compiled from tabulation of cases.

259. Fraser and Allen, "Could Essiac Halt Cancer?" p. 20.

260. Rene's lack of recollection for detail during the 1977 interviews with *Homemaker's Magazine* researchers undoubtedly caused an overstatement of numbers.

261. Caisse, I Was *"Canada's Cancer Nurse,"* p. 11.

262. "Nurse Spurned in Ontario Claims U.S. Clinic Satisfied Cancer Treatment Helpful," *Evening Telegram*, January 5, 1937, p. 2.

263. "Local Support for Miss Caisse Shown in Large Meeting," *Muskoka Herald*, March 18, 1937, pp. 1–2.

264. "Sanity Discussed," *Varsity*, March 12, 1937.

265. "Local Support for Miss Caisse Shown in Large Meeting," *Muskoka Herald*, March 18, 1937, p. 2.

266. "Miss Caisse Cancer Work Petition Signed by 17,000," *Muskoka Herald*, March 25, 1937, p. 1.

267. Caisse, I Was *"Canada's Cancer Nurse,"* p. 4. (Cox misspelled his name as "Lockhead.")

268. "Visits Sir Fred Banting About Cancer Treatment," *Evening Telegram*, March 16, 1937.

269. "Again Ask Medical Recognition of Miss Caisse's Cancer Work," *Muskoka Herald*, March 18, 1937, p. 4.

270. Ibid.

271. "Personals," *Muskoka Herald*, April 22, 1937.

272. "Rene M. Caisse Cancer Treatment," *Muskoka Herald*, June 3, 1937.

273. "Cancer Clinic Being Enlarged," *Muskoka Herald*, May 6, 1937.

274. "Cheery Chatter," *Bracebridge Gazette*, December 16, 1937.

275. "Rene M. Caisse Cancer Treatment," *Muskoka Herald*, June 3, 1937.

276. Robert J. Boyer told the author in September 2001 that Rene would regularly do that when stories appeared about her activities.

277. "Agitation for Recognition of Miss Caisse Persists," *Muskoka Herald*, June 24, 1937.

278. "I Am Not Concerned About Money—Miss Caisse," *Huntsville Forester*, July 22, 1937.

279. "Province Tests Nurse's Cancer Treatment," *Evening Telegram*, July 26, 1937, p. 1.

280. "If Necessary, We'll Pass Act to Help Miss Rene Caisse—Hepburn," *Muskoka Herald*, July 29, 1937, p. 1.

281. "Province Tests Nurse's Cancer Treatment," *Evening Telegram*, July 26, 1937, p. 1.

282. "Reported Treatment for Cancer is being Referred to Banting," *Globe and Mail*, July 27, 1937.

283. "Ontario Asks Cancer Test by Scientist," *San Francisco Daily News* (UP), July 27, 1937.

284. "Banting on Cancer," *Canadian Comment*, March 1938, pp. 22–23.

285. Dr. G.J. Forster, letter to Dr. Faulkner, 1937. Archives of Ontario, RG10-106-32.9.

286. Canadian Mothercraft Society files, Toronto.

287. "Hepburn Permits Caisse to Practice," *Toronto Daily Star*, August 6, 1937.

288. Harry Corwin Nixon, a farmer from St. George, Ontario, would be premier during 1943.

289. Haylett, "Bracebridge Isolation Hospital, 1937," p. 19.
290. Advertisement, *Muskoka Herald*, July 15, 1937.

Chapter 7

291. "Californian Tests Caisse Treatment," *Muskoka Herald*, August 12, 1937, p. 1.
292. Emma Carson, MD, *'Essiac' Cancer Treatment Endorsed by Eminent Physician: Report on visit to Caisse Cancer Clinic, Bracebridge, Ontario, Canada* (Los Angeles, Cal., U.S.A. c1938), p. 2.
293. "Californian Tests Caisse Treatment," *Muskoka Herald*, August 12, 1937, p. 1.
294. Carson, *'Essiac' Cancer Treatment Endorsed by Eminent Physician*, p. 2.
295. Ibid., pp. 2–3.
296. Ibid., p. 7.
297. Ibid., p. 8.
298. "Physician Endorses Miss Caisse," *Huntsville Forester*, August 26, 1937.
299. Probably in preparation for the publication of her biography in 1966, Rene jotted the date August 12, 1937, on the first page of an undated, typed, five-page extract of Dr. Carson's report (no original seems to have survived), which became the entry about Dr. Carson's visit. Pages two to five of that extract were reprinted in I Was *"Canada's Cancer Nurse,"* pp. 12–15, and the report in the entry was dated August 12, 1937. This date was, of course, the first day of Dr. Carson's visit to the clinic. Reference to Dr. Carson's visit "including the months of June and July" are unsubstantiated.
300. Carson, *'Essiac' Cancer Treatment Endorsed by Eminent Physician: Report on visit to Caisse Cancer Clinic, Bracebridge, Ontario, Canada.*
301. "Attorney-General of New York and Rochester M.D. Observe Miss Caisse's Cancer Clinic," *Bracebridge Gazette*, August 26, 1937, p. 5.
302. "American Doctors Praise Miss Caisse's Work at Cancer Clinic," *Bracebridge Gazette*, September 2, 1937, p. 5.
303. Wallace Fonds, 2002, July 4, 1939, p. 1267.
304. Caisse, I Was *"Canada's Cancer Nurse,"* p. 11.
305. "Visiting Doctors Endorse Miss Caisse" [editorial], *Muskoka Herald*, September 2, 1937, p. 2.
306. "American Doctors Praise Miss Caisse's Work at Cancer Clinic," *Bracebridge Gazette*, September 2, 1937, p. 5.
307. Caisse, I Was *"Canada's Cancer Nurse,"* p. 12.
308. Research could not identify the organization, its location, or its proceedings.
309. "Prominent U.S. Doctor Commends Miss Caisse," *Muskoka Herald*, September 2, 1937, p. 1.
310. "American Doctors Praise Miss Caisse's Work at Cancer Clinic," *Bracebridge Gazette*, September 2, 1937, p. 5.
311. "Personals," *Bracebridge Gazette*, September 9, 1937.
312. The Dionne Quintuplets were born in Callandar, Ontario, May 28, 1934, about 160 kilometres north of Bracebridge.
313. Susan Pryke, *Huntsville: With Spirit and Resolve* (Huntsville: Fox Meadow Creations, 2000), p. 204.
314. The alliance would haunt Rene on July 1939, when a letter written by Dr. A.H. Jeffrey to Dr. Noble in January 15, 1938, was presented to the cancer commission noting, "She also took an active part in the recent provincial election on the side of the Liberals, which will have to be remembered by the party."

315. "An Open Letter To the Electors," *Muskoka Herald*, September 30, 1937, p. 5.

316. "The Miss Caisse Cancer Clinic," *Muskoka Herald*, September 30, 1937, p. 8.

317. Thomas, the brother of the famous "Grip" cartoonist John Wilson Bengough, who immortalized Sir John A. Macdonald in caricature, was known as the "Dean of Canadian Shorthand Reporters."

318. "Urges Public to Aid Miss Rene Caisse," *Muskoka Herald*, September 9, 1937.

319. This was career politician Earl Rowe's one-time try for provincial involvement after he resigned from the ill-fated Bennett federal government in 1935 and took on the leadership of the Ontario Conservative Party. Rowe did not unseat Hepburn's Liberals, quit, and later returned to the House of Commons in 1940.

320. Dr. Faulkner would continue as Thurlow Township's medical officer of health and die of health problems in 1944. One of his sons, Farley, became famous fighting communism at Massey Hall rallies in the 1950s.

321. "Says Bracebridge Clinic helps cancer sufferers," *Porcupine Advance*, September 2, 1937, pp. 1, 6.

322. The highly respected lawyer had come to her as a patient and obtained Essiac treatments for himself and his wife, Beatrice. Now a widower, he appeared to take a special interest in Rene and her problems.

323. Fraser and Allen, "Could Essiac Halt Cancer?" p. 20.

324. Glum, *Calling of An Angel*, p. 48.

325. This may refer to Dr. George McCullagh of Orono.

326. Rene M. Caisse, letter to the Hon. Mitch Hepburn, November 13, 1937. Archives of Ontario, RG 10-106.

327. Saywell, *Just Call me Mitch*, p. 97.

328. Robert Bothwell and William Kilbourn, *C.D. Howe: A Biography* (Toronto: McClelland and Stewart, 1979), p. 68.

329. "Slaght Candidate?" *Muskoka Herald* [editorial], February 14, 1935, p. 4.

330. The "experiences" referred to here occurred in March when the petition was delivered to them at Queen's Park.

331. Advertisement, *Bracebridge Gazette*, December 23, 1937.

Chapter 8

332. "Alliston Editor Supports Miss Caisse's Cause," *Bracebridge Gazette*, January 13, 1938.

333. Mutilated newspaper clipping, probably from February 1938, Archives of Ontario, RG10-106.

334. "Government May Demand Secret of Cancer Serums," *Muskoka Herald*, February 10, 1938, p. 1.

335. Ibid.

336. "Doctors Seek Law to Bare All Cancer 'Cures'," *Globe and Mail*, February 8, 1938, p. 1.

337. Glum, *Calling of an Angel*, p. 57.

338. "Demand Government Keep Promise Given to Miss Caisse," *Muskoka Herald*, February 17, 1938, p. 1.

339. "Government May Demand Secret of Cancer Serums," *Muskoka Herald*, February 10, 1938, p. 1.

340. "Labor Men Deplore Hepburn stand on Cancer," *Muskoka Herald*, February 17, 1938, p. 1.

341. "Comment," *Bracebridge Gazette*, January 14, 1937, p. 1.
342. "Demand Government Keep Promise Given to Miss Caisse," *Muskoka Herald*, February 17, 1938, p. 1.
343. "The Cancer Cure 'Purge'," *Muskoka Herald* [editorial], February 17, 1938.
344. "Notice of Application to Parliament," *Ontario Gazette*, February 22, 1938, p. 310.
345. "No Date Granted Yet for Presenting Petition," *Muskoka Herald*, February 24, 1938, p. 1.
346. One would wonder at Dr. Guyatt's reaction to this clashing opposition of his University of Toronto colleague.
347. "Warns of Cancer 'Secrets' Killing chances for Cure," *Evening Telegram*, February 28, 1938.
348. Clerk, Legislative Assembly, letter to McGaughey & Little, February 25, 1938.
349. "Rejected Bill Now to Come Before House," *Globe and Mail*, March 3, 1938.
350. "Miss Caisse's Private Bill," *Muskoka Herald*, March 3, 1938.
351. "Presentation Made to Dean O'Leary," *Muskoka Herald*, March 3, 1938.
352. "The Drastic Cancer Bill" [editorial], *Muskoka Herald*, March 17, 1938.
353. "Ontario Bill Launched to Compel Revelation of Cancer Serum Facts," *Evening Telegram*, March 9, 1938, p. 17.
354. "Demand Government Keep Promise Given to Miss Caisse," *Muskoka Herald*, February 17, 1938.
355. Herbert A. Bruce, "The Cancer Problem," *Journal of the* C.M.A., 12, March 1923, pp. 13–19.
356. Herbert A. Bruce, "Cancer Centres Abroad," in C.J.M. & S., 71, 1932, pp. 30–34.
357. Nancy R. Thompson (ed.), *A Good Town Continues: Bracebridge 1915-1999* (Town of Bracebridge, 125th Anniversary Committee, 1999), p. 384.
358. Lt. Gov. Herbert A. Bruce, letter to Dr. R.E. Wodehouse, Deputy Minister of Pensions and National Health, January 15, 1937.
359. Dr. J. G. Cunningham, letter to Dr. B.T. McGhie, January 14, 1937.
360. "Act Planned to Control Cancer Cures," *Globe and Mail*, March 5, 1938.
361. "Ontario Bill Launched to Compel Revelation of Cancer Serum Facts," *Evening Telegram*, March 9, 1938, p. 17.
362. "Ask Legislature to Force Secret of Cancer Remedies," *Muskoka Herald*, March 10, 1938, pp. 1+.
363. "Nurse Caisse May Close Up Cancer Clinic," *Globe and Mail*, March 10, 1938, p. 1.
364. "House Rules May Prevent Nurse receiving Authority to Treat Cancer Patients," *Evening Telegram*, March 1, 1938.
365. "Demand Government Keep Promise Given to Miss Caisse," *Muskoka Herald*, February 17, 1938.
366. "Kirby Cancer Act Put into Force; Miss Caisse Closes Bracebridge Clinic," *Muskoka Herald*, May 26, 1938, pp. 1+.
367. "Act Planned to Control Cancer Cures," *Globe and Mail*, March 5, 1938.
368. "No Date Granted Yet for Presenting Petition," *Muskoka Herald*, February 24, 1938, p. 1.
369. The huge number of petitioners cited has no rational basis in fact, and only a few sheets of the volumes have survived to count. Rene stated in her petition to the government of February 22, 1938, that she had twenty-eight thousand signatures, and it seems unlikely that in one month twice as many names could have been accumulated for submission to the legislature. Bracebridge had a population of less than twenty-five hundred, and

Ontario's was under 3 million.

370. "Kirby Cancer Act Put into Force, Miss Caisse Closes Bracebridge Clinic," *Muskoka Herald*, May 26, 1938, p. 1.

371. "Legislature Committee Votes Down Miss Caisse's Cancer Treatment," *Muskoka Herald*, March 31, 1938.

372. This detail of the March 24 debate has been drawn from the *Toronto Daily Star*, March 24, 1938; *Globe and Mail*, March 25, 1938; and *Muskoka Herald*, March 31, 1938.

373. "Committee Rejects Nurse's Special Bill," *Globe and Mail*, March 25, 1938, p. 15.

374. "Hints Cabal of Doctors Against Cancer Treatment," *Toronto Daily Star*, March 24, 1938, p. 1.

375. "Committee Rejects Nurse's Special Bill," *Globe and Mail*, March 25, 1938, p. 15.

376. "Hints Cabal of Doctors Against Cancer Treatment," *Toronto Daily Star*, March 24, 1938, p. 1.

377. Dr. Mahlon Locke, a foot doctor in eastern Ontario, managed an astonishing practice to which some two thousand patients per day attended for his "healing" foot "twists." He turned Williamsburg into a major centre for visitors seeking treatments for various medical conditions. The Ontario College of Physicians and Surgeons, the CMA, and the province were absorbed in the phenomena during 1927–1938 when the treatment lost its appeal.

378. Donald Carrick, who later worked with Arthur Slaght after graduation from 1934 to 1941, caught the political bug, becoming member of Parliament for Toronto's influential Trinity riding, 1954–1957.

379. "Legislature Committee Votes Down Miss Caisse's Cancer Treatment," *Muskoka Herald*, March 31, 1938.

380. Caisse, I Was *"Canada's Cancer Nurse,"* p. 22. (This is the only identified source for the balance of votes.)

381. "Hints Cabal of Doctors Against Cancer Treatment," *Toronto Daily Star*, March 24, 1938, p. 1.

382. "Turn Down Miss Caisse," *Muskoka Herald* [editorial], March 31, 1938.

383. "Committee Rejects Nurse's Special Bill," *Globe and Mail*, March 25, 1938, p. 15.

384. Caisse, I Was *"Canada's Cancer Nurse,"* p. 22.

385. Donald M. Fleming would become the Honourable Donald Fleming, serving in the House of Commons as minister of finance, attorney general, and minister of justice, 1957–1963.

386. "Police Seek Dr. Bruce's Assailants," *Globe and Mail*, March 31, 1938, p. 1.

387. "Ontario Delays Cancer 'Cure' Probe Hoping Ottawa May Take Action," *Globe and Mail*, March 31, 1938, p. 1.

388. Rene M. Caisse, letter to the Hon. Mitchell Hepburn, May 23, 1938.

389. Prime Minister Mitch Hepburn, letter to T.F. Stevenson, March 25, 1938.

390. Berry Rockwell, letter to Premier Hepburn, April 3, 1938.

391. "Miss Caisse Taking a Rest," *Muskoka Herald*, March 31, 1938, p. 1.

Chapter 9

392. A.G.L. McNaughton, "Investigation of Cancer Cures," National Research Council, Report. May 5, 1938, p. 3.

393. Ibid.

394. "Miss Caisse's Private Bill," *Muskoka Herald*, March 3, 1938.

395. "Ontario Delays Cancer 'Cure' Probe Hoping Ottawa May Take Action," *Globe*

and Mail, March 31, 1938, p. 1.

396. McNaughton, "Investigation of Cancer Cures," p. 1.

397. "Ontario Left to Act Along on Cancer Probe," *Muskoka Herald*, May 19, 1938, p. 8.

398. A.G.L. McNaughton, letter to L.P. Picard, October 17, 1938.

399. "Miss Caisse Will Not Re-open Clinic as Reported in Toronto Newspapers," *Muskoka Herald*, June 2, 1938, pp. 1+.

400. "Kirby Cancer Act Put into Force; Miss Caisse Closes Bracebridge Clinic," *Muskoka Herald*, May 26, 1938, pp. 1, 2, 8.

401. McGaughey & Little, letter to the Hon. Harold Kirby, May 25, 1938.

402. Rene Caisse, letter to the Hon. Mitch Hepburn, May 23, 1938.

403. MaGaughey & Little, letter to the Hon. Harold Kirby, May 25, 1938.

404. "Kirby Cancer Act Put into Force; Miss Caisse Closes Bracebridge Clinic," *Muskoka Herald*, May 26, 1938, pp. 1, 2, 8.

405. Some say that Dr. McInnis prescribed Rene's treatment for his Timmins colleague Dr. Herbert Minthorn, who developed cancer in his chest.

406. "Press Support for Miss Caisse," *Muskoka Herald*, June 16, 1938, p. 1.

407. "Miss Caisse's Cancer Clinic Closed as New Law Takes Effect," *Bracebridge Gazette*, May 26, 1938, p. 1.

408. "Miss Caisse Will Not Re-open Clinic as Reported in Toronto Newspapers," *Muskoka Herald*, June 2, 1938, pp. 1+.

409. M.F. Hepburn, letter to Chas. Naylor, June 1, 1938.

410. Frost's mother, Margaret, had been living with cancer since her breast surgery in 1918.

411. Frost & Frost. His younger brother Cecil was also entrenched in conservative matters.

412. Leslie M. Frost, letter to John Thornbury, June 4, 1938.

413. "Miss Caisse May Re-open Her Clinic," *Huntsville Forester*, June 9, 1938, p. 1.

414. Saywell, *Just Call Me Mitch*, p. 407.

415. "Cancer Clinic Still Closed," *Bracebridge Gazette*, June 30, 1938.

416. Editorial notes, *Muskoka Herald*, August 4, 1938.

417. "Laymen in Majority for Cancer Inquiry," *Toronto Daily Star*, June 27, 1938, p. 3.

418. "Cancer Clinic," *Muskoka Herald*, August 11, 1938, p. 1.

419. Shortly after her illness, she married and was soon widowed, but in the early 1930s was well enough to marry Norman King and manage his small grocery in their modest home on Lake Street while he worked at CGE. She died in 1943, after living all those productive years without any recurrence of cancer.

420. Mrs. Eustace Charles McGaughey, interview with the author, October 20, 1997.

421. "No Date Granted Yet for Presenting Petition," *Muskoka Herald*, February 24, 1938, p. 1.

422. Dr. A.W. Blair, letter to Dr. R.T. Noble, January 13, 1938, Wallace Fonds, 2002, July 4, 1939, p. 66.

423. Robert T. Noble, letter to the Hon. Mr. Justice Gillanders, September 13, 1938.

424. The secretary's father was the renowned Canadian organist Frederic Tristan Egener.

425. Ivan Slater, who worked at the Bird Woollen Mill information bureau, was asked to recommend anyone reliable to rush a package to Toronto safely. Ivan offered to go and took along his friend Jackson McIllmoyle.

426. "The Roundtowner," *Muskoka Herald*, September 29, 1938, p. 5.

427. Commission meetings detail, September to December 1938, in Wallace

Fonds, 2002.

428. This was probably Dr. Minthorn, MB, University of Toronto, 1908.

429. Rene M. Caisse, letter to the "Royal Cancer Commission" [sic], October 27, 1938.

430. Dr. & Mrs. Edward Ellis had been handling a personal tragedy since April, when their daughter Ann Carol had survived a fifteen-foot fall on the rocks at the town wharf but fractured her skull.

431. "Dr. Lawson to Probe Nursing Home Death," *Toronto Daily Star*, September 14, 1938.

432. "Caisse Cancer Treatment Not Connected with the Death of Emsdale Patient," *Muskoka Herald*, October 6, 1938, p. 1.

433. All further hearings were identified as "Second Day," "Third Day," etc.

434. F.G. Banting and J.L. Bowlby, 1938, National Archives of Canada, NAC, RE-77.

Chapter 10

435. "Social and Personal," *Muskoka Herald*, February 2, 1939.

436. Rene M. Caisse, letter to Dr. T.H. Callahan, January 13, 1939.

437. "Name Committee of 2 to Probe Caisse Claims," *Globe and Mail*, January 14, 1939.

438. Rene M. Caisse, letter to Mr. Egener, February 1, 1939.

439. Clinic details and interviews are taken from Proceedings of a Sub-Committee of the Commission for the Investigation of Cancer Remedies, February 4, 1939, in Wallace Fonds, 2002.

440. There is no record of the wording of the resume, nor did it seem to have been included in the documentation.

441. Bert Rawson served on town council from 1932 to 1935, when presumably his poor health discouraged him from seeking a further term.

442. "Benefited By Treatment Given By Nurse Caisse 22 Say at Cancer Probe," *Evening Telegram*, February 4, 1939.

443. "Cancer Commissioners Visit Rene Caisse Clinic," *Muskoka Herald*, February 9, 1939, p. 1.

444. One can picture Bob Boyer sitting outside the restricted area in Rene's clinic, gleaning information from each patient as he or she returned from the gruelling interviews.

445. "Cancer Commissioners Visit Rene Caisse Clinic," *Muskoka Herald*, February 9, 1939, p. 1.

446. "Social and Personal," *Muskoka Herald*, February 23, 1939.

447. "Patients Again Treated at Miss Caisse's Clinic," *Muskoka Herald*, March 16, 1939, p. 1.

448. Dr. T.H. Callahan, letter to Chairman and Commissioners [Commission for the Investigation of Cancer Remedies], February 1939. R.C. Wallace Papers.

449. It is presumed that Dr. Minthorn was receiving Essiac treatments, but he neglected to tell the commissioners of his personal trauma.

450. Dr. H.L. Minthorn, letter to Dr. T.H. Callahan, February 29, 1939. R.C. Wallace Papers.

451. Wallace Fonds, 2002, Proceedings of the Commission for the Investigation of Cancer Remedies, March 30 and 31, 1939.

452. Rene M. Caisse, letter to the Hon. Mitch Hepburn, April 19, 1939.

453. Wallace Fonds, 2002. Proceedings of the Commission for the Investigation

of Cancer Remedies, July 4, 1939, Exhibit 47, pp. 240–248.

454. Rene M. Caisse, letter to the Hon. Mitch Hepburn, April 19, 1939.

455. Wallace Fonds, 2002. Proceedings of the Commission for the Investigation of Cancer Remedies, July 4, 1939, Exhibit 46, p. 62.

456. Ibid., pp. 105–136.

457. Ibid., pp. 180–207.

458. Ibid., p. 190.

459. Ibid., p. 183.

460. Ibid., Exhibit 47, pp. 543–546.

461. Rene M. Caisse, letter to the Hon. Mitch Hepburn, April 19, 1939.

462. The legislature reopened on March 8, 1939, with George Drew as Tory opposition leader.

463. Harold J. Kirby, Minister of Health, letter to Rene M. Caisse, April 28, 1939.

Chapter 11

464. Wallace Fonds, 2002, The Commission for the Investigation of Cancer Remedies, Interim Report, December 31, 1939.

465. Wallace Fonds, 2002, Proceedings of the Commission for the Investigation of Cancer Remedies, July 4, 1939, p. 1243.

466. Caisse, I Was "Canada's Cancer Nurse," p. 23.

467. Wallace Fonds, 2002, Proceedings of the Commission for the Investigation of Cancer Remedies, July 4, 1939, p. 1246.

468. Ibid., Exhibit 46, p. 57.

469. Ibid., pp. 1327–1331.

470. Ibid., Exhibit 46, p. 212.

471. Nellie McVittie died in 1992, her ninety-ninth year.

472. Ibid., pp. 1349G–1339L.

473. Commission stenographers recorded his name as both "McVee" and "McDee."

474. Dr. McGibbon died of reported pneumonia on October 10, 1936.

475. Dr. Callahan, letter to Dr. Wallace, February 19, 1939.

476. Wallace Fonds, 2002, Proceedings of the Commission for the Investigation of Cancer Remedies, July 4, 1939, pp. 1387–1398.

477. Ibid, pp. 1387–1410.

478. It is not clear if Rene was present at this discussion.

479. Ibid., Exhibit 46, pp. 293–295.

480. Ibid., pp. 159–162.

481. Ibid, p. 1039.

482. The stenographic records of hundreds of written exhibits plus the spoken words at the February, March, and July meetings resulted in duplication and even more typed transcripts. Case histories are scattered throughout. The style of organization makes it difficult to verify details presented to the commissioners. The page numbering by the official stenographers, Newall & Co., presents various series of typed interwoven material throughout several volumes.

Chapter 12

483. Rene Caisse, letter to the Hon. Mr. Harold Kirby, November 2, 1939.

484. Mr. Justice Gillanders, letter to Dr. R.C. Wallace, November 16, 1939.

485. When he enlisted in active war service in June 1942 to serve with the Lorne Scots, the commissioners each donated two dollars for a departing gift. While at war, he and his wife, Norah, exchanged hundreds of letters, which, after his death in 1988, she edited for a book called *A Time Apart: Letters of Love and War 1941–1945*, c1999. In 2003, Charlotte Gray reprinted one of their letters in her book *Canada, A Portrait in Letters, 1800–2000*.

486. "Miss Caisse Disputes Commission's Report," *Muskoka Herald*, February 8, 1940.

487. Wallace Fonds, 2002, The Commission for the Investigation of Cancer Remedies, Interim Report December 31, 1939.

488. "When Will Cancer Commission Report be Given?" *Muskoka Herald*, January 4, 1940, pp. 1, 4.

489. "No CureYet for Cancer, Probe Finds," *Globe and Mail*, January 11, 1940, pp. 1, 2.

490. Evidence of the dates of the actual hearings can be identified in the resulting proceedings of the commission. Other biographical writings about Rene M. Caisse offer a variety of incorrect dates. There had been little publicity of the hearings, no public involvement, and no coverage in the Toronto newspapers. The Royal York Hotel has no record of the booking because only the food service records survive. There never was a final report of the July 1939 hearings, nor was there ever a final report of commission hearings. The original transcripts are not in any record group of the Ontario Archives. This information was confirmed by their staff in 1977. The author is grateful that Dr. R.C. Wallace ensured that the papers of the activities in which he was involved as principal of Queen's University were placed, however casually, in his files, later to be placed in the University's Archive. The author raises concern over public access and use of the personal medical information that is documented in these transcripts. In the author's opinion, future researchers should have a need to know the data contained therein. Objective analysis of the findings may offer positive value to cancer research as regards to the Caisse remedy.

491. R.A. Leonardo, letter to Royal Ontario Cancer Commission, January 10, 1940.

492. Rene M. Caisse, "Cancer," *Muskoka Herald*, January 11, 1940, p. 1.

493. "Cancer Methods Probed by Ontario Commission," *Muskoka Herald*, January 18, 1940, p. 1.

494. "The Cancer Commission Reports," *Muskoka Herald* [editorial], January 18, 1940, p. 4.

495. Redmond Thomas, "Comment," *Bracebridge Gazette*, January 18, 1940, p. 1.

496. "Cancer Methods Probed by Ontario Commission," *Muskoka Herald*, January 18, 1940, p. 1.

497. "Miss Caisse's Clinic To Remain Open," *Huntsville Forester*, January 18, 1940, p. 1.

498. "Miss Caisse Disputes Commission's Report," *Muskoka Herald*, February 8, 1940, pp. 1, 8.

499. "Miss Caisse Disputes Cancer Committee Report," *Muskoka Herald*, March 7, 1940, pp. 1, 5.

500. Wallace Fonds, 2002, Proceedings of the Commission to Investigate Cancer Remedies, March 29, 1940, pp. 2155, 2158.

501. "Miss Caisse Disputes Cancer Committee Report," *Muskoka Herald*, March 7, 1940, pp. 1, 5.

502. Some thirty years later, Rene would express her detailed theories in her

autobiography, I Was "Canada's Cancer Nurse," pp. 16–19.

503. "Undergoes Operation," *Muskoka Herald*, November 7, 1940, p. 1.
504. Rene told the commission that she had an operation for gallstones. The Haigmeier Clinic was also an appropriate place to find rest and counselling for the exhaustion and discouragement she had suffered.
505. "Opening Lingerie and Gift Shop," *Muskoka Herald*, November 21, 1940.

Chapter 13

506. "Appointments Made at First Council Meeting," *Muskoka Herald*, January 9, 1941.
507. "Rene M. Caisse Closes Cancer Clinic Here," *Muskoka Herald*, January 23, 1941, p. 1. (This issue was actually dated January 23, 1940.)
508. Archives of Ontario, Deptartment of Health, RG10.
509. "Walkerville Clinic to Fight Cancer," *Muskoka Herald*, June 27, 1935.
510. Dominion of Canada Patent Number 398359, August 5, 1941.
511. Rene dropped the periods later and used the letters RMC in her labelling.
512. L.P. Teevens, letter to McGaughey & Little, September 22, 1941.
513. "Miss Caisse Conducting Clinics," *Huntsville Forester*, July 24, 1941.
514. J.G. Gillanders, letter to Frank Kirby, November 7, 1941.
515. J.G. Cunningham, letter to Dr. J.T. Phair, November 29, 1941.
516. Saywell, *Just Call Me Mitch*, p. 481.
517. J.J. Heagerty, MD, letter to Dr. Ray G. Hulburt, May 23, 1941.
518. "Death Takes C. McGaughey in North Bay," *North Bay Nugget*, October 21, 1943, p. 1.
519. Mrs. Charles Eustace McGaughey, Charles's daughter-in-law, spoke with the author on October 20, 1997, and recalled that Charles Sr. died of cancer.
520. "McGaughey Funeral is Held Today," *North Bay Nugget*, October 22, 1943, p. 1.
521. "Called by Death," *Muskoka Herald*, October 28, 1943.
522. Mary McPherson, interview with the author, 1996.
523. Bliss, *Banting*, p. 298.
524. He would retire and later die in his Bracebridge home in October 1997.
525. Canadian Mothercraft Society, 13th Annual Report, December 1944.
526. Sid Rodaway and Diane Malott, "What is Uranium King Stephen Roman's motive for chasing a cancer cure?" in *Business World*, July/August 1979, p. 11.
527. "Last Respectful Tribute," *Porcupine Advance*, May 16, 1946, p. 1.
528. Saywell, *Just Call Me Mitch*, p. 529.
529. Heather Minthorn Bozzer, conversation with the author, July 30, 1996.
530. "Doctor's Widow Recalls Early Days of Practice," Timmins Press, July 27, 1962.
531. "Pioneer Doctor in Cobalt Camp Headed Academy," *Globe*, December 29, 1953.
532. Vera Goltz, interview with the author, February 14, 1997.
533. "Mrs. George Allen," *Muskoka Herald*, September 11, 1947.
534. "Mrs. Joseph Caisse," *Muskoka Herald*, February 19, 1948, p. 5.
535. Vera Goltz, interview with the author, February 14, 1997.
536. The Muskoka District Health Unit would move across the street to 253 James Street in 1960.
537. N.F. Fisher to Rene M. Caisse, September 6, 1950, and May 3, 1951.
538. Alicia Dujovne Ortiz, *Eva Peron* (New York: St. Martin's Press, 1996), p. 324. (Translated by Shawn Fields.)
539. The property was sold to an investor in 1962; Rene held the mortgage for another ten years, during which time the property was leased to various

businesses and residents.

540. Robert's father, George W. Boyer, was long-time publisher of the *Muskoka Herald* and as a young man had taken Rene to a dance or two. George's wife, E. Victoria, worked with the paper until her death in 1977 at ninety years of age.

541. The Very Rev. Michael J. O'Leary of Rene's parish was named Monsignor that year.

542. Robert J. Boyer, interviews with the author, 2001.

543. He would die in February 1958 at eighty-seven years of age. One son, Dr. Robert L. Noble, distinguished himself as an anti-cancer drug researcher and discoverer of Vinblastine, based on plants.

544. Frank Henry, interview with the author, 1997.

545. Vera Goltz, interview with the author, February 14, 1997.

546. "Seven-man Foundation in Ontario to Conduct Cancer Research Work," *Montreal Gazette*, March 31, 1944.

547. Ibid.

548. Archives of Ontario, Dept. of Health, RG10-38.

549. Dr. J.T. Phair, letter to Dr. Jenkins, National Health Office in Victoria B.C., July 18, 1946.

550. Son of former medical officer of health in the 1930s, Dr. J.T. Phair.

551. Dr. Mackinnon Phillips, letter to Robert H. Brown, April 14, 1958.

552. Dr. Treleaven, letter to Dr. Phillips, April 14, 1958.

553. Dr. Deadman, letter to Dr. Matthew B. Dymond, July 18, 1960.

554. Rene M. Caisse, letter to Dr. W.G. Brown, October 6, 1958.

555. C.J. Telfer, letter to Mackinnon Phillips, May 29, 1958.

556. Leslie M. Frost, letter to Rene M. Caisse, September 18, 1958.

557. Dr. W.G. Brown, letter to R.A. Farrell, October 20, 1958.

558. Dr. M.B. Dymond, letter to R.J. Boyer, January 15, 1959.

559. Nat Morris [pseud.], *The Cancer Blackout, a history of denied and suppressed remedies* (Chicago: Regent House, c1959). (The author, whose name was really Maurice Natenburg, also published other versions.)

560. Glum, *Calling of an Angel*, pp. 111–122.

561. Fraser and Allen, "Could Essiac Halt Cancer?" p. 36.

562. Tufts University anniversary document, c1959, described its twenty-five-year medical class reunion. A biography of Dr. Charles A. Brusch is recorded along with description of the Brusch Medical Center.

563. Professor Emeritus of Gastroenterology, Boston University.

564. Professor Emeritus of Surgery, Harvard Medical School, and former chief of medical service at the Boston City Hospital.

565. Copy of an undated typed report headed "The Brusch Medical Clinic, Cambridge, Mass." in Rene Caisse's writing. The source of the typed pages that comprise up to Case 8 is unknown. Details of the testing and results are found in a number of other reports and letters provided to me by an anonymous researcher.

566. Fraser and Allen, "Could Essiac Halt Cancer?" p. 38.

567. Philip C. Merker, letter to Dr. Charles Brusch, June 19, 1959.

568. Glum, *Calling of an Angel*, pp. 127–128.

569. Caisse, I Was "Canada's Cancer Nurse," p. 19.

570. He was also chief of the Department of Pathology at Harvard, among other appointments.

571. Fraser and Allen, "Could Essiac Halt Cancer?" p. 38.

Chapter 14

572. Several letters in Rene M. Caisse archive, Bracebridge Public Library.
573. Glum, *Calling of an Angel*, pp. 133–134. The location of these records is unknown.
574. Leo V. Roy, "Essiac," May 1, 1961. A three-page typed essay signed by Dr. Roy.
575. W.G. Cosbie, medical director of the Ontario Cancer Treatment and Research Foundation, letter to J.C.C. Dawson, MD, registrar of the College of Physicians and Surgeons, and Dr. Matthew Dymond, Ontario minister of health.
576. Shulman, Morton, *Coroner* (Toronto: Fitzhenry & Whiteside, 1975), pp. 28–29.
577. Dr. Roy was allegedly also offering "health foods, a short-wave electrical machine and serum injections" as a cancer cure. Dr. Roy was to redirect himself into natural healing and writing; in the 1970s he ordered large quantities of Rene's R.M.C. Kidney Tablets from Everett Pharmacy, Bracebridge.
578. Caisse, I Was "*Canada's Cancer Nurse.*"
579. Rene endured relentless pressure for decades; many of the dates and sequences of events have not stood up to authoritative research into primary sources, but have been a substantial base for the compilation of this work.
580. Caisse, I Was "*Canada's Cancer Nurse,*" p. 26.
581. Ibid., p. 9.
582. Ibid., p. 27.
583. Cox's booklet, including its inaccuracies, has been reset and reprinted many times and given wide distribution via various individuals and organizations.
584. Caisse, I Was "*Canada's Cancer Nurse,*" p. 29.
585. Alayne Austin, conversation with the author, March 2004. Alayne, daughter of Ivan Slater, is often told she is the spitting image of her great-aunt Rene, which she considers a compliment.
586. Patient information for R.M.C. Remedies required by the Department of National Health and Welfare, March 21, 1951.
587. Everett's Pharmacy, Bracebridge, sales bill, July 10, 1970.
588. Alayne Austin, conversation with the author, March 2004.
589. Rene M. Caisse (McGaughey), letter to Dr. C. Stock, PhD, February 14, 1974.
590. Fraser and Allen, "Can Essiac Halt Cancer?" p. 38.
591. Rene M. Caisse (McGaughey), letter to Dr. C. Stock, PhD, February 14, 1974.
592. Rene M. McGaughey, letter to Dr. Chester Stock, received by Dr. Stock March 27, 1974. Rene used various signatures.
593. Rene M. McGaughey, letter to Dr. Stock, April 4, 1974.
594. Sheep sorrel, or Rumex acetosella, a dog-eared sour grass, has long been identified as a remedy for cancer. "The Virginia Almanak, 1754," records that Mrs. Mary Johnson of Williamsburg, Virginia, was allowed by the General Assembly to use the herb in the treatment of cancer and presents her "receipt" for preparing the herbal remedy.
595. Rene M. McGaughey, letter to Dr. Stock, received by Walker Laboratory, May 9, 1974.
596. Rene McGaughey, letter to Dr. Chester Stock, June 15, 1974.
597. Chester C. Stock, letter to Rene M. Caissee [sic] McGaughey, June 10, 1975.
598. Rene M. McGaughey, letter to Dr. Stock, August 4, 1975.
599. Chester C. Stock, PhD, letter to Mrs. Rene McGaughey, August 25, 1975.

Chapter 15

600. Carroll Allen, notes to the author, July 2003.
601. Carroll Allen, interviews with the author, June 2003.
602. Fraser and Allen, "Could Essiac Halt Cancer?" p. 10.
603. Moss had been at the institute for three years, but was fired that November for accusing the institute of brainwashing the public into believing that Laetrile had no value in the treatment of cancer.
604. Ralph Moss succeeded in publishing numerous papers and books on cancer therapy for many years. In 1992, he wrote that Essiac "remains worth investigating, not just because of persistent anecdotal reports, but because most of its identifiable components have individually shown anticancer properties in independent tests." (Ralph W. Moss, *Cancer Therapy* (New York: Equinox Press, 1992), p. 146.)
605. "Sloan-Kettering fires supporter of Laetrile," *New York Post*, November 23, 1977.
606. Fraser and Allen, "Could Essiac Halt Cancer?" p. 40.
607. Ibid.
608. Carroll Allen, interviews with the author, June 2003.
609. Jane Hughes, taped telephone conversation with Rene Caisse, February 1977.
610. Dr. Charles Brusch, letter to Rene Caisse, April 6, 1977.
611. Mike Gluss, conversation with the author, March 8, 2004.
612. Carroll Allen, interviews with the author, June 2003.
613. H.W. Rowlands, letter to J. Shearer, June 7, 1977.
614. K.J.R. Wightman, letter to Jane Hughes, June 9, 1977.
615. R.M. Taylor, letter to Jane Hughes, June 9, 1977.
616. M. Shulman, letter to Jeffrey Shearer, June 25, 1977.
617. Shulman, *Coroner*, pp. 24–30.
618. Dr. Shulman went on to promote a drug he developed and took for his Parkinson's disease, and sought federal testing permission in 1997 for a drug for impotence that he was sure would cure certain forms of cancer. He felt he should get the Nobel Prize for the latter.
619. "Morton Shulman's last hurrah," *Ottawa Citizen*, July 30, 1997, pp. A1, A2.
620. Jane Hughes, memo to "All Staff," June 16, 1977.
621. "Homemaker's Magazine comments further on Essiac," *Herald Gazette*, October 12, 1977.
622. John Kirkvaag, "Essiac formula will be tested by the Respirin [sic] Corporation," *Herald-Gazette*, October 26, 1977.
623. Christopher Du Vernet, "Hope for hopeless in renewal of Caisse cancer treatment," *Herald-Gazette*, July 13, 1977, p. 12.
624. Carroll Allen, taped telephone conversation with Rene Caisse, October 21, 1977.
625. Eleanor Sniderman was the wife of Sam "the Record Man" Sniderman.
626. Dr. David Walde would continue as a principal oncologist in Sault Ste. Marie and in 2002 top his many awards with the Commemorative Medal for the Queen's Golden Jubilee.
627. Dr. K.J.R. Wightman, letter to Miss Caisse, July 18, 1977.
628. Lou Specht, "Ample animal testing with Essiac," *Gravenhurst News*, October 12 or 13, 1977.
629. "Homemaker's Magazine comments further on Essiac," *Herald-Gazette*,

October 12, 1977.

630. Carroll Allen, taped telephone conversation with two staff of Brusch Medical Clinic, July 1977.

631. "Lieutenant Governor Pauline McGibbon accepts Caisse cancer formula in trust," *Herald-Gazette*, August 17, 1977, p. 1.

632. "The Essiac" treatment," *Herald-Gazette*, August 24, 1977, editorial.

633. Lotta Dempsey, "Cancer 'secret' locked in bank," *Toronto Star*, August 15, 1977.

634. Karin Moser, "MDs defying law to try cancer cure," *Ottawa Journal*, September 6, 1977, pp. 1, 2.

635. Ibid, p. 2.

636. Carroll Allen, interviews with the author, June 2003.

637. Carroll Allen, taped telephone conversation with Dr. Charles Brusch, about October 19, 1977.

638. Carroll Allen, taped telephone conversation with Dr. David Walde, about October 19, 1977.

639. *Herald-Gazette*, October 12, 1977.

640. Carroll Allen, taped telephone conversation with Dr. David Walde, about October 19, 1977.

Chapter 16

641. Carroll Allen, taped telephone conversation with Rene Caisse, October 21, 1977.

642. Carroll Allen, taped telephone conversation between Carroll Allen, Rene Caisse, Julia Cunningham, and Nancy Merritt, October 21, 1977.

643. John Kirkvaag, "Possible cancer cure?" *Orillia Journal*, October 25, 1977, p. 1.

644. John Kirkvaag, "Essiac formula will be tested by the Respirin [sic] Corporation," *Herald-Gazette*, October 26, 1977, p. 1.

645. "1977 Report on Essiac," an undated press release by David Fingard and Dr. Phillip B. Rynard.

646. Agreement between Dr. Brusch, Valeen Taylor, and Resperin, May 21, 1982.

647. This "foundation" might have prompted Fingard to tell a *Herald-Gazette* reporter in March 1978 that he would approach MP Stan Darling about the idea of setting up a foundation dedicated to Rene Caisse. It is not known if it was to be in corroboration with Dr. Brusch, but it did not materialize. In conversation with the author in 1997, Darling recalled that Fingard never spoke with him about it.

648. Cynthia Law, "Two doctors unsuccessful with Essiac," *Herald-Gazette*, November 2, 1977, p. 1.

649. Ted Britton, "Results of Essiac testing finally released," *Bracebridge Examiner*, November 3, 1977.

650. Dr. David Walde, letter to Jane Hughes, October 17, 1977.

651. The young freelance journalist with various degrees from England would become a foremost Canadian historical biographer, journalist, and speaker.

652. Dr. K.J.R Wightman, in: Charlotte Gray, "Laetrile: Canada's legal position firm but pressure in the South grows," in *Canadian Medical Association Journal*, November 5, 1977, Vol. 117, pp. 1068–1074.

653. Ted Britton, "Results of Essiac testing finally released," *Bracebridge Examiner*, November 3, 1977.

654. Ibid.

655. "The Duke-Fingard Inhalation Treatment." Series of papers in British medical journals, 1937–1942. Archives of Ontario RG10.

656. "Hepburn nearly missed opening of legislature," *Ontario Intelligencer*, January 15, 1937.

657. "Boon for Needy, Respiratory Disease Sufferers May Get Free Clinic Treatment," *Winnipeg Free Press*, March 24, 1938, p. 8.

658. Archives of Ontario, RG3.

659. "Ontario Will Study Inhalation Treatment," *Globe and Mail*, May 9, 1938, p. 4.

660. Duke-Fingard Inhalation Hospital Information Sheet. Undated. RG 10, Archives of Ontario.

661. There were three Dr. McPhedrans practising at that time, all at 170 St. George. Dr. Frederick M. McPhedran would move to Philadelphia in the late 1950s to work as a consultant in respiratory diseases. Dr. Harris McPhedran became principal of the College of Physicians and Surgeons and in 1958 would order Rene to stop treating patients.

662. Dr. A.G. McPhedran, letter to the Hon. Mitchell F. Hepburn, March 18, 1941.

663. Harold Kirby, letter to R.H. Elmhirst with suggested reply for the prime minister to Dr. McPhedran's letter of March 18, 1941, April 5, 1941.

664. Lionel Venne, interview with the author at Elk Lake, July 1996.

665. Executive, December 1979, pp. 57–60.

666. Sid Rodaway and Diane Malott, "What is Uranium King Stephen Roman's Motive for chasing a cancer cure?" *Business World*, July/August 1979, p. 9.

667. Ibid., p. 10.

668. Dr. Matthew Dymond, MDCM, FCFP, LLD, of Port Perry, Ontario was appointed minister of health December 1958 and remained in that portfolio until he resigned in August 1969, having served in that capacity longer than any other Ontario health minister.

669. *Drug Merchandising*, March 1970, news item.

670. Rodaway and Malott, p. 10.

671. The author was a former historian of The Consumers' Gas Company, Toronto.

672. "Roman's investment could help save millions," *The Standard* [Elliot Lake], 1978.

673. "Results of Essiac tests to be released soon," *Kitchener-Waterloo Record*, June 18, 1981.

674. Rodaway and Malott, p. 10.

675. "Roman's investment could help save millions," *The Standard* [Elliot Lake], 1978.

676. This reference to sheep sorrel was not reported in the *Toronto Star*, but was overheard by a person in the audience who wishes to remain anonymous. This appears to be the first evidence of public knowledge of ingredients in the Essiac formula.

677. Lillian Newbery, "Cancer cures useless? MDs can't convince audience," *Toronto Star*, April 6, 1978, p. 1, A13.

678. Ian W.D., Henderson, letter to David Fingard, April 28, 1978.

679. Ian W.D Henderson, letter to Dr. M.B. Dymond, June 22, 1978.

Chapter 17

680. David Fingard, letter to Rt. Honourable [sic] William Davis, March 21, 1978.

681. "Group is trying to make Essiac legal in U.S.," *Herald-Gazette*, March 15, 1978.
682. Dr. H.D. Wilson in *International Zeitschrift for Klinicshe Pharmacology*, 3(1), January, 1970, pp. 61–2.
683. "Group is trying to make Essiac legal in U.S.," *Herald-Gazette*, March 15, 1978.
684. David Fingard, letter to Stan Darling, MP, March 21, 1978.
685. "Detroit News," *Herald-Gazette*, June 21, 1978.
686. Pat Judson, "Essiac," press release to Detroit newspapers published in *Cancer Forum*, 1978.
687. M.B. Dymond, letter to Rene Caisse, undated, c1978.
688. F.G. Roman, letter to Rene M. Caisse, May 30, 1978.
689. Frank S. Miller served as MPP for Muskoka 1971–1985, and he was, among other portfolios, minister of health, 1974–1977, treasurer of Ontario, 1978–83, and premier in 1985.
690. Lang had known Rene since he was a young child.
691. Sandra Askin, interview with the author, October 19, 2001.
692. John Newton, *The Rene Caisse Story*, (Port Carling: Olive Enterprises (Muskoka) Limited, 1997). (30 min. video.)
693. Tom Valentine, "New Twists on the Essiac Cancer Cure," in *Search for Health*, Sept./Oct. 1992, p. 35.
694. Valeen C. Slater, "Rene Caisse McGaughey," c1979.
695. Rodway and Malott, pp. 14–15.
696. "Essiac — an ineffective cancer treatment," in "Issues," Health Protection Branch, Health and Welfare Canada, February 7, 1989. Note: This publication contains poorly researched and inaccurate biographical information on Rene Caisse and erroneously spells her name Renée Caisse.
697. Resperin's letter of instruction to patients, 1979.
698. "Will study effects on humans, Federal government approves Essiac test," *Herald-Gazette*, October 11, 1978.
699. Hope was well as of 1999 and was still corresponding with Rene's friend Mary McPherson.
700. Patrick McGrail stopped taking Essiac in 1980, and in 1984, at age seventy-six, was still doing well according Monique Begin, federal minister of health and welfare in a June 27, 1984, letter to MP Stan Darling.
701. After Rene's death, Mary supplied Dr. Brusch Essiac herbs until at least February 7, 1990.
702. "Rene Caisse remains hospitalized, remarkable results reported with Essiac," *Herald-Gazette*, December 20, 1978.
703. "Medicine woman dead at age 90," *Toronto Star*, December 29, 1978.
704. "Developer of Essiac dies," *Herald-Gazette*, December 28, 1978.
705. "Cancer herbalist dies," *Ottawa Citizen*, December 30, 1978.
706. "Caisse — a legendary woman," *Muskoka Free Press*, January 3, 1979.
707. "Rene Caisse buried Friday," *Muskoka Free Press*, January 3, 1979.
708. "Community remembers Nurse Rene Caisse (Mrs. McGaughey)," *Herald-Gazette*, January 4, 1979.
709. "Rene Caisse buried Friday," *Muskoka Free Press*, January 3, 1979.
710. "Is there still hope?" *Muskoka Free Press*, January 3, 1979.
711. "Estate of Rene Caisse McGaughey," *Herald-Gazette*, June 6, 1979, p. 19.
712. Mary McPherson, letter to Health For All (products), July 2, 1981.

Chapter 18

713. "Roman's investment could help save millions," *The Standard* [Elliot Lake], October, 1978.
714. Hugh MacMillan, letter to Hubert [sic] Sugg, January 16, 1979.
715. Valeen Taylor, letter to Hugh MacMillan, February 5, 1979.
716. Hugh MacMillan maintained his interest in Essiac since he obtained a quantity of the remedy from Rene for his mother during 1964–1965. MacMillan exhibited his small collection of Caisse mementos to the author at his home in Guelph.
717. Tom Cherington came to Bracebridge on August 12, 1981.
718. "Rene's fight goes on...," *Bracebridge Examiner*, August 19, 1981.
719. Lou Specht, "Rene Caisse in TV documentary," *Gravenhurst Leader*, August 19, 1981.
720. Cherington's morning show. CHCH-TV, Hamilton.
721. "Results of Essiac tests to be released soon," *Kitchener-Waterloo Record*, June 18, 1981.
722. "Briefing Information on Essiac," Health Protection Branch, Canada, April 9, 1981.
723. The Hon. Monique Begin, letter to Dr. M.B. Dymond, August 30, 1982.
724. "Essiac—an ineffective cancer treatment," in Issues, Health Protection Branch, Health and Welfare Canada, February 7, 1989. (Note: This publication contains poorly researched and inaccurate biographical information on Rene Caisse, and erroneously spelled her name Renée Caisse.)
725. The Hon. Monique Begin, letter to Stan Darling, MP, February 24, 1984.
726. Ibid.
727. Dr. E. Bruce Hendrick, letter to Mme Monique Begin, October 5, 1983.
728. Ibid., Health and Welfare Canada, Health Protection Branch, *Issues*, February 7, 1989.
729. Dr. M.B. Dymond, letter to Mary McPherson, May 2, 1985.
730. Ibid., October 30, 1986.
731. Ibid., July 14, 1987.
732. Ibid., October 30, 1986.
733. Gordon A. Mackay, telephone conversation with the author, August 14, 1996.
734. Dr. M.B. Dymond, letter to Mary McPherson, July 14, 1987.
735. Stan Darling, MP, letter to the Hon. Monique Begin, March 12, 1984.
736. Dr. M.B. Dymond, letter to Mary McPherson, July 14, 1987.
737. H.D. Wilson, letter to various customers, March 30, 1988.
738. "An ironic tragedy — Relative of Caisse cannot get Essiac," *Bracebridge Examiner*, March 2, 1988.
739. Dr. A. Klein, "Briefing Information on Essiac as an Herbal Tea," Health Protection Branch, Canada, March 17, 1988.
740. (The Rev.) Allen Spraggett, letter to the Hon. Jake Epp, June 20, 1988.

Chapter 19

741. Stan Darling, *The Darling Diaries* (Toronto: Dundurn Press, 1995), p. 255. (The ministers of national health and welfare were, in order of appointment, Monique Begin, David Crombie, Monique Begin, Jake Epp, and Perrin Beatty.)

742. The Hon. Jake Epp, letter to Mr. Darling, Response to Petition, June 27, 1988.

743. The Hon. Jake Epp, letter to Darlene Boyes and Patricia Van Heerde, December 8, 1988.

744. Joe Fullerton, "Essiac crusaders are unhappy with feds," *Bracebridge Examiner*, February 1, 1989, p. 1.

745. Dr. Philip B. Rynard died on November 20, 1980.

746. Dr. M.B. Dymond, letter to Dr. Charles A. Brusch and Mrs. Valeen Taylor, February 21, 1991.

747. Valeen C. Taylor, letter to Dr. M. Dymond, February 28, 1991.

748. Glum, *Calling of an Angel*.

749. "Essiac book not banned from Canada: Beatty," *Bracebridge Examiner*, May 10, 1989, p. A3.

750. Richard Thomas, *The Essiac Report* (Pagosa Springs, CO: Kali Press, 1996).

751. Cynthia Olsen, "Essiac A Native Herbal Cancer Remedy."

752. Mary MacPherson, discussion with the author, 1998.

753. It is said that Gilbert painted Rene's kitchen during a visit for Essiac.

754. Tom Valentine, "New Twists on the Essiac Cancer Cure," in *Search for Health*, Vol. 1, No. 1, Sept./Oct. 1992, p. 34.

755. "Preserving the Gift," *Herald-Gazette*, December 29, 1994, p. 1.

756. Stan Darling, letter to David Fingard, May 3, 1988.

757. Stan Darling, letter to Dr. Richard C. Graham, Health Protection Branch, Canada, June 1, 1988.

758. Stan Darling would have enjoyed seeing this biography of Rene, but he died of a stroke on April 11, 2004, at the age of ninety-two.

759. "Hull, Quebec — Cancer cure goes on trial," Spectator Wire Services, March 3, 1989.

760. Elaine Alexander of Flora Manufacturing died April 30, 1996, of what one report called bleeding ulcers, and another, cancer.

761. Doug Specht, "Plaque Honors 'Nurse Caisse'," *Herald-Gazette*, July 27, 1994.

762. See Appendix for brief history of the Cancer Remedies Act and repeal.

763. Legislative Assembly of Ontario, Debates, 8 October 1997, p. 12879.

Epilogue

764. Conference on Spontaneous Regression of Cancer, U.S. Dept. of Health, Education and Welfare, Bethesda, Md., 1974.

765. Kurt Pollak in collaboration with E. Ashworth Underwood, *The Healers, The Doctor, then and now* (Thomas Nelson & Sons, 1968), pp. 130, 131.

766. Caisse, I Was "*Canada's Cancer Nurse*," p. 8.

767. Fraser and Allen, "Could Essiac Halt Cancer?"

BIBLIOGRAPHY

Much of the information gathered and blended to write this biography came from the three significant Bracebridge newspapers that were published during Rene's lifetime, 1888–1978. Microfilms of the *Muskoka Herald*, *Bracebridge Gazette*, and the *Herald-Gazette* were searched in the Bracebridge Public Library and the Archives of Ontario. Other sources for useful material were the *Huntsville Forester*, *Gravenhurst Leader*, *Gravenhurst News*, and, more recently, the *Bracebridge Examiner*, as well as Toronto newspapers including the *Toronto Star*, *Globe and Mail*, and *Evening Telegram*.

Boyer, Patricia, et al. *Looking at Our Century*. Bracebridge: Herald-Gazette Press, 1975.

Boyer, Robert J. *A Good Town Grew Here*. Herald-Gazette Press, Bracebridge, 1975. 2nd edition with index, 2002.

Caisse, Rene M. *I Was "Canada's Cancer Nurse": The Story of Essiac*. New York: Maurine B. Cox. June 1966.

Carson, Dr. Emma. *"Essiac" Cancer Treatment Endorsed by Eminent Physician: Report on visit to Caisse Cancer Clinic, Bracebridge, Ontario, Canada*. Los Angeles, Calif., undated. Newspaper-style booklet, c1938.

Cosbie, W.G. *Toronto General Hospital 1819-1965: A Chronicle*. Toronto: MacMillan of Canada, 1975.

Darling, Stan. *The Darling Diaries*. Toronto: Dundurn Press, 1995.

Farmiloe, Dorothy. *Elk Lake Lore and Legend*. Little Current: Plowshare Press.

Bibliography

Fifield, James Clark. *American and Canadian Hospitals, a reference book giving historical, statistical and other information on the hospitals and allied institutions of the United States and possessions, and the Dominion of Canada.* Minneapolis: Midwest Publishers, 1933.

Fraser, Sheila Snow and Carroll Allen. "Could Essiac Halt Cancer?" in *Homemaker's Magazine,* June/July/August, 1977.

Glum, Dr. Gary L. *Calling of an Angel.* Los Angeles: Silent Walker Publishing, 1988.

Greenaway, Roy A. *The News Game.* Toronto: Clarke, Irwin, 1966.

Hamilton, Ross, ed. *Prominent Men of Canada.* Montreal: National Publishing Co. of Canada, 1931–32.

Issues, Health Protection Branch, Health and Welfare Canada. "Essiac—an ineffective cancer treatment," February 7, 1989.

Kalisch, Philip A. and Beatrice J. Kalisch. *The Advance of American Nursing* (Little, Brown & Co., Boston, 1978).

Kilbourn, William. *Toronto Remembered.* Toronto: Stoddard Publishing, 1984.

Loyal She Remains. Toronto: United Empire Loyalists' Association of Canada, 1984.

McClelland, James and Dan Lewis, eds. *Emerson 1875-1975, A Centennial History.* Manitoba: Emerson Chamber of Commerce, 1975.

McFarlane, Leslie. *A Kid in Haileybury.* Cobalt: Highway Book Shop, 1966.

McNaughton, A.G.L. "Investigation of Cancer Cures," National Research Council, Report. May 5, 1938.

Morris, Nat [pseud.]. *The Cancer Blackout: A History of Denied and Suppressed Remedies.* (Author's real name is Maurice Natenburg.) Chicago: Regent House, c1959.

Olsen, Cynthia. *Essiac A Native Herbal Cancer Remedy.* Pagosa Spring, CO: Kali Press, 1996.

Ortiz, Alicia Dujovne. *Eva Peron.* Translated by Shawn Fields. New York: St. Martin's Press, 1996.

Pollock, Dr. John. "History of Logging in the Lake Temiskaming-Montreal River Watershed," p. 12, in "They Came from All Walks of Life," Proceedings of the History Workshop, Temiskaming Abitibi Heritage Association, April 29, 1995. Haileybury: Rosanne Fisher Publishing. 1996.

Pryke, Susan. *Huntsville: With Spirit and Resolve.* Huntsville: Fox Meadow Creations, 2000.

R.C. Wallace Papers, Queen's University Archives.

Rene M. Caisse Archive, Bracebridge Public Library.

Rodaway, Sid and Diane Malott. "What is Uranium King Stephen Roman's motive for chasing a cancer cure?" in *Business World*, July/August 1979, pp. 7–15.

Saywell, John T. *Just Call me Mitch*. Toronto: University of Toronto Press, 1991.

Shulman, Morton. *Coroner*. Toronto: Fitzhenry & Whiteside, 1975.

Summertimes: In Celebration of One Hundred Years of the Muskoka Lakes Association. Erin: Boston Mills Press, 1994.

Tatley, Richard. *The Steamboat Era in the Muskokas*, Vol. II, *The Golden Years to Present*. Erin: Boston Mills Press, 1984.

The Toronto Star Centennial Magazine, The Hundred — A Celebration, November 1992.

Thomas, Richard. *The Essiac Report*. Los Angeles: The Alternative Treatment Information Network, 1993.

Wallace Fonds, 2002, Queen's University Archives, Proceedings of a Sub-Committee of the Commission for the Investigation of Cancer, February 3 & 4, 1939

Wallace Fonds, 2002, Queen's University Archives, Proceedings of The Commission for the Investigation of Cancer Remedies, July 4, 1939

Wallace Fonds, 2002, the Commission for the Investigation of Cancer Remedies, March 30 and 31, 1939.

Wallace Fonds, 2002, The Commission for the Investigation of Cancer Remedies, Interim Report, December 31, 1939.

INDEX

Numbers in bold indicate illustrations